Global Statement

Transitional Phase

In this phase, readers are beginning to integrate strategies to identify unknown words and to comprehend text. These strategies, combined with an increasing bank of sight words, enable readers to read texts such as novels, newspapers and websites with familiar content fluently and with expression. Transitional readers reflect on strategies used and are beginning to discuss their effectiveness.

Proficient readers have developed
demanding texts such as subject-
appropriate to the purpose and c
grammatical, cultural/world and
identify the target audience of a
question the text.

Key Indicators

USE OF TEXTS
- ◆ Reads and demonstrates comprehension of texts by:
  - – identifying the main idea(s), citing supporting detail
  - – selecting events from a text to suit a specific purpose
  - – linking ideas, both explicit and implicit, in a text, e.g. cause and effect.
- ◆ Locates and selects texts appropriate to purpose and audience, e.g. uses search engines, checks currency of information.

CONTEXTUAL UNDERSTANDING
- ◆ Recognises own interpretation may differ from that of other readers or the author/s.
- ◆ Recognises devices that authors and illustrators use to influence construction of meaning, e.g. visual clues, omissions.
- ◆ Recognises that authors and illustrators attempt to position readers.
- ◆ Recognises how characters or people, facts and events are represented, and can speculate about the author's choices.

CONVENTIONS
- ◆ Recognises an increasing bank of words in different contexts, e.g. subject-specific words, less common words.
- ◆ Explains how known text forms vary by using knowledge of:
  - – purpose, e.g. to persuade
  - – text structure, e.g. problem and solution
  - – text organisation, e.g. headings, subheadings, an index, glossary
  - – language features, e.g. conjunctions.

PROCESSES AND STRATEGIES
- ◆ Draws upon an increasing knowledge base to comprehend, e.g. text structure and organisation, grammar, vocabulary.
- ◆ Uses an increasing range of strategies to comprehend, e.g. creating images, determining importance.
- ◆ Determines unknown words by using word-identification strategies, e.g. reading on, re-reading.

USE OF TEXTS
- ◆ Reads and demonstrates compr
  - – explaining how the main ide
    intended audience
  - – selecting events from a text t
  - – linking ideas, both explicit an
- ◆ Locates and evaluates appropria
  audience, e.g. validity, bias.

CONTEXTUAL UNDERSTANDIN
- ◆ Recognises how one's values, a
- ◆ Discusses the target audience fc
  presentation to suit.

CONVENTIONS
- ◆ Recognises manipulation of tex
  narrative.
- ◆ Recognises the selection of lanc
  - – words to distinguish fact fron
  - – words/phrases that signal rela
  - – synonyms to denote connota

PROCESSES AND STRATEGIES
- ◆ Selects from a broad knowledge
  knowledge, grammar, vocabulary.
- ◆ Selects appropriate strategies fr
- ◆ Determines unknown words by

Major Teaching Emphases

ENVIRONMENT AND ATTITUDE
- ■ Create a supportive classroom environment that nurtures a community of readers.
- ■ Jointly construct, and frequently refer to, meaningful environmental print.
- ■ Foster students' enjoyment of reading.
- ■ Encourage students to take risks with confidence.
- ■ Encourage students to select their own reading material according to interest or purpose.

USE OF TEXTS
- ■ Provide opportunities for students to read a wide range of texts.
- ■ Continue to teach students to analyse texts, identifying explicit and implicit information.
- ■ Continue to teach students to make connections within texts, using both explicit and implicit information.
- ■ Model how concept knowledge and understandings can be shaped and reshaped using information from a variety of texts.

CONTEXTUAL UNDERSTANDING
- ■ Discuss how readers may react to and interpret texts differently, depending on their knowledge, experience or perspective.
- ■ Discuss how authors and illustrators have used devices to target specific audiences, e.g. quoting statistics.
- ■ Provide opportunities for students to challenge the author's world view.

CONVENTIONS
- ■ Continue to build students' sight vocabulary, e.g. less common words, subject-specific words.
- ■ Continue to build students' graphophonic and word knowledge, such as:
  - – recognising less common sound–symbol relationships
  - – recognising letter combinations and the different sounds they represent
  - – recognising how word parts and words work.
- ■ Jointly analyse texts where combinations and adaptations of text structure and text organisation have been used.
- ■ Teach students to identify the role of language features in a variety of texts.

PROCESSES AND STRATEGIES
- ■ Continue to build students' knowledge within the cues, e.g. orthographic, world knowledge.
- ■ Consolidate known comprehension strategies and teach additional strategies, e.g. synthesising, paraphrasing.
- ■ Consolidate word-identification strategies.
- ■ Continue to teach students how to locate, select and evaluate texts, e.g. conducting Internet searches, recognising bias.
- ■ Model self-reflection of strategies used in reading, and encourage students to do the same.

ENVIRONMENT AND ATTITUD
- ■ Create a supportive classroom
- ■ Jointly construct, and frequently
- ■ Foster students' enjoyment of r
- ■ Encourage students to take risk
- ■ Encourage students to select th

USE OF TEXTS
- ■ Provide opportunities for studer
- ■ Continue to teach students to a

CONTEXTUAL UNDERSTANDIN
- ■ Provide opportunities for studer
  create an interpretation of the
- ■ Provide opportunities for studer

CONVENTIONS
- ■ Continue to build students' sigl
- ■ Teach students to analyse how
- ■ Teach students to analyse how

PROCESSES AND STRATEGIES
- ■ Continue to build students' kn
- ■ Consolidate comprehension stra
- ■ Consolidate word-identification
- ■ Consolidate how to locate, sele
- ■ Model self-reflection of strategi

W9-CHC-280

s Reading Map of Development

Proficient Phase

a multistrategy approach to identify unknown words and comprehend
pecific textbooks, novels and essays. They are able to select strategies
mplexity of the text. Readers have a greater ability to connect topic,
ext-structure knowledge with what is new in the text. Proficient readers
ext. They draw on evidence from their own experience to challenge or

hension of texts by:
and supporting information relate to the author's purpose and the

suit a specific audience
implicit, in a text, e.g. thesis and supporting arguments.
teness of texts and information in texts in terms of purpose and

itudes and beliefs impact on the interpretation of text.
a specific text, and how the author has tailored the language, ideas and

structure and text organisation, e.g. historical account written as a

uage features such as:
opinion and bias, e.g. I think, It has been reported
ionships, e.g. similarly — to compare, on the other hand — to contrast
ions, e.g. thief, bandit, pickpocket.

base to comprehend, e.g. text structure and organisation, cultural/world

m a wide range to comprehend.
selecting appropriate word-identification strategies.

---

nvironment that nurtures a community of readers.
refer to, meaningful environmental print.
ading.
with confidence.
ir own reading material according to interest or purpose.

ts to read a wide range of texts.
halyse texts utilising information to suit different purposes and audiences.
G
ts to discuss how the ideologies of the reader and the author combine to
ext.
ts to identify devices used to influence readers to take a particular view.

t vocabulary, e.g. technical terms, figurative language.
uthors combine language features to achieve a purpose.
uthors manipulate texts to achieve a purpose, e.g. structure, organisation.

wledge within the cues.
tegies.
strategies.
t and evaluate texts.
s used in reading, and encourage students to do the same.

Accomplished Phase

Accomplished readers use a flexible repertoire of strategies and cues to comprehend texts
and to solve problems with unfamiliar structure and vocabulary. They are able to fluently
read complex and abstract texts such as journal articles, novels and research reports.
Accomplished readers access the layers of information and meaning in a text according to
their reading purpose. They interrogate, synthesise and evaluate multiple texts to revise and
refine their understandings

USE OF TEXTS
♦ Reads and demonstrates comprehension of texts using both explicit and implicit
  information to achieve a given purpose.
♦ Synthesises information from texts, with varying perspectives, to draw conclusions.
♦ Locates and evaluates appropriateness of texts and the information in texts in terms of
  purpose and audience.

CONTEXTUAL UNDERSTANDING
♦ Discusses reasons why a text may be interpreted differently by different readers, e.g.
  personal background of reader, author bias, sociocultural background.
♦ Discusses how the context (time, place, situation) of an author influences the construction
  of a text.
♦ Analyses the use of devices such as rhetoric, wit, cynicism and irony designed to position
  readers to take particular views.

CONVENTIONS
♦ Uses knowledge of one text form to help interpret another, e.g. literary features in
  informational texts.
♦ Recognises the effectiveness of language features selected by authors.

PROCESSES AND STRATEGIES
♦ Consciously adds to a broad knowledge base, as required, to comprehend.
♦ Selects appropriate strategies from a wide range to comprehend.
♦ Determines unknown words by selecting appropriate word-identification strategies.

Major Teaching Emphases and
Teaching and Learning Experiences
are not provided for this phase, as
Accomplished readers are able to take
responsibility for their own ongoing
reading development.

Reading Map of Development

First Steps Second Edition was developed by STEPS Professional Development
(proudly owned by Edith Cowan University) on behalf of the
Department of Education and Training (Western Australia).
It was written by:
Kevlynn Annandale
Ross Bindon
Kerry Handley
Annette Johnston
Lynn Lockett
Philippa Lynch

Second Edition

Addressing Current Literacy Challenges

Authors' Acknowledgements

The *First Steps* team from STEPS Professional Development gratefully acknowledges the contribution made by the following people.

To all the teachers and students who have been involved in trialling the materials and offering feedback as Critical Readers, Test Pilots or Navigator Schools, we give our grateful thanks for your hard work.

The authors of *First Steps* Second Edition gratefully acknowledge and value the work of the authors of the original edition, developed by the Education Department of Western Australia, and the efforts of the many individuals who contributed to that resource.

Contents

Chapter 8

Proficient Reading Phase

Chapter 9

Accomplished Reading Phase

CHAPTER 1
About Reading

As part of the *First Steps* second edition, the *Reading Map of Development* (formerly known as the *Reading Developmental Continuum*) is designed to help teachers map their students' progress and to offer suggestions for teaching and learning experiences that will assist with further development in reading.

This first chapter focuses on the beliefs about reading and reading instruction that underpin the *First Steps* reading material.

Defining Reading

Defining reading is no easier than defining literacy. What counts as effective reading varies from context to context according to what the reader wants and needs to achieve, what texts are being encountered, and what the dominant culture expects. One-dimensional definitions have an appeal of simplicity, but they ignore the complexity of the reading process and can often lead to narrow or skewed teaching.

Reading is one strand of literacy. In the *First Steps* resource, each strand is further broken down into smaller categories referred to throughout as substrands. The following table summarises how these substrands combine to capture the nature of reading, each one providing a different lens for consideration.

Substrand	Reading is . . .
Use of Texts: what students do with texts	• making meaning from texts
Contextual Understanding: how the context affects the interpretation and choice of language	• a social practice that is used to accomplish a wide range of purposes • questioning and critiquing texts
Conventions: structures and features of texts	• cracking the code that is letters, words, sentences and texts
Processes and Strategies: how students read, view, speak and listen	• the active, integrated problem-solving process of making sense of texts

Taken alone, none of the substrand definitions would adequately define reading in today's world. Instead, each is an essential component of a multidimensional definition of reading that provides signposts for understanding how the reading process unfolds, and how reading should be taught.

Luke and Freebody (1999) suggest that readers draw on a repertoire of practices when they read. These practices relate to the substrands.

Readers:
- participate in the meanings of texts;
- critically analyse and transform texts;
- break the code of texts;
- use texts functionally.

Understanding the Reading Process

Effective teachers have an understanding of how reading occurs and are able to plan teaching and learning experiences that support students in becoming more successful readers. Developing a clear understanding of the reading process is a challenge, as reading is often a silent, motionless, personal act involving cognitive and social processes that are interactive, and not always observable. Furthermore, beginning readers and skilled readers often go about the reading task in different ways.

First Steps uses a substrand framework and the Linguistic Cueing System schematic developed by Pearson (1976) as a basis to illustrate the multidimensional process of reading and to provide an impetus for recommended teaching approaches to support reading development. This resource looks at reading as an interactive process between:
- the context of the reading event;
- the knowledge within the cues;
- the use of reading strategies.

The Context of the Reading Event

Reading serves multiple purposes in people's lives. All reading takes place in a sociocultural context and for a particular purpose: the purpose and context of a reading event guides the reader to decide what is important and what must be understood to achieve success. Purpose and context drive the selection of reading strategies and enable the reader to access appropriate cues, often without being conscious of the connections being made.

Knowledge within the Cues

Efficient readers comprehend text by simultaneously drawing on a range of information sources, often referred to as semantic, syntactic and graphophonic cues. The cueing systems are not sequential or hierarchical and are equally important in contributing to the process of comprehending texts. It is critical that students from a very early age be provided with the opportunity to build knowledge and skills related to all three, which collectively make up an individual's prior knowledge or schema.

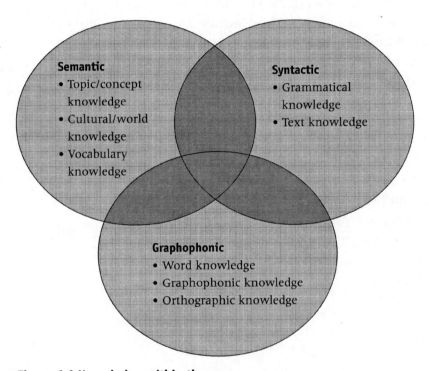

Semantic
- Topic/concept knowledge
- Cultural/world knowledge
- Vocabulary knowledge

Syntactic
- Grammatical knowledge
- Text knowledge

Graphophonic
- Word knowledge
- Graphophonic knowledge
- Orthographic knowledge

Figure 1.1 Knowledge within the cues

Semantic Cues

Readers draw on semantic cues to help them know if what they are reading makes sense. Semantic cues are associated with the overall meaning of a text, understanding both the words and the underlying messages. These cues include the reader's cultural and world knowledge, knowledge of the concept or topic, and vocabulary knowledge. They help readers to make personal associations with a text.

Syntactic Cues

Readers draw on syntactic cues to help them decide if the text sounds right. Syntactic cues are associated with the structure of the language; they include the reader's knowledge of grammatical features, of word order in sentences and of the organisation and structure of whole texts.

Graphophonic Cues

Readers draw on graphophonic cues to help them identify unknown words. Graphophonic cues focus on the relationships between sound and symbols. They include knowledge of letters and groups of letters, and the sounds associated with them. Graphophonic cues also include knowledge of print concepts and word structure.

Use of Reading Strategies

Many teachers work hard to ensure that all students build a bank of knowledge within the three cues. The sources of information within the cues include knowledge about:
- concepts and topics
- culture and the world
- vocabulary meaning
- words and word parts
- graphophonics
- orthography
- grammar
- text forms.

However, one of the most critical elements in supporting reading development is often neglected. The explicit teaching of a range of reading strategies is vital to ensure that students are able to successfully access their cues to support reading. Cues can only be used flexibly and independently through the application of such strategies. Strategies used to identify unknown words, to prepare for reading and to monitor and adjust reading are all imperative to successful reading.

Reading strategies include:

predicting   connecting   inferring   comparing
creating images   summarising/paraphrasing
synthesising   self-questioning   skimming   scanning
determining importance   re-reading   reading on
adjusting reading rate   sounding out   chunking
using analogy   consulting a reference

The process of comprehending text is an interaction between the author and the reader that occurs in a social and cultural context, and is driven by the purpose of the reader. These contextual elements contribute significantly to the reader's motivation and interest. The author contributes the words and an intended meaning in the text. The reader actively integrates a range of strategies, including word identification and comprehension, to interactively draw upon all knowledge available in the cues. Effective readers will have automated many of these strategies, so that they occur without conscious deliberation. By bringing in-head knowledge to interpret the information supplied by the author, the reader creates unique, personal meaning. Goodman (1996) says 'The sense you make of a text is the sense you bring to it'.

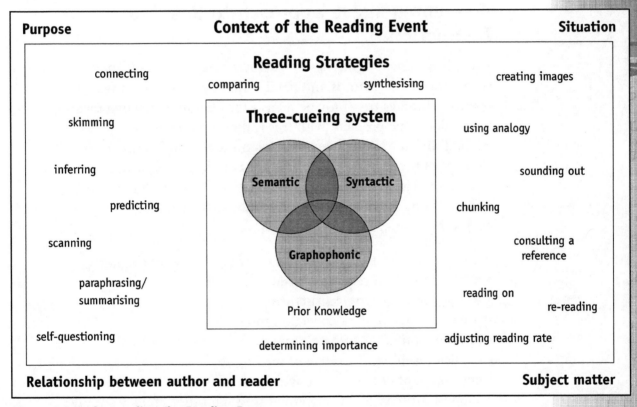

Figure 1.2 Understanding the Reading Process

Beginning or struggling readers may be unsure of the reading purpose, or may even misconstrue the reading act. They may have limited knowledge of the information within the graphophonic, syntactic and semantic cues, or they may have a narrow range of reading strategies to access these cues. If the text is too difficult, leading to mispronunciation of words and disconnected sentence fragments, the beginning reader will be unable to relate what is being read to meaningful oral language. Moreover, if the reader has English as an additional language, syntactic cues from the home language may interfere with the contribution of that cue to the reading act. Interference and inadequacies in one cueing source can weaken the interactive, rapid nature of the cueing system, and result in the erosion of fluency and comprehension.

A Comprehensive Approach to Reading Instruction

There is no single right way to teach reading, as students have such varied backgrounds and needs. However, there is a wealth of research findings that provide a basis for planning effective reading instruction. One problem with this is that researchers often view reading through a single lens, highlighting the one particular element of their study. This sometimes influences educators to take a weighted view of reading instruction, but by combining research findings from many lenses to inform the instruction, a comprehensive approach can be achieved.

A comprehensive reading approach is eclectic, incorporating:
- use of a range of reading procedures;
- use of varied grouping structures;
- use of a range of data-collection tools;
- introduction of a variety of texts;
- explicit teaching of a range of reading strategies;
- development of knowledge within all cues;
- support for reading development through other literacy strands;
- integration of reading instruction across the curriculum;
- use of a range of effective teaching and learning practices.

A Comprehensive Approach Uses a Range of Reading Procedures

(see *Reading Resource Book*, 2nd edn, Chapter 1)

The strategic use of a range of Reading Procedures ensures a strong foundation for a balanced reading program, as each procedure requires varying degrees of responsibility from the teacher and the student. Procedures such as Modelled Reading, Reading to Students and Language Experience allow the teacher to demonstrate how strategies can be used to help the reader make sense of the text. Shared Reading and Guided Reading provide opportunities for students to practise these strategies with guidance and support. Book Discussion Groups and Independent Reading sessions allow students time to apply what they have learnt about reading. Using a selective range of Reading Procedures ensures that explicit instruction and guidance at the point of need is balanced by regular opportunities for independent application of skills and strategies.

A Comprehensive Approach Uses Varied Grouping Structures

(see *Linking Assessment, Teaching and Learning*, Chapter 8)

The use of flexible grouping structures helps to meet the needs of each student in a class. Flexible grouping arrangements allow students to work with a variety of peers depending on the planned learning outcome. Students are grouped and regrouped according to the activity, to individual needs or to specific goals. Implementing a range of Reading Procedures will generally lead to a range of whole-class, small-group and individual learning opportunities for students. It is also important to consider other factors, such as the impact of ability grouping, the social dynamics of groups and the preferred learning styles of individuals.

A Comprehensive Approach Uses a Range of Data-Collection Tools

(see this book, Chapter 3; *Linking Assessment, Teaching and Learning*, Chapter 6)

It is important that teachers develop a repertoire of tools and methods for collecting data about students' reading development. A multifaceted approach to data collection will include a balance of observation, conversation and analysis of products. This type of approach will ensure that teachers are building an accurate picture of each student's strengths and needs. An accurate picture is necessary to make informed decisions about the most appropriate teaching and learning experiences that will support student development.

A Comprehensive Approach Introduces a Variety of Texts

(see *Reading Resource Book*, 2nd edn, Chapter 1)

In today's society readers are exposed to a vast range of texts, many made up of both print and visual features and conveyed through various media. Teachers can provide opportunities for students to access a wide range of texts by incorporating them into planned learning experiences. There will be times when newspapers, magazines or the Internet will be the most appropriate source of material, and other times when a reading series or a textbook will be more useful. Using a range of texts will provide students with opportunities to navigate texts that have different organisational features and to encounter varied language features and text structures.

A Comprehensive Approach Introduces a Range of Reading Strategies

(see *Reading Resource Book*, 2nd edn, Chapter 4)

The explicit teaching of multiple reading strategies allows readers to learn how to actively integrate their prior knowledge with new information in the texts being read. Explicit demonstrations, ongoing scaffolding, and opportunities to practise and apply a range of comprehension and word-identification strategies are essential. A long-term goal for all students is to be able to select and use a range of strategies flexibly and independently during any reading event.

A Comprehensive Approach Builds Knowledge within All Cues

Efficient readers make sense of text by drawing on a range of information sources interactively and simultaneously. These sources are often referred to as semantic, syntactic and graphophonic cues. It is critical to provide opportunities for students to build the knowledge within all three cues and to help them recognise how and when each information source can be helpful with word identification and comprehension.

A Comprehensive Approach Supports Reading Development through the Other Literacy Strands

All four strands of literacy — reading, writing, viewing, and speaking and listening — work in conjunction and are difficult to separate into discrete areas. It is important to show students how the strands are interrelated and how each one supports the others; e.g. learning about text structure in reading assists comprehension in viewing. It makes sense to ensure these links are explicit.

A Comprehensive Approach Integrates Reading Instruction across the Curriculum

Effective reading instruction involves the teaching and reinforcing of reading understandings, skills and strategies across all subject areas. The learning that has occurred during explicit reading lessons needs to be practised and consolidated independently in other learning areas; for instance, applying knowledge of text structure to comprehend a science text. Although many of these opportunities will be planned, further avenues will exist in the capture of teachable moments that arise in subject lessons. Dealing with unfamiliar vocabulary during mathematics, for example, allows the teacher to capitalise on the prior teaching of particular reading strategies.

A Comprehensive Approach Incorporates a Range of Effective Teaching and Learning Practices

(see *Linking Assessment, Teaching and Learning*, Chapter 7)

Finding a balance between time spent on teacher-directed, explicit instruction and student participation in discussions, activities or independent work is a juggling act that often troubles teachers. Too much or too little time spent in any of these areas tends to favour particular learning styles and to exclude some groups of students. It is critical to consider a variety of ways a concept, skill or strategy could be taught, and plan to incorporate a range of effective teaching and learning practices. Some practices are often complementary, and work effectively in a particular sequence; for instance, modelling, sharing, guiding and applying have been used prominently in reading as a means of moving students from a supportive to a more independent setting.

How a Comprehensive Approach Reflects the Beliefs Underpinning *First Steps*

F	Focused on strategies	Teachers: • explicitly teach students a range of reading strategies; • encourage students to be aware of, apply, monitor and adjust reading strategies; • encourage students to apply reading strategies across the curriculum.
I	Investigative	Teachers: • plan opportunities that involve students in problem solving to discover how texts work; • plan opportunities to engage students in authentic reading events that build upon existing foundations.
R	Reflective	Teachers: • provide time and support for students to reflect, represent and report on their reading, e.g. use of strategies; • model the process of reflection.
S	Scaffolded	Teachers: • support students' reading with a range of scaffolds such as modelling, sharing, guiding and conferencing; • provide specific and targeted feedback to guide students to independence.
T	Tailored	Teachers: • map the milestones of reading development and devise plans that meet the needs of students; • develop organisational structures that allow all students to participate at their developmental level, using a balance of small-group, whole-class and individual instruction.
S	Supportive	Teachers: • create an environment in which students feel safe to ask for help when they need it and to express themselves readily without fear of judgement or ridicule.
T	Tested	Teachers: • use a range of research-based reading procedures; • use a range of effective teaching and learning practices.
E	Embedded	Teachers: • create reading experiences that are engaging, authentic, and culturally and developmentally appropriate; • embed experiences in texts to build students' knowledge within the cues; • help students to make connections between their current understandings and what is new.
P	Purposefully practised	Teachers: • select experiences from across learning areas to allow students to consolidate and integrate new understandings and skills; • plan activities that are focused, scaffolded and contextualised.
S	Shared	Teachers: • understand that responsibility for implementing a balanced reading program needs to be shared among all stakeholders — teachers, parents, students and the school; • work collaboratively to develop appropriate programs to support students experiencing difficulty.

CHAPTER 2
Understanding the Reading Map of Development

The Reading Map of Development validates what teachers know about their students and is organised to help them link assessment, teaching and learning.

Although in practice literacy is an amalgam of the four strands of Reading, Writing, Speaking and Listening, and Viewing, individual maps are necessary to represent the complexity of each strand.

In addition, breaking each strand into substrands provides further opportunity for more specialised analysis. The organisation of the Reading Map of Development into the substrands provides a practical framework for looking at assessment, teaching and learning, and reflects current beliefs about how reading is defined.

The Reading Map contains behaviours, suggested teaching emphases, and a range of teaching and learning experiences for each phase of development. Together these features help teachers to make informed, strategic decisions about how to support students' literacy development.

How the Map Is Organised

There are six phases in the Reading Map of Development.
- Role Play
- Experimental
- Early
- Transitional
- Proficient
- Accomplished

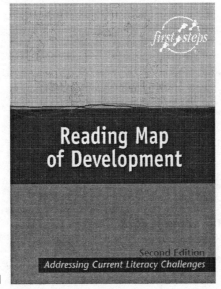

first steps

Reading Map of Development

Second Edition
Addressing Current Literacy Challenges

Figure 2.1

The same organisational framework is used for each phase.

PHASE NAME
The Phase Name is a description of a reader in that phase.

GLOBAL STATEMENT
The Global Statement:
• summarises the general characteristics of the typical reading behaviours in that phase;
• reflects students' current beliefs about reading;
• describes the types of texts with which students usually interact.

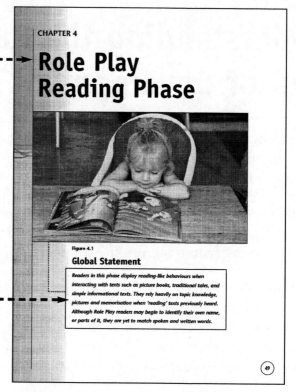

CHAPTER 4

Role Play Reading Phase

Figure 4.1

Global Statement

Readers in this phase display reading-like behaviours when interacting with texts such as picture books, traditional tales, and simple informational texts. They rely heavily on topic knowledge, pictures and memorisation when 'reading' texts previously heard. Although Role Play readers may begin to identify their own name, or parts of it, they are yet to match spoken and written words.

49

Figure 2.2 The Role Play Reading Phase Name and Global Statement

INDICATORS
Indicators:
• are organised under the substrand headings:
 – Use of Texts
 – Contextual Understanding
 – Conventions
 – Processes and Strategies
• describe reading behaviours.
Key Indicators:
• signify a conceptual leap in critical understandings;
• describe behaviours that are typical of a phase.
Other Indicators:
• describe behaviours that provide further details of the phase.

Role Play Reading Indicators

Role Play Reading Indicators

Use of Texts
◆ Listens to and demonstrates comprehension by talking about significant ideas from the text.
◆ Displays reading-like behaviour, e.g. holds book right way up, clicks mouse to see new window.
◆ Knows that print carries a message, but may 'read' their own writing and unfamiliar texts differently each time.
◆ Selects texts primarily for enjoyment, e.g. uses cover and illustrations.
• Attempts reading-like behaviours.
• Recognises significant environmental print, e.g. signs, logos, labels.

Contextual Understanding
◆ Makes links to own experience when listening to or 'reading' texts, e.g. points to illustrations, saying 'I had a party'.
◆ Identifies and talks about familiar characters or people from texts.

Conventions
◆ Recognises own name, or part of it, in print.
◆ Knows repetitive patterns in very familiar stories, e.g. Run, run as fast as you can . . .

• Uses some book language in retellings and play, e.g. Once upon a time . . .
• Is beginning to understand directionality of print, e.g. front to back when turning pages.
• Responds to and uses simple terminology such as book, right way up, front, back.
• Is beginning to recognise some letters by name or sound, e.g. Sam says 'That's my name.' pointing to 's' in a 'Stop' sign.
• Distinguishes print from drawings.
• May know the alphabet by rote, but may need a visual clue to connect a letter with its name.
• Identifies and supplies some simple rhyming words, e.g. hot, pot.

Processes and Strategies
◆ Relies upon knowledge of topic and text organisation, such as pictures, when 'reading'.
◆ Relies on the strategy of connecting to comprehend, e.g. connects text to self.
• Comments on specific features in pictures.
• Asks questions about signs, pictures and labels.

50

Figure 2.3 The Role Play Reading Indicators

MAJOR TEACHING EMPHASES (MTEs)

Major Teaching Emphases:

• are organised under the headings:
  – Environment and Attitude
  – Use of Texts
  – Contextual Understanding
  – Conventions
  – Processes and Strategies
• are suggestions of appropriate priorities for teaching at each phase;
• are designed to help teachers support and challenge students' current understandings.

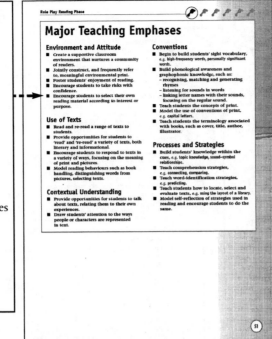

Figure 2.4 The Role Play Reading Major Teaching Emphases

TEACHING AND LEARNING EXPERIENCES

• Teaching and Learning Experiences are organised under the following headings:
  – Environment and Attitude
  – Use of Texts
  – Contextual Understanding
  – Conventions
  – Processes and Strategies.
• Each of these is divided into two sections: Teaching Notes and Involving Students.
  – Teaching Notes unpack the Major Teaching Emphases.
  – Involving Students contains a selection of developmentally appropriate activities that support the Major Teaching Emphases.

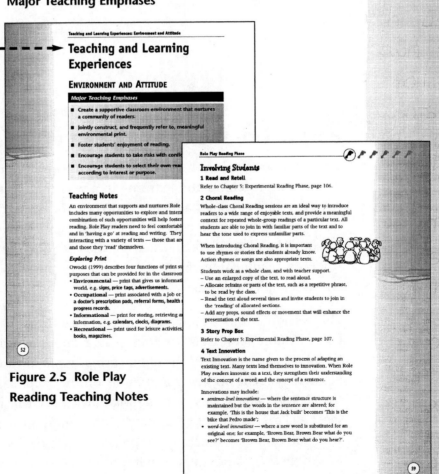

Figure 2.5 Role Play Reading Teaching Notes

Figure 2.6 Involving Students — Role Play Reading

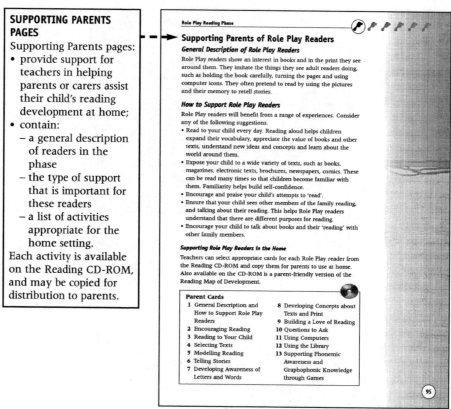

Figure 2.7 Providing parent support

How to Use the Reading Map of Development

The purpose in using the Reading Map of Development is to link assessment, teaching and learning in a way that best addresses the strengths and needs of all students. The process used to achieve this may vary from teacher to teacher; it may be dependent on a teacher's familiarity with *First Steps*, the data already collected about students' reading development, the time of the school year, or the school's implementation plan.

This section outlines a possible process (see Figure 2.8). As teachers become more familiar with linking assessment to teaching and learning, strategic decisions about using the map can be made. Some may focus on placing students on the map; e.g. **how many students and which ones, or using what indicators, which recording sheet and over what period of time?** Others may focus on the selection of Major Teaching Emphases and Teaching and Learning Experiences for individual, small-group and whole-class teaching.

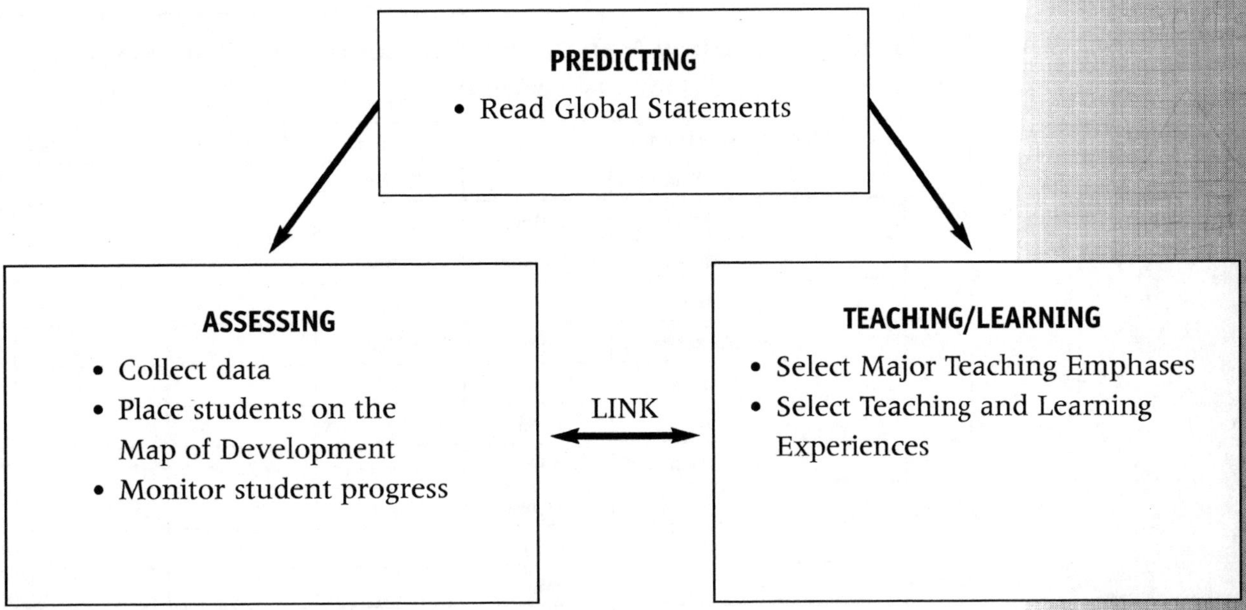

```
                    ┌─────────────────────────────────┐
                    │          PREDICTING             │
                    │                                 │
                    │     • Read Global Statements    │
                    └─────────────────────────────────┘
            ↙                                             ↘

┌──────────────────────────────┐          ┌──────────────────────────────┐
│          ASSESSING           │          │      TEACHING/LEARNING        │
│                              │          │                              │
│   • Collect data             │          │   • Select Major Teaching     │
│   • Place students on the    │  LINK    │     Emphases                  │
│     Map of Development       │  ←────→  │   • Select Teaching and       │
│   • Monitor student progress │          │     Learning Experiences      │
└──────────────────────────────┘          └──────────────────────────────┘
```

Figure 2.8

Suggested Process for Using the Reading Map of Development

Predict

Many teachers begin to use the Reading Map of Development by making predictions about each student's phase of development. Predictions are made by reading through the Global Statements. Teachers are then able to use this information, together with their professional judgement, to make an educated guess in each case. The initial predictions, recorded on a class profile sheet, allow teachers to immediately begin linking assessment, teaching and learning.

These predictions can be used to begin selecting Major Teaching Emphases from appropriate phases for whole-class, small-group or individual teaching. The MTEs will then guide the selection of teaching and learning experiences to support students' development.

It is critical that teachers begin to collect data to confirm or amend their initial predictions.

First Steps Reading Map of Development: Class Profile Sheet

Year Level: _____   Teacher: _____

	Role Play	Experimental	Early	Transitional	Proficient	Accomplished
1		Dixie	Ivy	William		
2		Gerard	Heather	Donna		
3		Thomas	Monique	Kerry		
4		Grant	Josh	Simone		
5		Stephen	Tim	Louise		
6		Annabelle	Michael	Jack		
7		Sui-Lee	Nikki			
8		Sian	Thi Chan			
9			Jayne			
10			Bradley			
11			Philip			
12			Jonathan			
13			Kris			
14			Ivan			
15			Tania			
16			Jacqui			
17						
18						
19						
20						
21						
22						
23						
24						
25						
26						

Major Teaching Emphases can be selected from a range of phases.
- Whole-class focus, e.g. **Early Phase**
- Small-group focus, e.g. **Experimental** or **Transitional**
- Individual student focus

Figure 2.9 Sample of a Class Profile

Collect Data

The Indicators on the Reading Map of Development provide a focus for data collection, which can be carried out on a continual basis using a range of tools in a variety of contexts. A balance of conversation, observation and analysis of products will ensure that information is gathered across all four substrands. Encouraging the involvement of students and parents or care givers in the data collection will provide further information about students' reading development and interests (see Chapter 3).

Place Students on the Reading Map of Development

The Reading Map of Development can be used as a framework for recording a wide range of information gathered about students' reading behaviours. A number of recording formats have been designed, and have been successfully used by teachers. Samples of these are provided on the Reading CD-ROM.

Information about the behaviours displayed can be recorded in a range of ways. The development of a system, such as highlighting or dating, is an individual or school preference. Marking the selected recording sheets in some way is referred to as 'placing the student/s on the Map of Development'.

There are a number of points that should be considered when placing students on the Map of Development.

- Indicators for each phase should be interpreted in conjunction with the Global Statement of the phase and with the indicators from the surrounding phases.
- With the exception of Role Play readers, students are considered to be in the phase where they exhibit *all* Key Indicators.
- When students display *any* of the indicators of the Role Play Reading phase, they are considered to be in that phase.
- For most students in the class, it will only be necessary to record information about the Key Indicators.
- It is important that any student behaviours (indicators) recorded have been displayed more than once, and in a variety of contexts.

FIRST STEPS READING MAP OF DEVELOPMENT: INDIVIDUAL STUDENT PROFILE SHEET

Student's Name: Celia Stone Year: One Teacher: Ms Teather School: Mt Yokine

ROLE PLAY		EXPERIMENTAL		EARLY	
USE OF TEXTS		**USE OF TEXTS**		**USE OF TEXTS**	
• listens to and demonstrates comprehension by talking about significant ideas from the text		✓ reads and demonstrates comprehension of texts by: ✓ recalling some ideas explicit in a text ✓ identifying the topic of a text ✓ selecting a limited number of explicit events to retell a text ✓ linking two ideas explicit in a text, e.g. *an action and its result*		• reads and demonstrates comprehension of texts by: - recalling key information explicit in a text - identifying the main idea explicit in a text - selecting events to retell a text, sometimes including unnecessary events or information - linking explicit ideas in a text, e.g. *compares a character at different points in the text*	
• displays reading-like behaviour, e.g. *holds book right way up, clicks mouse to see new window*		✓ demonstrates that print remains constant, e.g. *transfers knowledge of familiar words from one context to another*	4/6	✓ locates and selects texts appropriate to purpose, interest and readability, e.g. *uses library systems, skims contents page*	9/9
• knows that print carries a message but may 'read' their own writing and unfamiliar texts differently each time		✓ maintains the storyline when 'reading' familiar texts although limited words are read accurately			
• selects texts primarily for enjoyment, e.g. *uses cover and illustrations*		✓ with assistance, locates and selects texts appropriate to purpose or interest			
CONTEXTUAL UNDERSTANDING		**CONTEXTUAL UNDERSTANDING**		**CONTEXTUAL UNDERSTANDING**	
• makes links to own experience when listening to or 'reading' texts, e.g. *points to illustrations saying "I had a party."*		✓ expresses an opinion about a text, but may not always be able to justify it	4/6	✓ expresses and justifies personal responses to texts, e.g. *"I didn't like ... because..."*	
• identifies and talks about familiar characters/people from texts		✓ identifies the role of the author and illustrator of a text	3/3	• understands that authors and illustrators select information to suit a purpose and audience	
		✓ talks about the ways different people / characters are represented in texts, e.g. *The girl in this story plays football.*	3/3	• recognises how characters/people and events are represented and offers suggestions for alternatives	
CONVENTIONS		**CONVENTIONS**		**CONVENTIONS**	
• recognises own name or part of it in print		✓ recognises a small bank of known words in different contexts, e.g. *personally significant words*	4/6	• recognises a bank of frequently used words in different contexts, e.g. *high frequency words, personally significant words*	
• knows repetitive patterns in very familiar stories, e.g. *Run, run as fast as you can*		✓ identifies the letters of the alphabet by name or sound	4/6	• recognises all letters by name and their regular sound	
		✓ demonstrates understanding of the concepts and conventions of print, e.g. *left to right, top to bottom, capital letters*	3/3	• explains how known text forms vary by stating: - purpose, e.g. *procedures instruct* - some elements of organisation, e.g. *procedures have headings* - some elements of structure, e.g. *procedures list materials and steps*	
PROCESSES AND STRATEGIES		**PROCESSES AND STRATEGIES**		**PROCESSES AND STRATEGIES**	
• relies upon knowledge of topic and text organisation such as pictures when 'reading'		✓ draws upon a limited knowledge base to comprehend, e.g. *topic knowledge, sentence patterns and sound / symbol relationships*	4/6	• draws upon a small knowledge base to comprehend, e.g. *sight vocabulary, concept and text structure knowledge*	
• relies on the strategy of connecting to comprehend, e.g. *connects text to self*		✓ uses a limited range of strategies to comprehend, e.g. *predicting, comparing*	4/6	✓ uses a small range of strategies to comprehend, e.g. *self questioning, adjusting reading rate*	9/9
		✓ determines unknown words by using word identification strategies, e.g. *predicting using beginning letters and/or pictures*	4/6	✓ determines unknown words by using word identification strategies, e.g. *decoding using phonemes, onset and rime*	9/9
				• focuses on decoding words accurately when reading an unfamiliar text, which may result in limited fluency, expression and loss of meaning	

Teacher's Notes:
Enjoys visiting the school library-spending many lunch times @ library
Always keen to share her books with teachers likes talking about them.

Figure 2.10 Sample of a Student Profile

Link Assessment, Teaching and Learning

Placing students on the Reading Map of Development is just the beginning of the assessment, teaching and learning cycle. It is crucial that teachers continue to analyse student profiles so they will be better able to plan appropriate teaching and learning experiences.

Once a student's phase of development has been determined, the Major Teaching Emphases provide the first step in linking assessment, teaching and learning. These are provided at each phase of development, and are suggestions of appropriate priorities for students 'in that phase'.

Once Major Teaching Emphases have been selected for an individual, a small group or a whole-class focus, appropriate Teaching and Learning Experiences can be chosen from the corresponding phase in the Reading Map. The *Reading Resource Book* and other teacher resource material can provide further support for the chosen MTEs.

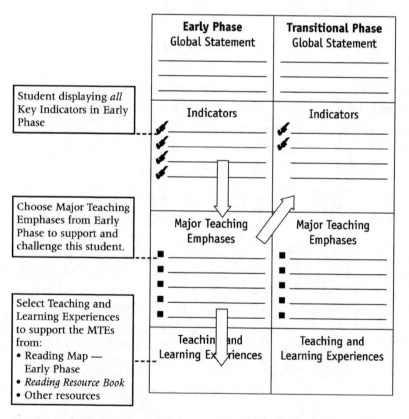

Figure 2.11 Choosing appropriate Major Teaching Emphases and Teaching and Learning Experiences

Monitor Student Progress

The Reading Map of Development can be used to monitor students' progress over time. It is crucial that teachers update the profiles of each student often enough to drive teaching and learning in the classroom so that student needs are constantly being met.

Decisions about the monitoring and updating process are a personal choice. Some teachers choose to focus on four or five students at a time; others choose to focus on the indicators from a particular substrand, or on students from a particular phase. These options help to make the monitoring and updating process manageable.

Frequently Asked Questions

Can I start using the Major Teaching Emphases and the Teaching and Learning Experiences before I have placed students on the Reading Map of Development?

Yes. The best way to start is to predict the phase of development of each student based on the Global Statement. Once this has been completed, you are able to choose the Major Teaching Emphases from the predicted phase. You can then select appropriate Teaching and Learning Experiences and use these as a springboard for collecting data in an ongoing manner.

Does a student have to display all Key Indicators of a phase to be 'in that phase'?

Yes. The phase in which the student is displaying all the Key Indicators is considered to be the student's phase of development.

There is, however, an exception to this when looking at students in the Role Play reading phase. When students display any of the indicators in the Role Play phase they are considered to be in that phase.

Do I need to place all students on the Map of Development?

It is important to be clear about your purpose for placing students on the Map of Development, and this will guide your decision about which students to choose. You may decide that for some students it is sufficient to predict using the Global Statement, and then use this information to select MTEs and Teaching and Learning Experiences. For others in the class you may gather information only about Key Indicators to create individual profiles. For a selected few, you may gather information about both Key Indicators and Other Indicators to create more detailed records of development.

How much evidence do I need to collect before an indicator can be marked or highlighted?

It is important to have sufficient evidence to determine whether a student consistently displays a particular behaviour. The most effective way to do this is to see the behaviour displayed several times in a range of contexts. Your professional judgement will help you decide whether the evidence you have is strong enough to mark the indicator. When in doubt, leave it out and wait until you have confirmation that an indicator is being displayed.

When would I use Other Indicators?

The Other Indicators list additional behaviours you may notice *some* students displaying. You may choose to use them when you are looking for more detailed information about a student.

How long should a student be in a phase?

There is no definitive time span. Some students may progress quickly through a phase, while others remain in the same one for a length of time. Each student is unique, and no two developmental pathways will be the same. Providing developmentally appropriate teaching and learning experiences will assist students to move along the Reading Map of Development.

How often do I need to update each student's progress on the Map of Development?

Data collection and analysis is an ongoing process, and the frequency of the collation of this information onto the map is your decision. However, it is crucial that you consider updating the profiles often enough to drive teaching and learning in the classroom so that student needs are constantly being met.

From which phase do I choose the Major Teaching Emphases?

Major Teaching Emphases are chosen from the phase where a student is displaying all Key Indicators; for example, if a student displays all of the Key Indicators in the Early Phase, the Major Teaching Emphases will come from the Early Phase. Major Teaching Emphases are designed to support students' current understandings and challenge them to begin displaying behaviours from the next phase.

Within a phase, which Major Teaching Emphases do I choose?

Any of the MTEs in the phase where students display all the Key Indicators will be appropriate. To select the most appropriate, you may take into consideration:

- the students' interests, strengths and needs;
- any 'gaps' in previous teaching;
- the grouping arrangements;
- links to other literacy strands and what is being taught in other learning areas.

The Major Teaching Emphases are designed to be revisited many times in different contexts, using different texts. This selection and revisiting process continues until students consistently display all key indicators in the next phase.

How do I use the Student Self-Assessment pages?

The Student Self Assessment pages are designed to be completed by the students. These pages can be completed over time either independently or with teacher support. This could happen during student conferences, reflection sessions or as part of an interview. These pages provide a springboard for individual goal setting.

Why are there no activities for students in the Processes and Strategies substrand in the Map of Development?

The activities for the Processes and Strategies substrand are in the *Reading Resource Book*. The rationale for this is that all readers make use of a range of processes and strategies that are not hierarchical, and are therefore not phase-specific. The activities in the *Reading Resource Book* can be applied across a range of phases to develop efficient use of the processes and strategies being introduced or consolidated.

Can I use the Map of Development with students who have English as an Additional Language?

Yes, the map can be used with EAL students. However, there are different considerations for those who are print-literate in another language and those who are not.

For students who are print-literate in a language other than English

Students who speak, read and write languages other than English may already be aware that each language has its own features. Some of these understandings can be transposed from one language to another; others cannot. This means that such students may have a well-developed understanding of language as a system, but not in those aspects of language that are peculiar to English.

When using the Map of Development with these students, consider the following.

- Their thinking and cognitive ability usually far outstrips their ability to read in English.
- Their understanding of oral texts is usually more advanced than their ability to express themselves in English.
- Their competence in using social language may mask difficulties they are experiencing with the language of learning.
- They tend to use elements of their own language as a bridge to learning the English language system, e.g. **directionality of print**.
- Their competencies may vary according to the similarity or difference between their home language and specific aspects of English.

For those not print-literate in a language other than English

Young students who have not learnt to read and write in any language seem to follow a pattern of development similar to that of students learning to read and write English as their first language.

Older students may progress in a similar way, but may make conceptual leaps and so progress more quickly than their younger counterparts. This is due to their maturity and greater cognitive development. They may not display behaviours from the Role Play and Experimental phases.

In using the *Reading Map of Development* to record a student's behaviours, patterns will emerge indicating strengths and needs. The behaviours exhibited may extend across a number of phases; therefore, it may not be appropriate to identify an EAL student as being in one particular phase. In order to tailor instruction appropriately, you may need to select Major Teaching Emphases from more than one phase of the map. (See *Linking Assessment, Teaching and Learning*, Chapter 4, for further information about *First Steps* and Diversity.)

CHAPTER 3
Collecting Data to Assess Reading Development

Chapter 6 of *Linking Assessment, Teaching and Learning* provides detailed information about beliefs of assessment and evaluation that underpin the *First Steps* resource. The data-collection tools listed in that chapter are generic, and can be applied to all areas of literacy. The focus of this chapter is on how data-collection tools can be used specifically to make judgements about students' reading development; the ideas and suggestions provide support for teachers when placing students on the *First Steps* Reading Map of Development.

Planning for success in reading requires teachers to find out what individual students know and can do. It is useful to ask the following questions.
• What information is needed?
• What are the most efficient and valid ways to collect the information, and who should collect it?
• How can the information be collected?
• How can the information be recorded?
• What can be done with the information?
• How can the information be shared with others?

Different data-collection tools will provide different perspectives on reading performance, so it is important to use a range. Decisions teachers make about which assessment tools to use, and how and when to use them, impact on the quality of the judgements made. These decisions can also impact on the messages given to students about 'what counts' in reading. It is important to develop efficient and valid ways of assessing reading, and to involve students, parents or care-givers, and other teachers in the process of collecting and recording data.

What Are the Most Efficient and Valid Ways to Collect Reading Information?

Data can be collected in several ways and can be grouped under the following broad headings.
• Focused Observation
• Reading Products
• Conversations

Focused Observation	Reading Products	Conversations
Formal and informal observation	Self-assessment Think-alouds Work samples Retells Surveys and questionnaires Tests Cloze procedure Oral reading	Conferences Interviews

Focused Observation

Powerful assessment takes place when teachers are observing students at work in regular classroom activities. Assessment need not be a separate procedure; it can happen as part of everyday teaching and learning. Observation involves much more than simply watching or listening to students in the classroom; it involves systematic collection of observable data and analysis of that information. It is one way of finding out what students know and can do in reading. It allows teachers to assess specific strategies students use — or understandings they demonstrate — either during reading experiences or in other learning areas. Focused observations in reading can be carried out in either an informal or a formal way — or both.

1 Informal Observations

Informal observations are unplanned. The teacher simply notes reading behaviours as they naturally happen.

2 Formal Observations

Formal observations are planned with a predetermined focus; this could be the reading behaviours to be targeted, or the students that will be observed. The teacher also decides when and how often formal observations will occur, and how they will be recorded.

What Information Can Be Collected?

Focused observations can provide teachers with information about student attitudes and student performance in the substrands. The following questions may provide a focus for observation.

- Is the student actively engaged in the reading? e.g. concentrating on the task, responding to something that is read, looking carefully at the pictures.
- Does the student use any avoidance strategies to get out of reading? e.g. leaving the room, wandering around, losing books or leaving them at home.
- Are there any behaviours that may signal problems? e.g. subvocalising, pointing to each individual word, fidgeting.
- Does the student self-select texts for silent reading? Does the student select a variety of texts?
- In Book Discussion Groups, does the student comment on the interpretation of the text and provide justification for opinions?
- What strategies is the student using to identify unknown words?

Reading Products

The assessment of both process and product is important when making decisions about supporting students' reading development. Teachers can assess not only the final products that are a result of learning, but also products that have been created during the process of learning. The *Reading Map of Development* can provide teachers with the support necessary when analysing selected work products.

As well as using focused observation for assessment in a classroom, teachers can consider what further information can be gathered from oral, written or visual work products. The following products are detailed.

1 Self-Assessment Products

2 Think-alouds

3 Work Samples

4 Retells

5 Surveys and Questionnaires

6 Tests

7 Cloze Procedures

8 Oral Reading

1 Self-Assessment Products

Self-assessment is a critical part of developing a student's responsibility for his or her own learning. Self-assessment can provide teachers with insights into reading development that otherwise might not be apparent. With teacher support and guidance, students can develop the skills necessary for them to assess their own reading. There are a variety of tools that can be used to encourage students to reflect on and make judgements about their learning; these include reading logs, goal-setting frameworks, and journals.

READING LOGS

A Reading Log, in its simplest form, is a place in which to record texts that have been read. The purpose of the Reading Log — together with the age and experience of the student — will determine the way it is used and structured. The sample in Figure 3.1 provides a suggestion of the types of entries that can be made. Further formats can be found on the Reading CD-ROM.

Reading Log

Name **Troy**

Type of Text	Title	Date
newspaper/magazine	Fishing Monthly	12/3
	Soap	10/10
comic	Asterisk	19/7
poetry	Weird and Wacky Poems	
biography		
mystery		
adventure	Harry Potter 1	2/8
	Harry Potter 2	30/8
historical fiction	Smithy	28/2
science fiction	Up in the Stars	5/4
	Journey Forward	15/4
procedural (how to)		
Jokes	Greatest Jokes Ever	3/2
	Greatest Animal Jokes Ever	10/6

Figure 3.1

What Information Can Be Collected?

Reading Logs provide teachers with information about a student's use of texts, including insights into a student's interests, preferences, attitudes or understandings.

PERSONAL READING GOALS

Setting reading goals and assessing the achievement of those goals is another form of self-assessment suitable for all students. It can provide the teacher with valuable information about reading strategies, and can assist students to develop independence in reading.

Reading goals can be recorded in many ways. They may be written in students' Reading Journals or recorded on goal-setting sheets. Once a goal is recorded, the teacher and the student can work together to monitor it. The cumulative record of goals can provide evidence of successful learning; it shows both teacher and student the specific reading strategies and understandings that have been learnt. It also clearly demonstrates the progress that is being made towards improving reading. For students who are just beginning to set reading goals, goal-setting frameworks can provide support.

Me as a Reader

Name: _____

How do you feel as a reader? Make this face look like that.

The kinds of reading I like to do are _____

_____

I like reading when _____

_____

I am getting better at _____

My New Reading Goal

Now I want to get better at _____

Figure 3.2 A sample goal-setting framework

My Reading Goal

I will re-read when I lose the meaning in my reading

Michelle reads her goal regularly during the week, and she and her teacher focus on using the identified strategy during lesson times.

She shades separate rings on the target to show progress towards achievement of her goal. She demonstrates achievement of the goal using Think-alouds, and through discussion with the teacher in lesson times.

When the goal is reached, it is dated and a new goal is set.

Figure 3.3 A personal goal record sheet

Reading Strategies and Goals

I use these reading strategies.

- _____
- _____
- _____
- _____
- _____
- _____

I'm working on these reading strategies.

- _____
- _____
- _____
- _____
- _____
- _____

Figure 3.4 Strategy and goal records indicate what has been learnt

What Information Can Be Collected?

Reviewing students' reading goals will provide information about processes and strategies they are using to comprehend texts.

READING JOURNALS

Reading journals allow students to record their personal expectations, reactions and reflections about texts before, during and after reading. These journals can be organised and used in many different ways, depending upon the purpose. The different types of reading journals include the following:
- Response Journals
- Dialogue Journals
- Reflective Journals
- Metacognitive Journals
- Summative Journals

Reading journals provide a framework for students to:
- record responses to texts;
- reflect on their selection of texts;
- record relevant background knowledge and experiences;
- clarify their thoughts about authors' messages and purposes;
- share thoughts with others.

All journal writing requires clear guidelines, and there should be regular opportunities to make entries during class time; however, so that this will not become tedious, they can be made every second or third day. All types of entries need to be modelled extensively before students use them independently, although the emphasis will be on content and meaning, not on mechanics and spelling. Until students are familiar with journal writing, teachers can brainstorm and chart possible sentence starters or questions as prompts for responses.

If journals are being used as a data-collection tool, they need to be collected and analysed on a regular basis.

Response Journals

Response Journals can be a record of thoughts and questions about the texts being read; they allow students either to respond to the message of the text or to focus on their personal reading strategies and goals. Adhesive notes are an excellent way for students to record their thoughts as they read; alternatively, they can be provided with frameworks to help focus their responses. Formats can be found on the Reading CD-ROM.

My Reading Response Journal	
My favourite part of the story. My favourite character.	I liked it. ☺ It was all right. 😐 I didn't like it. ☹

Figure 3.5 A sample Response Journal framework

Reading Response Journal Prompts

- What are some similarities or differences between the character in the book and yourself?
- Has anything similar to what happened in the book happened to you? Explain.
- What do you think will happen next?
- What makes you think that?
- What is the problem the central character must solve?
- Describe one of the scenes from the story.
- What is unclear or puzzling about the story?
- Why did the central character behave in the way he/she did?
- Retell the story.
- Compare the text with previously read books or movies.
- What were turning point/s in the book?
- What questions do you have for the author?

Figure 3.6 Prompts assist the student to question and understand

Dialogue Journals

Dialogue Journals are 'conversations' in writing conducted by the student with either a peer or the teacher; they allow students to correspond with others about their reading. The student writes a response to the text message and the teacher or peer writes a short reply.

Learning How to Learn in Reading

Choose a text you have recently finished reading.

Record the strategies you used in your reading.

Record the way you solved any problems you had.

Share your process with a friend, explaining exactly what you did.

Figure 3.7 A sample reflective framework

Reflective Journals

Reflective Journals can focus on particular reading activities. A prepared framework helps students to reflect on the processes, feelings and outcomes of the activities.

Metacognitive Journals

Metacognitive Journals provide a framework to help students think about and become aware of their own thought processes when constructing and comprehending texts.

'What have I learnt?' and 'How did I learn it?' are two key questions for them to consider.

Thinking About Your Reading

1 I found this text to be: Easy/Difficult (circle one)

2 The best part of this reading was _____

_____

_____

3 Strategies I used well were _____

_____

4 Something I want to work on for the future is

_____

_____

Figure 3.8 A sample framework for a Metacognitive Journal

Summative Journals

Summative Journals may be completed at the end of a theme, a unit of work or a specified period of time. Students reflect on a series of past reading events and consider future application of new learning.

What Information Can Be Collected?

Any type of journal entry provides a source of information about any of the four substrands of reading.

OTHER SELF-ASSESSMENT FORMATS

Many self-assessment tools are available commercially. Teachers can use — or adapt — those that will suit their teaching styles, their students and the teaching context. Consider the following.

Two Stars and a Wish provides students with a simple framework for reflecting on positive aspects of their work (the stars) as well as focusing on an area for improvement (the wish). It also provides a simple framework for peer assessment.

Two Stars and a Wish

Two stars and a wish for _____

Figure 3.9

Student self-assessment formats are provided for each phase of the Reading Map of Development. These will:

- support teachers as they involve students in the data-collection and reflection processes;
- support students to reflect on their own reading and to set reading goals;
- reflect the Indicators of each phase, but have been written in student-friendly language;
- are designed to be completed by students.

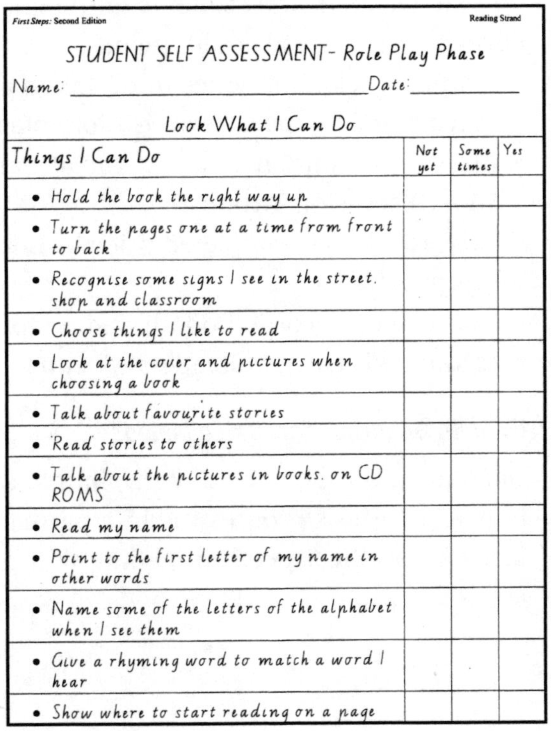

First Steps: Second Edition   Reading Strand

STUDENT SELF ASSESSMENT - Role Play Phase

Name: _____ Date: _____

Look What I Can Do

Things I Can Do	Not yet	Some times	Yes
• Hold the book the right way up			
• Turn the pages one at a time from front to back			
• Recognise some signs I see in the street, shop and classroom			
• Choose things I like to read			
• Look at the cover and pictures when choosing a book			
• Talk about favourite stories			
• Read stories to others			
• Talk about the pictures in books, on CD ROMS			
• Read my name			
• Point to the first letter of my name in other words			
• Name some of the letters of the alphabet when I see them			
• Give a rhyming word to match a word I hear			
• Show where to start reading on a page			

Figure 3.10

2 Think-alouds

Think-alouds are articulations of a reader's thoughts before, during and after reading. They may be the student's spontaneous reactions to the text, or may be encouraged or requested by the teacher.

The analysis of a student's Think-aloud can provide insights into the strategies being used to comprehend text. Although Think-alouds are not exact replications of a reader's complete thinking, they do alert teachers to the hidden processes taking place in the reader's mind.

PROCEDURE

- Model and explain how to 'think aloud'.
- Have students read the text, stopping at a predetermined place to think aloud.
- Record and then analyse the thoughts.

What Information Can Be Collected?

When analysing a Think-aloud, the teacher will be looking for patterns in the student's responses. These patterns will reveal the processes and strategies the student is using to comprehend text.

3 Work Samples

A range of work samples from everyday classroom practice can provide teachers and students with concrete evidence of reading development. These could include:
- comprehension activities undertaken as part of strategy instruction, e.g. book reviews, story maps;
- annotations students have made as part of their preparation for Book Discussion Groups;
- role task sheets completed prior to Book Discussion Groups (see Figure 3.11);
- oral reading recorded on an audio tape;
- productions such as Readers' Theatre.

What Information Can Be Collected?

Depending on the task, a work sample can assist teachers to see how a student is progressing in a particular substrand or can help identify specific aspects of reading that need emphasis in following lessons.

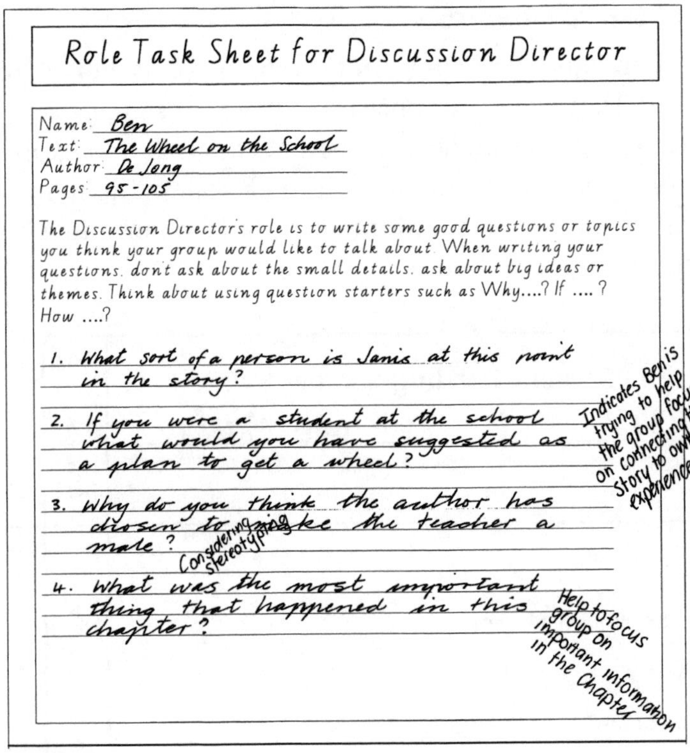

Role Task Sheet for Discussion Director

Name: _Ben_
Text: _The Wheel on the School_
Author: _De Jong_
Pages: _95 - 105_

The Discussion Director's role is to write some good questions or topics you think your group would like to talk about. When writing your questions, don't ask about the small details, ask about big ideas or themes. Think about using question starters such as Why....? If ....? How ....?

1. What sort of a person is Janis at this point in the story?

2. If you were a student at the school, what would you have suggested as a plan to get a wheel?

   Indicates Ben is trying to help the group focus on connecting the story to own experiences

3. Why do you think the author has chosen to make the teacher a male? *Considering stereotypes*

4. What was the most important thing that happened in this chapter? *Help to focus group on important information in the chapter*

Figure 3.11

4 Retells

Retelling focuses students on meaning, as they are involved in reconstructing a text. It is an effective activity from which to observe or ascertain the level of comprehension; it requires students to focus on choosing and sequencing relevant information from literary or informational texts. For further explanation about retelling, see 'Read and Retell' activities, Chapters 5–7, Use of Texts, Involving Students.

What Information Can Be Collected?

Oral or written retells can provide teachers with valuable information about any of the four substrands:

- in Use of Texts, e.g. selecting and sequencing the ideas or events, using explicit and/or implicit information to make inferences;
- in Contextual Understanding, e.g. retelling a text from a different point of view;
- in Conventions, knowledge of text form, e.g. text structure and organisation, language features;
- in Processes and Strategies, the strategies used to comprehend text, e.g. identifying important information, summarising, paraphrasing.

5 Surveys and Questionnaires

Reading surveys and questionnaires can take many forms and address a range of topics. They typically consist of a series of statements or questions about which the students or parents are asked to express agreement or disagreement (sometimes using a scale). The items to be included on the survey or questionnaire will be determined by the type of information required.

Student Reading Survey Name: _Shana_ Date: _March_	Always	Sometimes	Not at all
1 I like to read.		✓	
2 I like other people to read to me.	✓		
3 I can read by myself.	✓		
4 When I come to a word I don't know, I can figure it out.		✓	
5 I can tell what a story has been about after it has been read.	✓		
6 I like to choose my own books to read.	✓		
7 I like to read at home.		✓	

Figure 3.12 A sample student reading survey

Parent Questionnaire – Reading

Child's name: _Frances_   Date: _24 April_

1 Does your child imitate 'adult' reading behaviour? e.g. holding the book, turning the pages.

Always   —X——   Sometimes   Not yet

2 Does your child recognise his or her own name, or some of the letters?

Always   —X——   Sometimes   Not yet

3 Does your child select favourite books to be read?

Always   —X——   Sometimes   Not yet

4 Does your child enjoy listening to stories, and ask for them to be read and re-read?

Always —X—   Sometimes   Not yet

5 Does your child like to read at home?

Always   —X—   Sometimes   Not yet

Figure 3.13 A sample parent questionnaire about reading

What Information Can Be Collected?

Surveys and questionnaires can be used to ascertain students' reading attitudes and interests, or to glean information about their home reading practices.

6 Tests

Testing is another way of gathering data about a student's reading development, and should be used in conjunction with other data-collection tools. Several types of tests are available, but generally they can be categorised under the following headings.

CRITERION-REFERENCED TESTS

Criterion-referenced tests are designed to measure how well students have learnt a specific body of knowledge or certain skills. Therefore, they can provide information related to strengths and weaknesses.

NORM-REFERENCED TESTS

Norm-referenced tests are often referred to as Standardised Tests. They are the formalised tests in which scoring, norms and administration have been established as a result of each having been given to a large number of students. They are administered under specific conditions adhering to the directions set out in the examiner's manual. The performances of other students are presented as norms for the purpose of comparing achievement.

TEACHER-MADE TESTS

Many teachers devise their own tests to measure student progress in reading. These are generally criterion-referenced, and measure the students' mastery of what has been taught. The advantage they have over other types is that they can be tailored to a specific group of students or to specific information the teacher is seeking.

What Information Can Be Collected?

Tests give information about a student at a particular time, situation and place. The information may or may not be able to be generalised to apply to other situations, times or places.

Tests may provide information about particular aspects of any of the substrands. The analysis of errors and misunderstandings they present can provide teachers with direction for planning an effective reading program.

7 Cloze Procedures

Cloze involves deletion of words from a passage according to various criteria. In order to complete the cloze, students use the context of the passage to supply words to fill the spaces.

Cloze passages are purposeful practice activities that assist students to value contextual information. When they discuss and justify their choice of words to complete a cloze, they are further focused on this contextual information.

PREPARING THE TEXT

Students should be familiar with the cloze procedure before completing any tasks that will be used for assessment and evaluation.

Cloze should always be done with a text that has content familiar to the students so that they are able to use prior knowledge to help 'cloze' it. A text that provides lots of context clues will assist their word selection. The first and last sentences — perhaps even the first two or three sentences — and all punctuation should be left intact to allow the reader to establish the gist of the passage. When preparing the final text, each deleted word should be replaced with an underlined blank space. Spaces should be of equal length to avoid giving visual clues, unless this is the focus of the cloze passage.

When using cloze activities as an assessment tool, selection of words for omission will depend on the information being sought. Words can be deleted either randomly or selectively, but selective deletion has a greater instructional benefit.

Random Deletions

Random deletions are made at regular intervals, such as at every fifth or seventh word. Proper nouns, dates, sums of money or numbers are not usually deleted unless there are sufficient clues in the text to help readers identify the word. If the random selection falls on one such word, the following one should be chosen instead.

Selective Deletions

Selective deletion includes:
- deleting content words such as nouns, main verbs, adjectives or adverbs in order to provide information about a student's knowledge of the topic or use of semantic cues;
- deleting structural words such as conjunctions, prepositions and auxiliary words to provide information about a student's use of syntactic cues;

• deleting initial, medial or final consonants from some words to provide information about a student's use of graphophonic cues.

ORAL CLOZE

Shared Reading provides a suitable context to introduce oral cloze. Environmental print in the classroom such as labels, instructions, rhymes, songs or language experience stories could also be used for oral cloze activities. The procedure is as follows.

• Words are selected for omission, and covered.
• The teacher reads aloud the chosen text, pausing to encourage students to complete sentences or phrases with appropriate and meaningful words, and to justify their choices.

WRITTEN CLOZE

Students must read the whole text before they begin filling the spaces.

• To ensure that insertions make sense, in the passage, students should be encouraged to think what would make sense and then to check that it does. Synonyms that retain the meaning are acceptable. Students should be encouraged to discuss the reasons behind their word choice, and the context clues they used to determine the selection.
• The completed passage must be read to check for meaning. At this stage, students may read silently or orally.
• Scaffolding is provided for the reader by proceeding from oral to written cloze, by moving from whole-class to small-group to individual work, or by providing examples or options for the words deleted.

What Information Can Be Collected?

Cloze passages are particularly useful if teachers are seeking information in the Conventions or Processes and Strategies substrands. By structuring passages that require students to do different things with language, information can be gained about understandings of word meanings (semantics), language patterns (grammar or syntax) and the relationships between letters and sounds (graphophonics).

8 Oral Reading

Oral reading is highly complex, drawing on the reader's ability to understand the meaning of a text and convey that meaning to an audience. Oral reading is a useful assessment tool, as it provides a window into the mind of the reader. By analysing students' oral reading miscues, teachers can get some idea of the strategies they are using successfully, those they may be overrelying on and those that need developing.

Oral reading can be either rehearsed or unrehearsed. Rehearsed oral reading gives students an opportunity to practise reading the text aloud before reading it 'in public'; the aim of this is to convey meaning to an audience through expression and fluency.

Unrehearsed oral reading, on the other hand, usually involves the student in reading a passage that is unfamiliar, but that may have been read silently beforehand.

What Information Can Be Collected?

Oral reading is an opportunity to observe how students apply what they know about reading. It enables the teacher to collect information about the Processes and Strategies substrand. As the student reads, the teacher is able to determine the strategies and cues the student is using and those requiring further development. Teachers often use a Miscue Analysis or Running Record to record unrehearsed oral reading.

MISCUE ANALYSIS

A miscue analysis (Goodman & Burke 1972) is a detailed diagnostic procedure for recording, analysing and interpreting deviations from a text read aloud. (A miscue is defined as any departure from the text.) Terms such as 'mistake' or 'error' have negative connotations, whereas a miscue, although a deviation from the text, can contribute to the meaning — or, at the very least, preserve it. A miscue analysis is often conducted in conjunction with teacher questioning and a retell of the text to get a fuller picture of the students' understanding.

Completing a miscue analysis can, however, be time-consuming, so many teachers limit its use to specific students considered to be at risk, or perhaps involving all students at major milestones in the school year. The procedure involves the following steps.

- Select a text and invite the student to preview it. It must be an unfamiliar text at a level that the student can read independently, but of sufficient length and difficulty that a number of miscues will be made. It should be self-contained, so that a cohesive interpretation can be made.
- Photocopy the text to record the miscues. If this is impractical because of copyright considerations, the lines of print being too close together, or there being so few words on a page that paper is wasted, the text may be typed. Some teachers choose to number

each line of the text for easy reference. Alternatively, miscues can simply be recorded without the text being copied out.

- If desired, a tape recorder can be set up in a quiet place, away from distractions. This makes it possible to return to the reading and complete or refine the recording of miscues at a later time.

- Ask the student to begin reading the text. If problems arise with the reading, encourage the student to persevere and try to solve them. Only after an extended pause should any prompt be offered, and then simply to say, 'Just do whatever you usually do when you come to a word you don't know'.

- Use a coding system to record the miscues. Leave an introductory section of the text unmarked to give the reader an opportunity to establish some familiarity and fluency with the passage.

Type of error	Coding
Substitution	Write word above
No attempt made	Underline
Insertion	Write word
Omission	Circle omission
Self-correction	Write word used and SC
Reversal	Arrow both words

- At the conclusion of the oral reading, it is appropriate to ask the student to retell the text and to answer some questions.

- Analyse enough of the miscues to gain an understanding of how the student is reading — it may not be necessary to analyse them all. The focus is not on the number of miscues, as all readers make them, but on the effect they have on meaning. They can be sorted according to the semantic, syntactic and graphophonic cues being used.

- Analyse the retelling and the answers to the questions, possibly including comments about the student's attitude, comprehension, understanding of concepts or use of reading strategies.

Analysis of Miscues

Student: *Peter Cook*	Date: *24-11-2004*					
Student wording	Text wording	Type of miscue	Meaning lost	Meaning retained	Self-corrected	Instructional ideas
house	home	substitution		✓		
turtle	table	substitution	✓			Visual/imagery/cloze
—	the	omission		✓		

Figure 3.14

Conversations

As well as using focused observation and the collection of products, teachers can also consider what further information can be gathered through conversations.

Both incidental conversations and scheduled conferences will provide valuable information that may not be collected in other contexts. Teachers who ensure they are having conversations with individual students on a regular basis can gain a deeper understanding of their reading development.

Information about the following types of conversations is detailed.
1 Conferences
2 Interviews

1 Conferences

There are a variety of ways to involve students in reading conferences. These include:
• one-on-one conferences — teacher and student;
• peer conferences — student and student;
• small-group conferences — students;
• three-way conferences — student, teacher and parent.

Each of these situations can provide a teacher with a data-collection opportunity; however, the one-on-one conference can also provide the opportunity for individual instruction.

Effective one-on-one conferencing centres on building relationships with individual students. For conferences to be successful, students need to know what is expected of them; for example, what their role will be, the conference structure, and the records that will be kept. Each student–teacher conference will be unique, but it can be helpful to have a planning framework, such as shown below.

Teacher–Student Conference Framework

Identify the focus for the conference.

What are you reading?

Where are you up to?

How can I help you?

What was your reading goal? Have you achieved it?

Hear input from the student: read some of the text; share thoughts about incidents or characters.

Offer praise: emphasise strengths.

Ask questions.

Give directions for the future: offer suggestions. Set a new reading goal, if appropriate.

Complete closure.

The following charts indicate the roles of teacher and student in building a successful reading conference.

The Role of the Teacher

Select a particular focus.

Encourage the student to talk.

Introduce new strategies and processes.

Provide feedback to students.

Record information after each conference.

Review students' reading goals and assist them to set new ones.

Use the information from conferences to plan future learning.

The Role of the Student

Be prepared.

Have current reading material and topics for discussion.

List some things about the text that may be confusing, thoughtful, insightful or unanswered. Be willing to discuss these.

Review the reading goal. Discuss problems or successes in achieving the goal.

Discuss any reading problems the teacher can help with.

Be prepared to set a new reading goal.

What Information Can Be Collected?

Reading conferences can be used to gain information in any of the four substrands, depending on the focus of the conference. Suggested comments and questions for each one are given below.

USE OF TEXTS

Tell me about the books you have been reading, Why did you choose this book? Describe the main character of this story.

CONTEXTUAL UNDERSTANDING

Are any of the characters in this book like people you know? Is there anything you wanted to find out about . . . that isn't in this book?

CONVENTIONS

When you were looking for information about . . ., what features of the text did you use to help? Show me a word, a letter, a capital letter.

PROCESSES AND STRATEGIES

What do you do when you come to a word you don't know? What do you think happened before? What do you predict will happen next? What do you do when your reading doesn't make sense?

2 Interviews

Interviews are one-on-one, prepared question-and-answer conversations between a teacher and a student or between a teacher and a parent.

Teacher–student interviews provide an opportunity for teachers to actively listen to students and encourage them to verbalise their thought processes. Teachers can design questions to focus on different aspects of reading — such as knowledge, attitude, strategies or task completion — depending on the purpose and the desired outcomes of the interview. However, planning questions that elicit useful information and encourage students to do most of the talking is a challenge; effective questions should be focused, open and probing, and encourage answers of more than one word.

Further examples of reading interview questions can be found on the Reading CD-ROM.

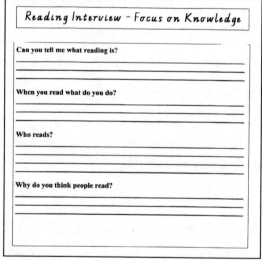

Reading Interview – Focus on Knowledge

Can you tell me what reading is?

When you read what do you do?

Who reads?

Why do you think people read?

Figure 3.15 One example of reading interview questions

Interviews with parents or caregivers can also provide useful information about students' reading outside school. In all interviews, it is important to consider the following points.

- Explain the reasons for the interview and limit questions to those that will yield the most useful information. This way, parents won't feel 'interrogated'.
- Let the parents know that you will be taking notes, and the reasons for this.
- Be sensitive to parents' levels of literacy.

Sample questions for a parent–teacher interview are shown in Figure 3.16.

Parent/Teacher Interview - Reading

Child's Name:_____
Parent/s name/:_____
Date:_____

What are your child's special interests?

How do you currently help your child with reading?

What are your child's strengths in reading?

What does your child read at home?

Does your child enjoy being read to?

Does your child read signs or other print in the environment?

Does your child talk about the things they see in books? On TV? On the Web?

What questions about helping your child become a better reader would you like to ask me?

Figure 3.16

What Information Can Be Collected?

Interviews can provide information about any of the four substrands, depending on the questions being asked. The previous questions are suggested as a guide only, and can be modified to suit different students or teaching contexts.

How Can Information About Reading Be Recorded?

Teachers use a range of ways to record the information they gather about students' reading development. The use of computers or palm pilots often helps streamline the time it takes to record information.

The following ways of recording information, on paper or electronically, are detailed.
1 Anecdotal notes
2 Checklists
3 Rubrics
4 Annotations
5 *First Steps* Reading Map of Development

1 Anecdotal Notes

Anecdotal notes are short, objective, factual descriptions of observations recorded at the time an event or activity occurs, or soon thereafter. Behaviours listed on the *First Steps* Reading Map of Development will provide a focus for observations.

- Making useful anecdotal notes takes time and practice. They should record an accurate description of the situation and information about students' strengths and weaknesses, and include comment and questions that may guide further observations.
- Notes should be written daily, and as soon as possible after an observation has been made. They can be written during a variety of reading procedures; e.g. **Guided Reading, Book Discussion Groups, Reading Conferences.**
- The recording format should suit the teaching situation, the students and the teacher's personal style; e.g. **grids, adhesive notes, the *First Steps* Reading Map of Development.** Two examples of grid formats are shown in Figures 3.17 and 3.18.
- The notes should be examined and analysed regularly to be sure that comments are being made for every student on a variety of reading behaviours in different contexts.

Cross-Curriculum Grid

Teacher: _Ms Handley_   Class: _5_   Date: _August_

Student	Mathematics	Technology and Enterprise	Social Studies	Science	Art and Music
Susan				15/4 Used scanning strategy to locate information in text	
Richard		8/3 Used knowledge of text organisation to locate information in an explanation			
Janette			26/6 Used text structure knowledge to link cause and effect		

Figure 3.17

Observation Grid

Teacher: _Janet Johnston_   Class: _Year 4 (8/9 year olds)_   Date: _Weeks 4/5, March 2-16_

Focus: _Reading Group 1_

Name: _Jack Bradley_	Name: _Mary Smith_	Name: _Peter Tan_
1 March Selected a new form for silent reading – Adventure stories Will need to check whether he enjoyed the genre – conference time???	8 March Remembered to use the punctuation correctly in guided reading group (changed voice to show someone speaking) 10 March Noticed a pattern between two stories we have been studying (the symbolism of light and dark representing good and evil).	12 March Recognised the way the illustrator had stereotyped the Princess – giving her blonde hair, blue eyes.
Name: _Suzie Lee_	Name: _Hans Jensen_	Name: _Elise Steckis_
10 March Suggested predicting using the cover and title before reading in guided reading group. Will need to reinforce this as she tends to rush in without thinking about what will be in the text.	2 March Oral reading was fluent with correct phrasing and intonation. Might ask Hans to work with Stephanie – having problems with phrasing. 8 March Showed Stephanie how to chunk phrases together to improve fluency.	12 March Made a text-to-self connection when reading in guided reading group.

Figure 3.18

2 Checklists

A checklist is a list of skills or behaviours to be checked off as they are observed. However, it is critical to acknowledge that checklists, whether teacher-made or commercially produced, are static. Most may not be applicable to every student in one classroom at the same time.

Name: Riley Williams Teacher: Anne Finlay Year Level: 1				
Concepts and Conventions of Print Checklist	Observed			Comment
Book handling: • front cover • title • turns pages from front to back • holds right way up • points to print/pictures	✓ ✓ ✓ ✓ ✓	✓ ✓ ✓	✓ ✓	
Concepts of print: • directionality — left/right, — top/bottom	✓	✓	✓	
Letter and word knowledge: • identifies first and last letters of a word • identifies first and last words on a page • matches some spoken and written words • knows that numerals and letters are different	✓ ✓			

Conventions of print:
• identifies — (.), (?),
           — upper case letter,
           — lower case letter
	✓			

Notes:

Figure 3.19 A sample checklist

3 Rubrics

Rubrics are recording frameworks that feature short, descriptive statements along a continuum of excellence. Teachers or students determine the quality of a performance against a set of predetermined criteria; for example, a retelling rubric may assess performance using criteria such as selection and sequencing of ideas and events, introduction to the characters, and setting the scene. Rubrics can be scored using either a numerical system or descriptive words or phrases, such as 'well-developed', 'partially developed', 'not developed'. Rubrics can be reused, adding levels of achievement as students' skill level increases or adding additional criteria for new concepts, skills or attitudes they display.

There are many publications and websites that offer ready-made rubrics; however, many teachers wish to create their own. Students also can be involved in the creation of rubrics, as ultimately it is their work that is being judged.

CREATING A RUBRIC

- Deciding on the criteria.

  Teachers may involve students in brainstorming the criteria.
  If students have not had experience in generating criteria for
  evaluation, teachers may wish to show them some models of
  completed work. Characteristics of effective and not-so-effective
  samples can be listed and discussed for inclusion as criteria on the
  completed rubric.

- Articulating the qualities.

  It is often easier to decide on the two extremes first; that is, what
  makes 'best' performance and what makes 'worst' performance.

- Deciding on the number of gradations.

  It is a good idea to have an even number of gradations, as this
  eliminates the tendency to rank in the middle.

- Deciding on the labelling to be used for the gradations and
  considering whether there will be a corresponding numerical
  value for each.

Some teachers prefer to use 'neutral' words for the gradation labels;
others prefer words that signal excellence, such as Lead, Bronze,
Silver and Gold rather than Unsatisfactory, Satisfactory, Competent
and Excellent.

Teachers may wish to involve students in self- or peer-assessment,
using the completed rubric, before work is formally submitted for
teacher evaluation.

Rubrics can be 'holistic' or 'analytic' in nature; holistic rubrics
evaluate the task as a whole, while analytic rubrics evaluate each
separate criterion. The tables that follow illustrate holistic and
analytic rubrics for oral reading.

Holistic Rubric for Oral Reading	
Level of Achievement	**Description**
4	Oral reading is fluent and conversational, demonstrating appropriate pace and phrasing. Self-corrects, with minor interruptions to the flow of reading.
3	Oral reading is uneven, alternating between fluent, smooth reading and slowed pace. Some self-corrections impede the flow of reading.
2	
1	

Analytic Rubric for Oral Reading				
Criteria	Quality			
Oral reading	4	3	2	1
Fluency	Fluency is consistent and conversational.			Reading is slow and laborious.
Voice quality				
Phrasing				
Unfamiliar words				

4 Annotations

Annotations are short descriptions of judgements made about a student's work recorded directly onto the work sample. Annotations may be completed at the time of the event, but this can be done at a later time if the work sample, such as written work, is portable.

Annotations need to be objective, factual comments, and should lead to the recognition and interpretation of individual patterns of learning over time.

5 The First Steps Reading Map of Development

The *First Steps* Reading Map is an excellent framework for recording information about reading development. Some teachers choose to record observations, the outcomes of conversations, or their analysis of products directly onto the Reading Map; this can be done by writing comments on adhesive notes, highlighting the indicators or recording the date when behaviours were displayed. Others prefer to use another recording method first — such as a checklist, miscue analysis or rubrics — and then transfer the information onto the Reading Map.

The following recording formats can be found on the Reading CD-ROM, and may be photocopied for classroom use.

1 Class Profile Sheet
2 Individual Student Profile Sheet — Key Indicators only
3 Individual Student Profile Sheet — all indicators
4 Class Profile Sheets — Key Indicators only
5 Class Profile Sheets — all indicators

CHAPTER 4

Role Play Reading Phase

Figure 4.1

Global Statement

Readers in this phase display reading-like behaviours when interacting with texts such as picture books, traditional tales, and simple informational texts. They rely heavily on topic knowledge, pictures and memorisation when 'reading' texts previously heard. Although Role Play readers may begin to identify their own name, or parts of it, they are yet to match spoken and written words.

Role Play Reading Indicators

Use of Texts

- ◆ Listens to and demonstrates comprehension by talking about significant ideas from the text.
- ◆ Displays reading-like behaviour, e.g. holds book right way up, clicks mouse to see new window.
- ◆ Knows that print carries a message, but may 'read' their own writing and unfamiliar texts differently each time.
- ◆ Selects texts primarily for enjoyment, e.g. uses cover and illustrations.
- • Attempts reading-like behaviours.
- • Recognises significant environmental print, e.g. signs, logos, labels.

Contextual Understanding

- ◆ Makes links to own experience when listening to or 'reading' texts, e.g. points to illustrations, saying 'I had a party'.
- ◆ Identifies and talks about familiar characters or people from texts.

Conventions

- ◆ Recognises own name, or part of it, in print.
- ◆ Knows repetitive patterns in very familiar stories, e.g. Run, run as fast as you can . . .

- • Uses some book language in retellings and play, e.g. Once upon a time . . .
- • Is beginning to understand directionality of print, e.g. front to back when turning pages.
- • Responds to and uses simple terminology such as book, right way up, front, back.
- • Is beginning to recognise some letters by name or sound, e.g. Sam says 'That's my name.' pointing to 's' in a 'Stop' sign.
- • Distinguishes print from drawings.
- • May know the alphabet by rote, but may need a visual clue to connect a letter with its name.
- • Identifies and supplies some simple rhyming words, e.g. hot, pot.

Processes and Strategies

- ◆ Relies upon knowledge of topic and text organisation, such as pictures, when 'reading'.
- ◆ Relies on the strategy of connecting to comprehend, e.g. connects text to self.
- • Comments on specific features in pictures.
- • Asks questions about signs, pictures and labels.

Major Teaching Emphases

Environment and Attitude

- Create a supportive classroom environment that nurtures a community of readers.
- Jointly construct, and frequently refer to, meaningful environmental print.
- Foster students' enjoyment of reading.
- Encourage students to take risks with confidence.
- Encourage students to select their own reading material according to interest or purpose.

Use of Texts

- Read and re-read a range of texts to students.
- Provide opportunities for students to 'read' and 're-read' a variety of texts, both literary and informational.
- Encourage students to respond to texts in a variety of ways, focusing on the meaning of print and pictures.
- Model reading behaviours such as book handling, distinguishing words from pictures, selecting texts.

Contextual Understanding

- Provide opportunities for students to talk about texts, relating them to their own experiences.
- Draw students' attention to the ways people or characters are represented in text.

Conventions

- Begin to build students' sight vocabulary, e.g. high-frequency words, personally significant words.
- Build phonological awareness and graphophonic knowledge, such as:
  - recognising, matching and generating rhymes
  - listening for sounds in words
  - linking letter names with their sounds, focusing on the regular sound.
- Teach students the concepts of print.
- Model the use of conventions of print, e.g. capital letters.
- Teach students the terminology associated with books, such as cover, title, author, illustrator.

Processes and Strategies

- Build students' knowledge within the cues, e.g. topic knowledge, sound–symbol relationships.
- Teach comprehension strategies, e.g. connecting, comparing.
- Teach word-identification strategies, e.g. predicting.
- Teach students how to locate, select and evaluate texts, e.g. using the layout of a library.
- Model self-reflection of strategies used in reading and encourage students to do the same.

Teaching and Learning Experiences

ENVIRONMENT AND ATTITUDE

Major Teaching Emphases

- Create a supportive classroom environment that nurtures a community of readers.

- Jointly construct, and frequently refer to, meaningful environmental print.

- Foster students' enjoyment of reading.

- Encourage students to take risks with confidence.

- Encourage students to select their own reading material according to interest or purpose.

Teaching Notes

An environment that supports and nurtures Role Play readers includes many opportunities to explore and interact with print; a combination of such opportunities will help foster an enjoyment of reading. Role Play readers need to feel comfortable in taking risks and in 'having a go' at reading and writing. They benefit from interacting with a variety of texts — those that are read to them and those they 'read' themselves.

Exploring Print

Owocki (1999) describes four functions of print supporting real-life purposes that can be provided for in the classroom.

- **Environmental** — print that gives us information about the world, e.g. signs, price tags, advertisements.
- **Occupational** — print associated with a job or profession, e.g. a doctor's prescription pads, referral forms, health records, patient progress records.
- **Informational** — print for storing, retrieving and organising information, e.g. calendars, clocks, diagrams.
- **Recreational** — print used for leisure activities, e.g. picture books, magazines.

Role Play readers can be provided with opportunities to explore the print that serves these various functions. Consider the following ideas.

Environmental

- *Labels* using full sentences can be attached to students' belongings and work.

Figure 4.2 Sample classroom labels

- *Everyday print* in the environment can be referred to both inside and outside the classroom so that students can begin to understand the purpose of written language, and the way it works. This can be done by talking about everyday print, encouraging students to bring in examples, preparing charts of community signs and taking students for walks around the community, pointing out and reading environmental print.
- *Charts* can be displayed at eye level so that they are easier for students to refer to. These may include alphabet and number charts, or a class list including photographs next to each name.

Occupational

- *Corners* can contain appropriate literacy materials; e.g., a supermarket could have advertising brochures, signs for 'specials' and print-outs from a checkout; a doctor's surgery might have magazines, pamphlets and health record charts. Establishing a corner in preparation for an excursion or a field trip, or as a result of it, gives the students a context and a purpose for exploring literacy.

Possible options for occupational corners could be:

author's or illustrator's studio
construction site
pet store
post office
hospital
museum
restaurant
science laboratory
weather station
airport
hairdresser's salon
travel agency
veterinary clinic

**Figure 4.3 'Anything You Want Restaurant'
created at a Pre-primary Centre**

Informational

- *Calendars* and *planners* can help to develop concepts of terms such as the days of the week, yesterday, today, tomorrow, week, month and year, as well as to record forthcoming events.
- *Word Walls* can include the names of the students in the class, as well as words they are currently learning or have recently learnt.

Recreational

- *A writing or word-study centre* can promote active inquiry into how letters and words work. Boards with magnetic letters, pocket charts with letter cards, and writing materials such as coloured paper, pencils, envelopes, tape and stamps can be included.
- *Songs, poems* and *rhymes* can be written on charts and read together. Pictures can be attached to help students identify them.
- *Reading corners* should include a variety of materials, such as literary and informational texts, picture dictionaries, electronic books, book and tape sets.

Interacting with Print

Encourage students to interact with and make use of the print provided in the classroom.

- Create opportunities to 'read the room'. Taking students on a 'print walk' around the room gives them the opportunity to 'read' and revisit charts they have made and words they have learnt. The print walk is also an opportunity to play games, such as matching words or phrases.

- Write daily messages for the students. Place these on the door and use them each morning as a stimulus for discussing print.
- Write and share sentences about planned cross-curriculum activities; for instance, 'Today we will make some very colourful masks. We will use lots of bright paper'. These sentences can provide another opportunity for students to interact with and discuss print.
- Write letters to individual students, mailing them in the class postbox. Invite students to take the letters home and 'read' them with an adult.
- Model the use of environmental print for different purposes, such as copying words, looking for letters, reading for pleasure or using a calendar to find a date.

Fostering Enjoyment of Reading

Take every opportunity to foster students' enjoyment of reading.
- Read to students every day from a variety of literary and informational texts, including electronic sources such as CD-ROMs, websites and software programs.
- Provide opportunities for them to select their own materials.
- Give students time and opportunities to 'read' to peers or themselves.
- Involve them with reading buddies from another class.
- Encourage students to bring favourite books from home to 'read' to friends.
- Make use of the school and local libraries.
- Encourage participation in book fairs.
- Invite guests, such as grandparents or visiting authors, to read to the class.
- Provide an enticing reading corner.

Encouraging Risk-Taking

Role Play readers can be encouraged to become risk-takers by being asked to:
- offer opinions about texts read aloud;
- use personal experience to make connections to ideas in the text;
- use a variety of strategies to comprehend;
- use a variety of cues to comprehend;
- join in saying favourite parts of a text when being read to;
- have a go at reading and writing.

For further information about Environment and Attitude, see:
- *Linking Assessment, Teaching and Learning*, Chapter 5: Establishing a Positive Teaching and Learning Environment;
- *Reading Resource Book*, 2nd edn, Chapter 1: Use of Texts.

USE OF TEXTS

Major Teaching Emphases

- Read and re-read a range of texts to students.

- Provide opportunities for students to 'read' and 're-read' a variety of texts, both literary and informational.

- Encourage students to respond to texts in a variety of ways, focusing on the meaning of print and pictures.

- Model reading behaviours such as book handling, distinguishing words from pictures, selecting texts.

Teaching Notes

In this phase students need many opportunities to interact with a variety of texts, both literary and informational, to help them become familiar with the language of books and reading. It is important that Role Play readers have frequent opportunities to listen to skilled readers and to respond to texts.

The foci for helping readers in this substrand are organised under the following headings.
- Variety of Texts
- Responding to Texts
- Reading Behaviours

Variety of Texts

Role Play readers benefit from having texts read and re-read to them. These could include songs, poems, rhymes, fairy or folk tales, traditional or modern stories, reports, procedures, timetables or environmental signs. They could be class-made, or published materials such as books, tapes, CD-ROMs or software programs.

Responding to Texts

After Modelled and Shared Reading of texts, Role Play readers can be provided with opportunities to respond in various ways; for example:
- asking questions of the author or illustrator;
- retelling the text from memory or by referring to the pictures;
- drawing or painting;
- making a model; or
- answering questions orally.

Responding to text can also involve students in answering questions about it. There are many ways of organising and discussing types of questions; e.g. **Bloom's Taxonomy (Bloom 1956), Question–Answer Relationships (Raphael 1986), Three Level Guides (Herber 1970) or Open and Closed Questions.**

Whichever questioning hierarchy is used it is wise to include questions that require different levels of thinking and begin to help students — particularly EAL students — recognise the nature of each one. The focus in this phase is on identifying explicit information; however, Role Play readers also benefit from opportunities to discuss information implicit in the text.

Raphael (1986) categorises questions as Right There (Literal), Think and Search (Inferential), Author and You (Interpretive) and On Your Own (Critical/ Evaluative), providing a useful framework for ensuring that different types of questions are used in the classroom.

Literal
Literal questions focus on what the author said. The answer is 'right there', explicitly stated in the text or pictures. Common literal questions begin with 'who', 'when', 'where' or 'what', and it is important that teachers follow them up with clarifying questions, such as 'How did you know that?' or 'Can you show me where . . . is in this picture?' so that students get the idea of substantiating answers by returning to the text.

Inferential
The answers to these questions can be found in the text but are not necessarily explicitly stated or in the one place; they are the Think and Search questions. They show relationships such as cause and effect, compare and contrast, or sequence. They are also sometimes 'how and why' questions: the student is required to 'put the answer together'; for example, 'What happened after . . .?', 'Why did Mr Jones . . . when he saw . . .?', 'How are . . . and . . . alike?'

Interpretive
These are the Author and You questions. They require the student to base the answer on the text, but also to draw on previous personal experience to reach a reasonable answer; examples are 'How is . . . different from or similar to people you know?' or 'Is this book like any other book you know? How?' The answer must not be a wild guess; it must be probable in light of the text, not just possible from the reader's experience.

Critical/Evaluative

These questions go beyond the text, asking for students' own opinions or judgements. They are the On Your Own questions, as the answers are not found in the text, although it does provide a starting point for discussions about the underlying messages. For example, critical questions after reading 'Little Red Riding Hood' could be 'Should Little Red Riding Hood's mother have let her go into the forest by herself?'; 'Should children be punished for not obeying their parents?'; 'Was the woodcutter right to kill the wolf?'

Reading Behaviours

Role Play readers benefit from regular opportunities to see, hear and 'have a go' at practising reading behaviours. In Modelled and Shared Reading sessions, often using an enlarged text, teachers can focus on demonstrating many aspects of reading, such as:

- reading behaviours and book-handling skills — turning the pages, looking at the words and pictures, holding the book the right way up;
- reading behaviours and electronic text-handling skills — clicking on an icon for more information, responding to on screen prompts;
- how to select a text — looking at the cover, flicking through the pages, choosing favourites to read again;
- concepts of print — pointing out that we talk about the pictures but read the print;
- how to identify important information in a text — looking at the pictures, making connections to things they know, ignoring banners and advertisements in Internet text;
- asking questions about and commenting on the text — 'I wonder why the . . .?', 'Do you . . .?';
- how to make predictions about what will happen;
- highlighting the point that texts with different purposes are constructed differently — informational texts may have photographs and tell facts.

> For further information about the Use of Texts substrand, see *Reading Resource Book*, 2nd edn:
> - Chapter 1: Use of Texts
> - Chapter 4: Processes and Strategies.

Involving Students

1 Read and Retell

Refer to Chapter 5: Experimental Reading Phase, page 107.

2 Choral Reading

Whole-class Choral Reading sessions are an ideal way to introduce readers to a wide range of enjoyable texts, and provide a meaningful context for repeated whole-group readings of a particular text. All students are able to join in with familiar parts of the text and to hear the tone used to express unfamiliar parts.

When introducing Choral Reading, it is important to use rhymes or stories the students already know. Action rhymes or songs are also appropriate texts.

Students work as a whole class, and with teacher support.
– Use an enlarged copy of the text, to read aloud.
– Allocate refrains or parts of the text, such as a repetitive phrase, to be read by the class.
– Read the text aloud several times and invite students to join in the 'reading' of allocated sections.
– Add any props, sound effects or movement that will enhance the presentation of the text.

3 Story Prop Box

Refer to Chapter 5: Experimental Reading Phase, page 108.

4 Text Innovation

Text Innovation is the name given to the process of adapting an existing text. Many texts lend themselves to innovation. When Role Play readers innovate on a text, they strengthen their understanding of the concept of a word and the concept of a sentence.

Innovations may include:
• *sentence-level innovations* — where the sentence structure is maintained but the words in the sentence are altered; for example, 'This is the house that Jack built' becomes 'This is the bike that Pedro made';
• *word-level innovations* — where a new word is substituted for an original one; for example, 'Brown Bear, Brown Bear what do you see?' becomes 'Brown Bear, Brown Bear what do you hear?'

– Select a simple story, rhyme or song that can be easily modified.
– Read the text several times until the students are familiar with the particular rhyme, rhythm or repetitive pattern.
– When working as a whole class and using a big book or an enlarged text, place sticky notes on words to be replaced in the original text.
– Invite students to make suggestions for alternative words to fill the spaces created by the sticky notes.
– Jointly select words and write them on the sticky notes, continuing until all spaces have been filled.
– Read the newly created text together.

This procedure can be adapted, as follows.
– Copy the text so that students can make further innovations, leaving spaces for their choice of words.
– Provide time for them to illustrate their innovations.
– Publish the innovations, and use them for further reading.

5 Picture Book Activities

Teachers can help build young students' understandings about texts by examining the links between illustrations and text in picture books.

– Randomly select illustrations from the text.
– Allow students time to share comments about the illustrations.
– Read the print corresponding to each illustration.
– Discuss whether the illustrations just support the text or tell something more. Guide the students to notice differences and similarities in written and pictorial text.

6 The Reading Olympics

This activity is particularly appropriate in any year of the Olympics, but it can be renamed to coincide with other sporting events. It involves students finding texts that satisfy specific criteria. It has the potential to involve family members as students 'go for gold' in finding texts to enter in the Reading Olympics.

– Discuss the meaning of 'going for gold' and the idea of creating records; that is, finding texts that meet a certain criterion.
– Discuss the criterion for the week, or a similarly allocated period. Criteria can be chosen to link to the current teaching focus; for instance:
  – the greatest number of words in a title;
  – the author's name with the most letters;
  – the largest book (in size, not thickness);

- the greatest number of pages;
- the greatest number of times a specific letter appears on a page, e.g. 'n';
- the longest sentence on a page;
- the longest word in a text;
- the greatest number of a type of punctuation mark on a page, e.g. commas.
- Invite students to 'go for gold' for a specified amount of time.
- At the end of the Reading Olympics, create a display showing the criterion, the entries, and the winning text.
- Award 'medals', for the winning text; these can be cut from card and attached to lengths of ribbon.

7 Sequencing Activities

Sequencing activities provide a meaningful context for Role Play readers to 'read' and 're-read' familiar text, focusing on the meaning of words and pictures.

- After students 're-read' a well-known text, have them sequence a series of pictures from it. The pictures could be either student- or teacher-made.
- Where sequences vary, have students return to the text to justify their choices.
- Organise students to use the pictures to retell the text to others.

As a variation, illustrations from textless picture books can be used. Students sequence the pictures, and so create the story to tell to others. Pictures illustrating parts of well-known poems, rhymes or songs can also be used for this activity.

8 Wall Stories

Wall Stories are large representations (including illustrations) of the main events of a text; they are an effective way of helping Role Play readers focus on the meaning of words and pictures. Literary texts with simple storylines are a great source for Wall Stories, as are songs, poems, rhymes and language-experience activities.

Students are able to reconstruct a text they have heard, working either as a small group or with the whole class.

- Read a chosen text to the students.
- Pair students to orally retell the text.
- Work with them to elicit and record the main events of the text on a chart or on large cards. (Alternatively, sequence prepared cards that list the main events.) When students are unsure of

information or disagree about a main event, model the process of returning to the text to clarify meaning.

– Organise students to work in small groups to illustrate the main events.

– Jointly sequence the completed cards and read the newly created text with the students.

Display the wall story and refer to it frequently during classroom print walks.

9 Dramatisation

Students develop a deeper understanding of texts when given the opportunity to express interpretations through a creative medium such as drama, art or writing. Dramatising favourite texts helps Role Play readers to focus on meaning. A student's level of understanding of a text can often be determined by observing a dramatisation.

Providing an interesting range of items, such as puppets, dress-up clothes and simple props, will often encourage students to dramatise familiar texts.

• It is easy to make simple puppets. One option is to use pictures from the text glued to ice-cream sticks or similar items. Finger puppets can be made by cutting the fingers from old gloves and using markers to draw the characters on the finger sections. Alternatively, cut-outs of the characters can be glued onto the gloves.

• Dress-up clothes can include hats, scarves, capes and aprons.

• Simple props can be masks, swords, wands, telephones and boxes.

Role Play readers can participate in dramatisation activities following the reading aloud of a text by the teacher. They can use any of the items mentioned above to:

• dramatise events, problems or solutions, such as Little Red Riding Hood meeting the wolf in the forest, the Gingerbread Man climbing onto the fox's back, or Prince Charming arriving at the door with the glass slipper;

• have a telephone conversation between two characters, such as Goldilocks and Baby Bear;

• retell the text.

Dramatisation efforts can be captured on video or digital camera and used for enjoyment, reflection and sharing.

10 Who Am I?

Solving Who Am I? riddles encourages Role Play readers to return purposefully to the text to find explicit information.

– After a shared reading, ask students to solve Who Am I? riddles that focus on characters from the text.
– Begin with broad, open clues and progressively add more specific clues, using those that focus on feelings, actions and speech as well as attributes; e.g. **I live near a forest where I like to go to pick flowers. I spoke to a stranger when I was told not to. I have a special red coat. My grandmother is sick in bed. I said, 'Oh granny, what big eyes you have.' Who Am I?**
– Model how to use the clues and the text to solve the riddle; e.g. **I think the Who Am I? is Little Red Riding Hood. In this picture she is walking through the forest wearing her red coat and she is picking some flowers. I remember that Little Red Riding Hood's grandma was sick, because it says so in the story.**
– When students are familiar with creating Who Am I? clues, guide them as a group to create their own.

Whole-class riddles could be created as part of Modelled or Shared Writing sessions.

11 Text Less

Creating text for textless picture books or story CDs allows Role Play readers to focus their attention on illustrations as a means of communicating a story. As these texts have no words, information about the setting, characters and events must be drawn from the illustrations. Using textless picture books is beneficial to Role Play readers, as it gives them an opportunity to practise oral storytelling and confirm their understandings of narrative story structure.

– As a whole class, examine the cover and the title of the book and discuss the clues they give to the contents of the text.
– Together look at each page of the text, asking students to share what they think is happening. Where necessary, elicit storylines by asking leading questions, such as 'What do you think is happening on this page?', 'What names could we give these characters?', 'What problems is . . . having?', 'What do you think . . . will say now?'
– Revisit each page, encouraging students to create the story as each one is turned.
– As they create the story, write it on strips of paper or, if desired, a chart. This can be 're-read' several times.

CONTEXTUAL UNDERSTANDING

Major Teaching Emphases

- Provide opportunities for students to talk about texts, relating them to their own experiences.

- Draw students' attention to the ways people or characters are represented in text.

Teaching Notes

Students in this phase can begin to develop an understanding that texts present particular experiences that may or may not be similar to their own. While it is desirable for them to have the opportunity to talk about these similarities and differences, the enjoyment of reading should not be replaced by overanalysis. In discussions, it is important to be sensitive to the text, the students, the context and the desired outcomes of the lesson. In this phase, the focus is on facilitating the exploration of each student's thinking, while refraining from influencing opinions.

In Modelled and Shared Reading sessions, begin to demonstrate how to relate what is being read to one's own experiences; for example, 'In this text, the family has a dog. It reminds me of the dog that I had as a child'.

The foci for helping Role Play readers to develop contextual understanding are organised under the following headings.
- Discussions about Texts
- Discussions about the Way People or Characters Are Represented in Texts

Discussions about Texts

For students to understand texts, they need to make connections between their own experiences and those presented in the text. This can be achieved in various ways.
- Encourage students to make such connections; e.g. **Has anything that happens in the story ever happened to you?**
- Have them compare events and people in texts with their own lives; e.g. **Is the family in this book like yours? How is your family the same or different? What do you do when you . . .?**

- Encourage them to share opinions about why a particular book is liked or disliked.
- Encourage them to think about whether a particular text could be true, and give their reasons; e.g. **Do you think this could really happen?**
- Invite them to imagine themselves in the text; e.g. **Who would you like to be? Why? What might you have done?**

Discussions about the Way People or Characters Are Represented in Texts

Role Play readers benefit from opportunities to have ongoing conversations about choices authors and illustrators make. This could include recognising and discussing how characters or people have been represented in a text; for example, the gender of the characters, the author's choice of details and the illustrator's use of colour.

It could be achieved in a range of ways.
- Invite students to talk about the story told in the words and that told in the pictures; e.g. **How do the pictures support the text?**
- Have them talk about why they think the illustrator has chosen to illustrate the text in a particular way; e.g. **Jane Dyer has chosen to use big pictures with rounded lines in her illustrations in this book. Why do you think she did that?**
- Encourage them to make comparisons between the people or characters in a text and people in real life; e.g. **Do you know any people who are like the characters in the story? Who are they? How are they the same? How are they different?**
- Encourage them to think about how people or characters are represented in texts; e.g. **In this book the children have been drawn with blond hair. Do all children have blond hair? What other hair colours could have been used?**
- Support them in reflecting on the names given to characters; e.g. **Why might the author have chosen Buster as the name for the boy in this story?**

For further information about the Contextual Understanding substrand, see *Reading Resource Book*, 2nd edn, Chapter 2: Contextual Understanding.

Involving Students

1 Goodies and Baddies Rating Scale

Refer to Chapter 5: Experimental Reading Phase, p. 116.

2 Catalogue Searches

Searching through catalogues allows students to make connections and comparisons between what they know about the world in which they live and the ideas portrayed in texts. The focus for Catalogue Searches is the decisions authors make when creating catalogue advertisements.

– Provide students with a collection of advertising catalogues either from a particular time of the year, such as summer, or focused on selling similar products, such as toys, books, children's clothes, camping gear.
– Have them skim through the catalogues. Discuss the types of items that are for sale.
– Involve them in discussion of which images are presented in the different catalogues. Focus their thinking by asking leading questions.
  – Who can you see in the pictures?
  – In what way are the people in the pictures the same?
  – How do you think the people in these pictures feel?
  – Who might be interested in the things in this catalogue but are not represented here?
  – Would you like these sorts of clothes/games/food?

3 Possible Predictions

Possible Predictions is an activity in which students are encouraged to make predictions about characters' actions or story outcomes. Making comparisons between personal predictions and what happens in the text assists readers to relate their personal experiences to the text.

– Read the text aloud, stopping at a preselected point: this should either be at a significant 'crossroad' or offer a variety of options as to what might happen next.
– Invite students to think about what they have heard so far and to make a prediction of what actions, events and/or outcomes might happen next. Encourage them to supply reasons for their predictions.
– Discuss the predictions and reasons with the whole group.

- Record the predictions under headings representing common ideas or themes.
- Continue to read aloud, discussing the choice or the pathway chosen by the author.
- Refer to the students' predictions and discuss how the outcome would have been different if their predictions had been part of the text.
- Speculate on why the author may have chosen the particular pathway that was published.

4 Changing Places

Inviting students to choose which character to change places with enables Role Play readers to make connections to the characters or people in a text. In this activity, students are required to justify why they chose a particular character.

- After reading a text, invite students to choose anyone in it with whom they would like to change places.
- Invite them to share the names of these characters, and give their reasons. Encourage them to return to the text to justify their choices; for example:
  - 'I'd like to be Cinderella, but only at the end when she married the prince'; or
  - 'I'd like to be the third little pig. He was clever, because he built his house with bricks and he tricked the wolf'.

5 Like or Unlike?

Like or Unlike? is an activity that helps students to make connections and comparisons between what they know about the world in which they live and the way characters or people are represented in a text.

- Select a main character or person from a text.
- Before reading the text, invite students to share what they know about that type of person or thing in real life; for example, ask: What do we know about grandmothers/smart children/ princesses/wolves?
- Record responses on a class chart.
- Ask students to draw their impressions or ideas of the character.
- Have them share their portraits with the whole class, discussing the characteristics they have included.
- Read the text to the class.
- Discuss how the character has been represented in the text. Record student responses on the class chart.

– Draw students' attention to any differences or similarities between what they know and how the characters may have been represented in the text.

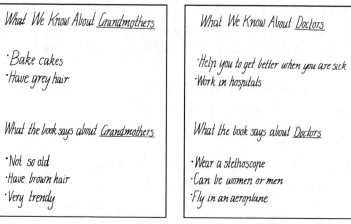

Figure 4.4 Whole-class generated Like or Unlike? charts

6 Hidden Pictures

Hidden Pictures is an activity that allows students to decide how the characters or people in a text could be represented. Creating a drawing of characters or people before the text has been read or viewed helps Role Play readers to understand that authors and illustrators make decisions to present a certain view of the world, which may differ from their own.

– Read an unfamiliar text without showing students the illustrations.
– After reading, allocate students a character or person from the text; ensure they have still not seen the illustrations.
– Ask them to draw the character or person.
– When the drawings have been completed, discuss:
  – what was heard in the text to help make decisions — 'In the story it said he had blond hair';
  – what was inferred from the text to help make decisions — 'He was laughing all the time, so I drew a happy face'.
– Invite students to share their drawings.
– Provide time for them to compare their drawings with the text illustrations.
– Discuss the similarities and differences.

7 Text Innovation

Text Innovation is the name given to the process of adapting an existing text. By completing innovation activities with a contextual understanding focus, students are encouraged to adapt characters, character traits, or setting. They will also consider the impact of their changes on the storyline.

- Select a text for innovation.
- Read it to the students several times.
- Select a feature that could be innovated upon. These could include:
  - changing the gender of one of the characters;
  - changing a character trait — instead of a mean character, have a kind character;
  - changing the setting of the text — 'Little Red Riding Hood' is set at the beach.
- Jointly innovate on the original text to create a new one, either oral or written. Discuss how any changes impact on the rest of text; e.g. **When we changed the characters from being mean to being kind, what else did we have to change?**
- Encourage students to make comparisons between the original text and the new version, sharing and explaining their preferences.
- If the innovation has been written, invite students to illustrate the new text and make it into a big book, a slide show or a wall story.
- As a whole class, work with students to re-read the newly created text.

8 Text Detective

Text Detective is an activity that requires students to consider the information provided in a title and in names of characters when making inferences. As with Hidden Pictures, completing this activity helps Role Play readers understand that authors and illustrators sometimes present a view of the world that may differ from their own.

- Before reading the text or showing the cover, read the title to students.
- Have them discuss what they suppose the author, in choosing the title, wanted them to think the text was about.
- Introduce the names of the characters.
- Have students share inferences about each character, based on their names and the title.
- Read the text to students. Discuss the characters, and make comparisons between what the students had inferred and what was in the text.
- Discuss how much information the title and the characters' names had given them before the text was read.

CONVENTIONS

Major Teaching Emphases

- **Begin to build students' sight vocabulary,** e.g. high-frequency words, personally significant words.

- **Build phonological awareness and graphophonic knowledge,** such as:
  - **recognising, matching and generating rhymes**
  - **listening for sounds in words**
  - **linking letter names with their sounds, focusing on the regular sound.**

- **Teach students the concepts of print.**

- **Model the use of conventions of print,** e.g. capital letters.

- **Teach students the terminology associated with books, such as cover, title, author, illustrator.**

Teaching Notes

Creating a rich oral-language environment that includes reading aloud, reciting poems and rhymes, singing songs and playing with language is a starting point for developing understandings about written language. Modelled and Shared Reading and Writing provide a springboard for exploring many of the concepts and conventions of print involved in written language. In this phase, draw students' attention to concepts and conventions of written language — for instance, that print is read from left to right.

The following suggestions are not intended to be prescriptive. Consider the needs of the students and the requirements of any curriculum or syllabus documents before making decisions about what to teach and when.

The foci for supporting Role Play readers to develop understandings about Conventions are organised under the following headings.
- Sight Vocabulary
- Phonological Awareness and Graphophonic Knowledge
- Concepts of Print
- Conventions of Print
- Book Terminology

Sight Vocabulary

Sight vocabulary is the bank of words a reader is able to automatically decode, pronounce and understand in the contexts in which they are used. Such words are called 'sight words' because efficient readers need to instantly recognise them on sight to maintain the speed and fluency required to make sense of the author's message. Many of these words have irregular spellings, making them difficult to decode.

It is estimated that 100 words make up about half of all we read (Fry et al. 1984); they make up what is known as the high-frequency vocabulary. If students are to become fluent readers, they need to learn to recognise them quickly and easily.

Sight vocabulary for Role Play readers could include:
• personally significant words, such as their names, and the names of classmates, their teacher, and family members;
• high-frequency words, such as words from the Dolch list (Dolch 1939), the Basic Sight Vocabulary (Holdaway 1980), or Fry's 300 Instant Sight Words list (Fry et al. 1984).

Phonological Awareness and Graphophonic Knowledge

Understandings to be developed in relation to phonological awareness include the following.
• Word awareness: spoken language is made up of words that represent objects, emotions and concepts.
• Syllable awareness: some words have a single syllable and others have more than one.
• Phonemic awareness: words are made up of individual sounds, or phonemes.

Within phonological awareness is phonemic awareness (see *Reading Resource Book*, 2nd edn, Chapter 3). When developing phonemic awareness, the following progression may be considered.

• Isolating phonemes: alliteration, position (first, last), generating words with a given sound.
• Blending phonemes: putting sounds together to form words, using individual phonemes (c a t), or onset and rime (c at).
• Segmenting phonemes: isolating sounds, hearing and counting sounds in words, producing sounds.
• Manipulating phonemes: adding, deleting or substituting sounds.

Understandings to be developed in relation to graphophonic knowledge include:
- learning alphabet letter names;
- learning that letters in words represent sounds.

It is recommended that letter names be used when students first begin to ask about print, as they are constant, whereas sounds vary. The letter 'A' will always be 'A', but it represents different sounds in 'Amy', 'Anne', 'Audrey' and 'Arnold'. Sounds can also vary according to accent or dialect. When beginning to formally introduce letters, it is important to use both the letter name and the regular sound, such as /a/ in cat, /b/ in big, /t/ in mat.

Concepts of Print

The following concepts of print are important for Role Play readers to know.
- A book has a front and a back.
- A book has a 'right way up'.
- Books are read from front to back.
- A page is turned to reveal the next part of the book.
- The left-hand page is read before the right-hand page.
- Print is read from left to right and a page is read from top to bottom.
- Print is different from pictures.
- Pictures support text.
- The concept of first and last can be applied to letters in a word or words on a page.
- Spaces indicate the boundaries of words.
- There is a match between spoken and written words; that is, print is speech written down.
- Terms such as 'letter', 'sound', 'word' and 'sentence' are different concepts.
- Numerals and letters are different.
- Print is constant.

The concepts of print relating to text in books may vary from those relating to text in other media; for example, a series of exchanged emails is read from bottom to top, and screen pages are rarely left and right. However, Role Play readers need to learn about the concepts they will encounter most often. Variations can be pointed out as new media are introduced.

Conventions of Print

In drawing Role Play readers' attention to conventions of print, it is important to include:

- punctuation marks, such as full stops and question marks;
- upper case and lower case letters;
- text organisation — for example, a story has an illustration and print, but a report may have a photograph and print.

Book Terminology

The terminology associated with books, such as 'illustration', 'photograph', 'title', 'cover' and 'spine', is important to further develop the conventions of reading. Talking about the differing roles of the author and the illustrator will benefit Role Play readers.

For further information about the Conventions substrand, see *Reading Resource Book*, 2nd edn, Chapter 3: Conventions.

Involving Students

1 Word Walls

A Word Wall is a designated space in the classroom devoted to displaying words. As words are discovered, introduced and discussed word walls are constructed jointly with the students. Words can be sorted according to the current teaching focus. For Role Play readers, the first words to be placed on the Word Wall will usually be the names of the students in the class.

- Create the Word Wall jointly with students. Begin by displaying enlarged letters of the alphabet (both upper and lower case).
- Add students' names one at a time, pointing out distinctive features such as initial letters and length.

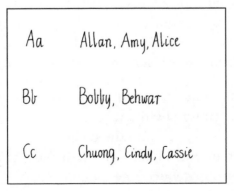

Aa	Allan, Amy, Alice
Bb	Bobby, Behwar
Cc	Chuong, Cindy, Cassie

Figure 4.5

- As students become more aware of sound–symbol relationships, group the names according to the sound of the initial letter.

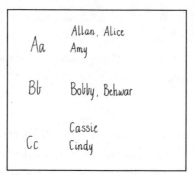

Figure 4.6

– As students' understandings about print develop, add other words significant to them, such as family names and high-frequency words.

<table>
<tr><td>Aa</td><td>Allan, Alice, and, at
Amy</td></tr>
<tr><td>Bb</td><td>Bobby, Behwar, bed, but</td></tr>
<tr><td>Cc</td><td>Cassie, cat, can
Cindy
Chuong, chop</td></tr>
</table>

Figure 4.7

– Read, refer to and use the words on the Word Wall during daily print walks, when modelling, or during writing activities.

2 Word-Sorting Activities

Word-sorting activities develop students' ability to identify and categorise words according to selected criteria. These activities provide an excellent opportunity for Role Play readers to interact with words and letter combinations in a problem-solving context. They can also be used to develop phonological awareness, graphophonic understandings, or sight-word recognition.

Word-sorting activities can be organised in a range of ways.
- *Closed sorts* use criteria chosen by the teacher.
- *Open sorts* require students to choose the criteria.
- *Guess my sort* involves an individual, a group or the teacher sorting the words. Another group deduces the criteria.

Word-sorting activities can be completed using individual word cards provided in envelopes, words on overhead transparencies on an overhead projector, pocket charts and word cards, or even

physical sorting activities that require students to move around the room holding word cards.

In the Role Play reading phase, the focus is on the pictorial representation of words rather than on written language. Picture cards may have the words printed on them, but these students will focus mainly on the pictures and will not be expected to read the words. They may begin to look at features such as beginning letters or the number of letters in a word.

Role Play readers can be involved in a range of word-sorting activities.

- *Picture sorts* focus students' attention on sorting items into categories. They can begin by sorting picture cards, such as pictures of animals and pictures of people.
- *Beginning-letter sorts* focus attention on beginning letters; for example, words that begin with the letter 'b' and words that don't.
- *Number-of-letters sorts* focus attention on the length of words.
- *Sound sorts* focus attention on words that have a particular sound; for example, sorting the pictures into words that have the /k/ sound and those that don't.

Physical word sorting involves students moving around the classroom holding or wearing a word or picture card.

- Provide each student with a word or a picture on a large card.
- Instruct them to move around the room looking for other students' words that would match theirs in some way. These students form a group.
- At the conclusion of a whole-class sort, ask students to stay in the groups they formed. Each group is then asked to hold up their cards and explain why they are together.

3 Star of the Day

Star of the Day helps students to recognise their own names and assists in developing understandings about written language.

- Write each student's name on a strip of card, making the strip length relative to the length of the name (Bob would have a short card, Annaliese a long one). Place the names in a container.
- Each day select one card; that student becomes the Star of the Day. Have other students ask questions to find out the background and interests of the Star of the Day.

– Generate discussion about the written aspects of a student's name, such as Nikki:
  – use the term 'word' to describe Nikki's name;
  – use the term 'letter' to describe what makes up the name;
  – count the letters;
  – clap the syllables;
  – compare it with other names;
  – identify the different letters;
  – look at the first and other letters using the terms 'capital' and 'small letter' or 'upper and lower case' to describe them;
  – write 'Nikki' in front of students and pointing out the left-to-right progression;
  – write the name on another card, cut the letters apart and have several students, including Nikki, reassemble the name using the original strip as a model;
  – add the word to the word wall.
– Repeat this, using each student's name over successive days.

4 Secret Messages

Secret Messages is an activity that involves students in basic decoding. The messages can be created using the sight vocabulary or graphophonic understandings being introduced at the time. Role Play readers will find it easier to decipher messages that use a combination of words and pictures.

Modelling the process for solving the messages is critical at this phase.

– Think of a simple, meaningful sentence or message, such as 'Look in the box'.
– Write a series of clues that will enable students to decode the message; for example, 👀 = look.
– Work with students to jointly solve the message.
– Keep a copy of all activities to build up a permanent collection for future use.

Figure 4.8 A sample secret message

5 Magic Words

Magic Words (Hoyt 2000) is an activity that provides an opportunity for students to identify sight words or to focus on parts of words, such as single letters. The use of a familiar text projected onto a wall with an overhead projector is the context for Magic Words. Students use a piece of card and a 'little magic' to isolate selected letters or words from a whole text.

– Read and re-read a text with the whole class.
– Select a criterion for the magic words; for example, 'I am looking for a word with the letter "s" in it'.
– Demonstrate how to 'lift' words from the screen by using a piece of white card. Place the card on the selected word on the screen, ensuring it fits the word. Slowly move the card away from the screen, isolating the selected word. As if by magic, the word is now 'floating' on the white card.
– Have students examine the magic word to decide if it fits the criterion.
– Allow them time to take turns lifting words with identified criteria, such as:
  – words with a particular letter
  – long or short words
  – punctuation marks.

6 The Letter Can

The Letter Can is an activity using a bag, a container or a box to stimulate Role Play readers to continue to develop their graphophonic understandings in the home setting. It involves selecting students to take a Letter Can home and return it to school filled with items beginning with the nominated letter. This is an excellent way of involving parents or caregivers in the learning process.

– Decorate a can (with a lid) with bright paper, such as alphabet adhesive paper.
– Include in the can instructions for parents or caregivers.

> Please help _____ to fill this can with items that begin with the enclosed special letter and return it to school tomorrow. Items can be three-dimensional or pictures from magazines. Please ensure that your child knows the name of each item in the can. Thank you for your assistance.

– Also include the special letter inside the can. The same letter may be used for a number of days.
– The following day, when the Letter Can is returned, discuss the items included and make a list of them.
– Send the can home with a different student each day. Add any new items to the list.
– Create an alphabet centre to display the labelled items that students have brought along.

7 Alphabet Hunt

This activity uses a collection of commercially produced alphabet books, friezes or charts to support the development of graphophonic understandings. Students may be invited to bring alphabet books from home to add to the class collection.

– Form groups of four to work with an adult. Provide each student with a different alphabet book.
– Provide each student with a sheet of paper that is to be folded in quarters.
– Place all the letters of the alphabet in a 'mystery' bag or box and invite all students to select one. Students then write their selected letters in each of the four squares.
– Have students look through their alphabet books to find the pages with their selected letters.
– In one square on the paper, students draw the object from their book page, such as a dog. An adult helper should write the name of the drawn object for each student.
– All students then swap alphabet books, find the pages in the new books that have their selected letters and draw the pictures from those books in another square of the paper. This process continues until students have four different pictures for their selected letter; for example, a door, a duck, a daffodil and a dog.
– Provide time for students to share their finished pages and discuss the pictures. They can suggest any other objects that could have been drawn.
– Once a page has been created for each letter of the alphabet, collate the pages to make a class alphabet book.

Model how to use these personally created books as a reference during writing.

8 Cloze Activities

Cloze activities encourage students to use context clues to predict the missing parts of a text; they are easily prepared by deleting

words or parts of words. Activities designed for Role Play readers can focus on either whole words or beginning letters.

When working with students to complete cloze activities, it is important to model how to gain the full benefit of context clues by always reading to the end of a sentence before trying to 'cloze' it.

It is beneficial for students to have the opportunity to discuss answers and justifications, allowing them to hear about strategies used by others, and alternative choices. The following list provides options of cloze activities suitable for Role Play readers.

Oral cloze
When reading a familiar book to students, pause every so often and have the students say the next word.

Key-word picture cloze
After reading a familiar text, write sentences from it on strips, leaving out a key word (preferably a noun). On small cards, draw or paste pictures to match the words that have been deleted. Have students work in small groups, with an adult, to fill the gaps using the picture cards.

Whole-word cloze
After reading a familiar text, rewrite it as a chart, deleting some of the words. Write the deleted words on small cards or large sticky notes. Jointly select appropriate cards or sticky notes to fill the gaps.

Graphophonic clues cloze
After reading a familiar big book with the students, use large sticky notes to cover all but the first letter of selected words. Have the students use their knowledge of the text and the initial letter to predict the word that will 'cloze' the sentence.

For directions on preparing cloze activities, see the section 'Cloze Procedure' in Chapter 3.

9 Elkonin Boxes

Elkonin Boxes (Elkonin 1973) supports students in identifying the number of sounds in a word, which is not always the same as the number of letters; for instance, 'bike' has four letters but only three sounds.

– Draw up an Elkonin Box on an overhead transparency. Ensure that the box has the same number of spaces as there are sounds in a chosen word.

- Begin by asking students, for example, 'What sound do you hear first in "cat"?'
- When they respond with the sound, not the letter name, place a counter in the first space.
- Repeat this procedure for each sound in the word, saying 'What sound do you hear next?'
- Place a counter in the second and third spaces respectively when each sound is identified. Finish by counting the number of sounds.

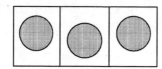

Figure 4.9

As an extension, Elkonin Boxes can be used to help students identify the location of particular sounds in a word. This could be done by giving a word such as 'bat', and then asking the students to put a counter in the space where they hear the sound /t/.

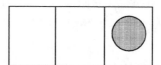

Figure 4.10

Once students are familiar with Elkonin Boxes, they can use them individually to help with the development of phonological awareness. Readers can use pictures of objects instead of the written word.

10 Sound Hunter

Participating in Sound Hunter helps students to make connections between letters and sounds; it is best introduced and practised in the context of a text. Texts such as books, charted songs and poems, modelled writing examples or written messages can provide contexts for Role Play readers to develop their graphophonic understandings by hunting for words. Students' names can also make a good starting point for this activity.

- Choose a specific focus. For Role Play readers, it may be an initial sound, a final sound or a particular letter.
- Select a text that clearly exhibits the chosen focus.
- Read the text for enjoyment.
- Revisit the text, hunting for the chosen focus, such as words with the letter 'm'. Students circle or underline the letters.

My family like to go shopping on Monday.

Figure 4.11

– Discuss the words and the sound (or sounds) represented by the focus letter.
– Challenge students to then find as many examples as they can in the resources provided, which could be other books, charts or magazines.
– Create a chart of the words found by the students. Leave room for more words to be added to it.
– Revisit, discuss and add to the chart on future occasions.

11 Rhyming Words Card Game

The Rhyming Words card game helps students to recognise, match and generate rhymes. The game is best played in groups of three or four students with adult support.

– Select pairs of rhyming words that are familiar to students and can be easily illustrated; e.g. **cat and mat, dog and frog, car and star**.
– Make a pack of cards with a picture on each one. Add the corresponding words. Familiarise students with the pictures before they begin the game.
– Shuffle the cards and deal five to each player. Place the remaining cards face down on the table.
– Have students look at their cards to see if they have any rhyming pairs. If they have, these cards are placed on the table and named; e.g. **'I've got star and car'**.
– Invite Player A to ask the student on his or her left for a card to make a match: 'Have you got a word that rhymes with cat?' The adult supervising the group can support any students that may need help answering the question. If Player A gets a matching rhyming card, the two are put on the table and the player has another turn. If not, the player chooses a card from the central pile.
– Direct the next player to choose a card from his or her set and repeat the procedure: 'Do you have a word that rhymes with . . .?'

12 Letter Poetry

Letter Poetry (Hoyt 2000) provides a structure for the creation of simple poems using words with a specified focus. It supports Role Play readers in developing their understandings of sound–symbol relationships, and is best introduced as a whole-class activity where the teacher has the opportunity to model the process and thinking involved in creating a letter poem.

- Select a focus letter, such as 'm'.
- Have students brainstorm words that begin with the focus letter.
- Record the words on sticky notes, blank cards or a whiteboard.
- Introduce a framework for creating a poem.
- Manipulate the brainstormed words, jointly selecting the best fit for each space in the framework.
- Read the poem several times; talk about the letter and the sound.
- Select a group of students to illustrate the poem. Display their work in the classroom.
- Create and collate further poems for other letters.
- Revisit the poems regularly.

```
_ _ _ is for _ _ _ .
a_ _ _ _ and a _ _ _ _ ,
A _ _ _ _ a _ _ _ _ ,
and the _ _ _ on
the _ _ _ .
```

```
I like _ _ _ _ ,
I like _ _ _ _ ,
I like _ _ _ _ ,
but I don't like _ _ _ .
```

```
_ _ _ is for _ _ _
who likes _ _ _ ,_ _ _
and _ _ _ .
_ _ _ doesn't like _ _ _ ,
_ _ _ and _ _ _ .
```

```
A _ _ _ _ is big.
A _ _ _ _ is big.
A _ _ _ _ is big,
but a _ _ _ _ is small.
```

Figure 4.12 Letter-poetry frameworks

13 What Comes Next?

What Comes Next? is an adaptation of the game that was known as Hangman. However, What Comes Next? requires students to guess the letters in the correct order rather than randomly.

Role Play readers can begin playing 'What Comes Next?' by focusing on their names, then move on to other words that are significant to them.

As a daily activity for Role Play readers, What Comes Next? can provide a context for reinforcing graphophonic understandings or concepts of print, such as:

- a word is a unit of print with a space either side;
- a word is written from left to right;

- words can vary in length;
- a word has an initial letter;
- a word is made up of a series of letters in a sequence;
- letters together represent the specific sounds in a word.

– Write students' names on individual cards. Cut each card according to the length of the name: Joe will have a short card, while Josephine has a long one.
– Choose one name; e.g. **Josephine**. Write the initial J followed by 8 dashes, J _ _ _ _ _ _ _ _.
– Make sure that the length of the space for the name matches the length of the student's name card.
– Say 'Guess whose name this is. Does anyone know the first letter?'
– If Josephine has the only 'J' name in the class, and she responds, bring her to the front of the class to match her card with the blank model. Fill in the letters and count them. Comment on the length of the name.
– If four students have names that begin with J (Joe, Jamal, Jonathan, Josephine), they will probably all think the name is theirs; bring them to the front one by one to check who is correct. Ask them to measure their name cards against the blank model. Joe and Jamal are too short, but the name could be either Jonathan or Josephine.
– Add the second letter of the chosen name: Jo_ _ _ _ _ _ _.
  Ask students if that helps them to guess. Add the third letter: Jos _ _ _ _ _ _; at this stage it will be evident that the name is Josephine.
– Count the letters in both Josephine and Jonathan to show that Josephine actually has one more letter.
– Choose a different name every day, so each student gets a turn.
– When students have learnt to focus on letters within names, replace the name cards of different lengths with cards of the same length.
– Add names or words to the class list or word wall.

14 Hidden Messages

Hidden Messages is an activity that helps students to understand there is a message contained in print; they will enjoy the intrigue of finding messages hidden around the room. The messages can provide a meaningful context for reinforcing any concepts of print being addressed; book characters, classroom pets or class toys may all be possible 'writers' of hidden messages.

– Write a series of messages addressed to students and hide them somewhere in the classroom.

– 'Discover' the first message hidden in the room.
– Read the message to students, taking the opportunity to discuss concepts and conventions of print included in it. The message needs to contain an instruction, such as 'Look under the bookshelf'.
– Direct a student to carry out the instruction.
– Work with students to continue in this way until the final message is found. The final one can be specific; for example, 'Today we will read a story about a very naughty bear. What might he be doing?'

15 Bright Balloons

Bright Balloons can provide a meaningful, fun context for reinforcing any concepts and conventions of print, vocabulary or graphophonic understandings being introduced. Personal messages to individual students can be written and placed inside a balloon; these may be for special occasions, or in recognition of good work. A message intended for the whole class can be photocopied. At the end of the day, the inflated balloons can be sent home, popped, and the message read.

Figure 4.13 Messages for Bright Balloons

16 Matching Activities

Matching activities help develop students' awareness of concepts of print such as one-to-one correspondence between spoken and written words, the constancy of the printed word, and directionality of print.
– Select a song, poem or rhyme to provide the context for the matching activity.
– Write the text, or parts of it, on sentence strips or word cards.
– Read the text several times, encouraging students to join in when predictable or repetitive refrains are read.
– Randomly distribute the word cards or sentence strips and have students match lines, phrases or words.
– Re-read the entire text together, checking that it makes sense.
– Leave the sentence strips and word cards in an accessible area, encouraging students to continue to match and reconstruct the text as they wish.

17 Segmenting Sentences into Words

In spoken language the speech stream is constant, with no obvious separation of words. In written language, however, each word is separated by a space. Some students have difficulty in transferring the notion of separate words to spoken language. Segmenting sentences into words is an activity that supports students in understanding this notion.

- Begin by explaining that when we talk, we use words. Give students some examples of words:
    - dog, tree, boy, Australia (names of objects, people, places)
    - pink, square, five (describing words — colour, shape, number)
    - run, jump, fly (action words).
- Ask students to provide some other words.
- Explain that when we speak to each other we usually use more than one word, and what we say is called a sentence. Give some examples of sentences, such as 'Tom has a new bike' or 'Mary sat on the chair'.
- Ask students to provide some other sentences.
- Choose a sentence to be repeated slowly word by word, clapping or tapping to indicate each individual word. Keep the activity short and fast-paced, providing a sense of fun and enjoyment.
- Use familiar rhymes or poems to reinforce the understanding of a sentence.

As an extension, write the students' sentences, pointing out the spaces between words. Where students can observe text being typed onto a computer screen, have them dictate a simple message, saying 'space' after each word.

18 Book Words

Creating a chart of the words used when talking about books — such as author, spine, illustrator, index, contents — will help Role Play readers understand and use the terminology. Add to the chart as new book words are learnt.

Figure 4.14

19 Generic Games and Activities

The games and activities listed in the table below are generic because they can be used to support the development of concepts and conventions of print, graphophonic understanding, and phonological awareness. The matrix includes the list of conventions that can be developed using each game or activity. All can be used to suit a range of purposes.

When using these activities it is important to:
- keep them fun and informal;
- use settings that encourage interaction among students;
- embed them in the context of work that is already being done in the classroom;
- ensure that the students are fully familiar with the way to play the games.

Generic Games and Activities	Sight Vocabulary	Graphophonic Understandings	Concepts of Print	Conventions of Print	Word Awareness	Syllable Awareness	Rhyme	Phoneme Isolation	Phoneme Blending	Phoneme Segmentation	Phoneme Manipulation
CONVENTIONS											
						Phonological Awareness					
								Phonemic Awareness			
I Spy . . .		•				•	•	•	•		
Bingo	•	•				•	•	•	•		
Snap	•	•					•	•			
Concentration	•	•					•	•			
Dominoes	•	•					•	•			
A Trip to the Moon						•	•	•			
I Say . . . You Say							•	•			
Play Ball		•	•	•	•	•	•	•			
Snap and Clap					•	•	•				
What Could It Be?		•				•	•	•	•		
Odd One Out	•					•	•	•	•	•	
Mystery Bag						•	•	•	•	•	
Hunting for Words	•	•			•	•	•	•			
Using Songs and Rhymes						•	•	•			
What Can You Show Us?	•	•	•	•	•	•	•				
Tic Tac Toe	•	•			•	•	•				

I Spy

- Begin by saying 'I spy with my little eye something that . . .' and continue with phrases such as 'begins with t', 'rhymes with bear', 'ends with at'.
- Students take turns to guess the word.

A variation of this is Where's Spot?, in which a toy dog is hidden. If students find I Spy too difficult, modify it to Where's Spot? Choose a hiding place (such as a box) and say, for instance, 'Spot's hiding somewhere that starts with b. Where could that be?' Have students go and look to see if Spot is in the place they have guessed.

Bingo

The format of a traditional Bingo game is used.

- Each student has a large card divided into rectangles, each one containing a randomly chosen letter, blend, picture or word. The students are also provided with counters, the number corresponding to the number of rectangles on the cards.
- A complete set of cards for the caller to use is also required.
- A caller draws cards from a box one at a time and calls out what is on each one.
- Students look for a match at each call; if they have one, they place a counter on it. The first to cover all rectangles calls out 'Bingo!'

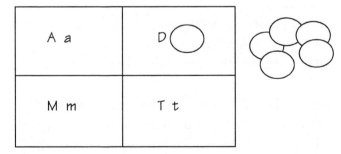

Figure 4.15

Snap

The format of a traditional Snap game is used.

- A set of cards where multiples of four cards match or are related in some way is made up (see Figure 4.16).

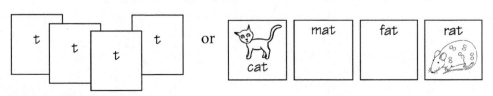

Figure 4.16

87

- All the cards are dealt to the players.
- In turn, each student overturns one card from his or her hand and places it face up on the table, so forming a central pile.
- When an upturned card matches one on the central pile, the first to place a hand on the central pile says Snap, and what the criterion for the Snap is, then takes all the cards in the pile.
- The round continues in this way until one student has all the cards.

Concentration

This is a game that invites students to exercise concentration and memory to locate matches in a given array of cards placed face down.

- All cards in the pack are placed in rows face down on the table.
- In turn, each student turns up two cards (one at a time), and attempts to match them according to predetermined criteria.
- If there is a match, the student identifies the criterion, keeps the cards and has another turn. If there is no match, the cards are replaced exactly where they were, face down.
- The game continues in this way until all the cards are matched. The winner is the student with the most matched pairs.

Dominoes

Make a set of dominoes that has two pictured objects on each card. The aim is to join in a line dominoes sharing a common element; for example, beginning with the same letter, rhyming, or ending with a common sound.

- The game is played in pairs or small groups.
- Each player is dealt the same number of dominoes.
- A student is selected to place the first domino on the playing surface.
- Players take turns to place a domino on the playing surface by selecting a card that will match the domino that is already there. A domino may only be added to the beginning or end of the line, and the player must identify the match. If a player cannot place a domino, the turn is missed. The first to place all his or her dominoes is the winner.

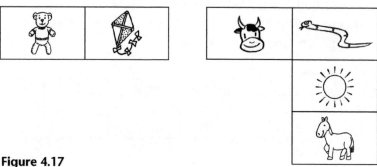

Figure 4.17

A Trip to the Moon

To play this, students sit in a circle.

- Begin the game by saying 'We're going on a trip to the moon. You can come if you bring something.' Each student is provided with a criterion for selecting the 'something'; for example:
  - 'You need to bring something that rhymes with van.'
  - 'You need to bring something that starts with s.'
- Students then take turns to say 'I will bring a . . .'. Provide feedback to each one about the choice.

I Say . . . You Say

I Say . . . You Say involves a student orally providing words that meet a criterion identified by the teacher.

- The teacher chooses a criterion for the game and shares it with the students. As an example: 'Today we are going to play I Say . . . You Say with words that begin with b. So let's begin. I say bat, you say . . .'.
- Students are selected in turn to provide a word to fill the space until it becomes difficult to find matching words.
- Another word or new criterion is then chosen to continue the game.

Play Ball

- Students sit or stand in a circle.
- A criterion is nominated for the type of word to be provided; for instance, words that rhyme with 'cat'.
- One student is given a ball and tosses it to another, saying a word that fulfils the criterion.
- Students continue to toss the ball to one another until no more words can be provided.
- The game then continues with a new criterion.

Snap and Clap

Snap and Clap makes use of rhythm and repetition to encourage students to focus on rhyming words. The focus is on providing the word to match the criterion, not on maintaining a complicated clapping and snapping pattern.

- Begin with a simple snap, clap rhythm, then say a word. Students are challenged to repeat the snap, clap rhythm and then to provide a rhyming word; for example:
  - snap, snap, clap — teacher says 'coat';
  - snap, snap, clap — student 1 says 'float';
  - snap, snap, clap — student 2 says 'boat'.

• This is continued until students cannot think of any more rhyming words; a new pattern with a new word is then chosen.

What Could It Be?

What Could It Be? involves the creation of clues that are presented orally for students to solve; for instance, 'I'm thinking of something in the room whose name has two parts. It is made of glass, and you can see through it. What could it be?'

The following examples illustrate how the clues can easily be changed to reflect a shift in focus.

• Using onset and rime: I'm thinking of an animal. The animal's name is /k/ /ow/. What could it be?'
• Using individual phonemes: 'I'm thinking of an animal. The animal's name is /k/ /a/ /t/. What could it be?'
• Using rhyming words: 'I'm thinking of an animal. The animal's name rhymes with 'bat'. What could it be?'
• Using initial sounds: 'I'm thinking of an animal whose name begins with 'm'. What could it be?'

Students can make up their own clues for others to solve.

Odd One Out

In Odd One Out students are asked to identify a word — or parts of a word — from a series that contains variation. In a series of three words, two should have something in common (phonologically), the third being the 'odd one out'. Depending on the words chosen, this activity can be used to develop a range of understandings related to phonological awareness, as shown in the following examples.

Syllable awareness: Listen while I say three words. Tell me which one has two parts.

Rhyme awareness: Listen while I say three words. Tell me which one doesn't rhyme with the others.

Matching phonemes: Listen while I say three words. Tell me which one does not begin with 'm'.

As a variation, do not give the criteria. Ask students to pick the odd one out and suggest why it does not belong; for example, 'Listen while I say three words. Which one does not belong?' However, when beginning to use this variation, make sure the words differ in one aspect only. If the focus is to identify initial sounds, the words used should have the same number of syllables, otherwise the students may not focus on the aspect being developed.

As an extension, incorporate written words into the activity.

Mystery Bag

Place some 'mystery objects' in a bag. Select one object at a time, but do not show it to the students. Provide clues to help them identify it.

The clues provided will be determined by the selected focus, such as initial phonemes, rhyming words, or onset and rime. The following statements illustrate the type that would be appropriate for Role Play readers.

• In the bag I can feel something whose name begins with 'f'. What could it be?
• In the bag I can feel something whose name rhymes with 'dish'. What could it be?
• In the mystery bag I can feel a f /ish. What could it be?

The procedure is then repeated with other objects.

Hunting for Words

Challenge students to go 'hunting' for words in the classroom, at home, or in the general environment. The words should fulfil a given criterion, such as words beginning with 'm', words ending with 't' or words with four letters.

Students copy the words into their 'spy pads', and later they share and discuss them as a class.

Using Songs and Rhymes

Collect, sing and chant songs and rhymes that focus on letter names and sounds, such as YMCA, or B-I-N-G-O or MICKEY MOUSE. Once students have learnt a new song, the tune can be used to create new verses that can support the development of phonological awareness.

The following innovations (Yopp 1992) illustrate how other familiar tunes can be used to motivate students to practise new graphophonic understandings being introduced.

Sung to the tune of 'Old McDonald Had a Farm'
What is the sound that starts these words —
Michael, man and meat? (*Wait for students' response.*)
/m/ is the sound that starts these words —
Michael, man and meat.
With a /m/, /m/ here and a /m/ /m/ there,
Here a /m/, there a /m/, everywhere a /m/, /m/.
/m/ is the sound that starts these words —
Michael, man and meat.

What is the sound that starts these words —
Sausage, sand and Sue —

What is the sound that starts these words —
Evan, edge and egg —

Sung to the tune of 'A-Hunting We Will Go'

A-hunting we will go!	A-hunting we will go!
A-hunting we will go!	A-hunting we will go!
We'll catch a fox and	We'll catch a cat
put him in a box	and put him on a mat
And never let him go.	And never let him go.

This one is great for rhyming words.

Sung to the tune of 'Twinkle Twinkle Little Star'

Listen, listen to my word.
Tell me all the sounds you heard:
   TREE (*Say the word slowly.*)
/t/ is one sound, /r/ is two,
/ee/ is the last in tree it's true.
Listen, listen to my word.
Tell me all the sounds you heard.

The Farmer in the Dell

We're looking for an /s/, We're looking for an /s/ . . .

If You're Happy and You Know It

If you're happy and you know it, shout out /b/.

What Can You Show Us? (Richgels et al. 1996)

- Display an enlarged text — for example, a poem or a song —
  to direct students' attention to different aspects of language.
- Students share with a partner what they notice about the text,
  such as capital letters, long or short words, known words,
  or particular sounds.
- Individual students can be asked to show the rest of the class
  something they notice in the text. They can do this by pointing to
  features, using highlight tape, or using a soluble marker on plastic
  laminate over the text.

Tic Tac Toe

Tic Tac Toe is played in the same way as Noughts and Crosses, but
for Role Play readers it uses pictures to create a sequence of three
(diagonally, vertically or horizontally). Player A may have to choose

pictures of words that begin with the letter 'b' and Player B may have to choose pictures of words that begin with the letter 's'.

It is helpful for Role Play readers to select their picture cards prior to playing the game.

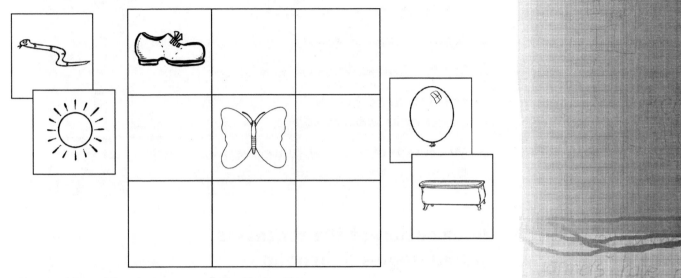

Figure 4.18 A grid and picture cards for Tic Tac Toe

Students play the game in pairs.
- Each pair is provided with a playing grid and a selection of picture cards.
- Each student selects five cards matching their given criterion (as given above).
- They then take turns to place their cards on the grid.
- The winner is the first to place three words horizontally, vertically or diagonally on the grid.

PROCESSES AND STRATEGIES

Major Teaching Emphases

- **Build students' knowledge within the cues,** e.g. topic knowledge, sound–symbol relationships.

- **Teach comprehension strategies,** e.g. connecting, comparing.

- **Teach word-identification strategies,** e.g. predicting.

- **Teach students how to locate, select and evaluate texts,** e.g. using the layout of a library.

- **Model self-reflection of strategies used in reading and encourage students to do the same.**

Organisation of the Processes and Strategies Substrand

The organisation of Processes and Strategies differs in several ways from that of the other substrands.

Both the Teaching Notes and the Involving Students sections are located in *Reading Resource Book*, 2nd edn, Chapter 4: Processes and Strategies.

The rationale for this difference in organisation is that reading processes and strategies are not hierarchical, and therefore not phase-specific. A variety of processes and strategies need to be introduced, developed and consolidated at all phases of development.

What varies from one phase to the next is the growth in:
- the number and integration of strategies;
- the awareness and monitoring of strategies;
- the efficiency in use and selection of strategies;
- the ability to articulate the use of the strategies;
- the awareness of how the use of strategies helps with making meaning;
- the ability to locate, select and evaluate texts.

Supporting Parents of Role Play Readers

GENERAL DESCRIPTION OF ROLE PLAY READERS

Role Play readers show an interest in books and in the print they see around them. They imitate the things they see adult readers doing, such as holding the book carefully, turning the pages and using computer icons. They often pretend to read by using the pictures and their memory to retell stories.

Supporting Role Play Readers in the Home

Role Play readers will benefit from a range of experiences in the home setting. Ideas for providing appropriate experiences are available on Parent Cards located on the *First Steps* Reading CD-ROM. Teachers can select appropriate cards for each Role Play reader from the Reading CD-ROM and copy them for parents to use at home. Also available on the CD-ROM is a parent-friendly version of the Reading Map of Development.

Parent Cards

1 General Description and How to Support Role Play Readers
2 Encouraging Reading
3 Reading to Your Child
4 Selecting Texts
5 Modelling Reading
6 Telling Stories
7 Developing Awareness of Letters and Words

8 Developing Concepts about Texts and Print
9 Building a Love of Reading
10 Questions to Ask
11 Using Computers
12 Using the Library
13 Supporting Phonemic Awareness and Graphophonic Knowledge through Games

---

CHAPTER 5

Experimental Reading Phase

Figure 5.1

Global Statement

In this phase, readers use memory of familiar, predictable texts and their developing sound–symbol knowledge to match some spoken words with written words. Experimental readers are focused on understanding and conveying the meaning of these texts rather than reading all words accurately. They read and comprehend texts with repetitive, limited and known vocabulary and supportive illustrations.

Experimental Reading Indicators

Use of Texts

◆ **Reads and demonstrates comprehension of texts by:**
  – **recalling some ideas explicit in a text**
  – **identifying the topic of a text**
  – **selecting a limited number of explicit events to retell a text**
  – **linking two ideas explicit in a text,** e.g. an action and its result.

◆ **Demonstrates that print remains constant,** e.g. transfers knowledge of familiar words from one context to another.

◆ **Maintains the storyline when 'reading' familiar texts, although a limited number of words are read accurately.**

◆ **With assistance, locates and selects texts appropriate to purpose or interest.**

Contextual Understanding

◆ **Expresses an opinion about a text, but may not always be able to justify it.**

◆ **Identifies the role of the author and illustrator of a text.**

◆ **Talks about the ways different people or characters are represented in texts,** e.g. The girl in this story plays football.

• Demonstrates that print and illustrations combine to carry the message.

• Compares self to characters and events in texts.

Conventions

◆ **Recognises a small bank of known words in different contexts,** e.g. personally significant words.

◆ **Identifies the letters of the alphabet by name or sound.**

◆ **Demonstrates understanding of the concepts and conventions of print,** e.g. left to right, top to bottom, capital letters.

• Responds to and uses terminology such as letter, sound, word.

• Demonstrates understanding of one-to-one correspondence between spoken and written words, e.g. points to individual words or word-like clusters.

• Recognises a word as a unit of print with space on either side.

• Uses knowledge of repetitive language patterns to predict words, e.g. Brown bear, brown bear, what do you . . .?

• Identifies simple grammatical symbols, e.g. capital letters, question marks.

• Associates familiar letters with regular sounds, e.g. M says 'mmm' in Michael, A says 'a' in Ann.

• Hears and articulates sound segments in some words, including onset and rime, e.g. cat — 'c' and 'at', string — 'str' and 'ing'.

• Identifies and supplies rhyming words when listening to text, e.g. I see a frog sitting on a . . .

Processes and Strategies

◆ **Draws upon a limited knowledge base to comprehend,** e.g. topic knowledge, sentence patterns and sound–symbol relationships.

◆ **Uses a limited range of strategies to comprehend,** e.g. predicting, comparing.

◆ **Determines unknown words by using word-identification strategies,** e.g. predicting using beginning letters and/or pictures.

• Asks for assistance with some words.

• Generates key words that describe a picture.

• Responses about the reading process reflect a limited understanding of the use of cues and strategies, e.g. 'How do you read?' answered by 'You look at the words and pictures and then you . . . read 'em'.

Major Teaching Emphases

Environment and Attitude
- Create a supportive classroom environment that nurtures a community of readers.
- Jointly construct, and frequently refer to, meaningful environmental print.
- Foster students' enjoyment of reading.
- Encourage students to take risks with confidence.
- Encourage students to select their own reading material according to interest or purpose.

Use of Texts
- Read and re-read a variety of texts both literary and informational, providing opportunities for students to do the same.
- Teach students to draw upon explicit information in the text to comprehend, e.g. by sequencing events.

Contextual Understanding
- Provide opportunities for students to share and justify opinions and feelings about texts, e.g. about characters, events, information.
- Discuss some of the decisions authors and illustrators make when creating texts, e.g. what characters will look like.
- Draw attention to the ways people or characters are represented in texts, and discuss alternatives, e.g. 'This giant is mean. How do we know this?'

Conventions
- Continue to build students' sight vocabulary, e.g. high-frequency words, personally significant words.

- Continue to build phonological awareness, graphophonic and word knowledge, such as:
  - segmenting words into sounds
  - linking letters with their regular sounds
  - recognising that a letter can represent different sounds
  - recognising how word parts and words work.
- Model the use of conventions of print, e.g. question marks, exclamation marks.
- Build students' knowledge of different text forms, e.g. purpose, structure and organisation.

Processes and Strategies
- Continue to build students' knowledge within the cues, e.g. text organisation, vocabulary knowledge.
- Consolidate known comprehension strategies and teach additional strategies, e.g. self-questioning, predicting.
- Teach word-identification strategies, e.g. decoding using phonemes, onset and rime.
- Continue to teach students how to locate, select and evaluate texts, e.g. using alphabetical order, introducing browsing techniques.
- Model self-reflection of strategies used in reading, and encourage students to do the same.

Teaching and Learning Experiences

ENVIRONMENT AND ATTITUDE

Major Teaching Emphases

- **Create a supportive classroom environment that nurtures a community of readers.**

- **Jointly construct, and frequently refer to, meaningful environmental print.**

- **Foster students' enjoyment of reading.**

- **Encourage students to take risks with confidence.**

- **Encourage students to select their own reading material according to interest or purpose.**

Teaching Notes

An environment that nurtures Experimental readers and develops their confidence is one that allows them to experiment with reading and to explore texts. As they are initially more interested in telling the 'story', Experimental readers need to feel comfortable in taking risks and not be expected to get all the words right; often their interests will far exceed their ability to accurately read the words. These readers benefit from opportunities to interact with a variety of texts: those they can read independently, those read to them, and those they just browse. A combination of such opportunities will help Experimental readers to see reading as enjoyable and purposeful.

Exploring Print

It is important to continue building students' knowledge of print by exposing them to a wide variety of texts and pointing out features of print they see around them. In the classroom, a print-rich environment can be created with the students so that they understand how print is used in meaningful ways in everyday life. Print can be grouped according to its function (Owocki 1999).

For example:

- **Environmental** — print that gives us information about the world, e.g. schedules, price tags and advertisements.
- **Occupational** — print associated with a job or profession, e.g. a mechanic's car manuals, service checklists, booking sheets.
- **Informational** — print for storing, retrieving and organising information, e.g. clocks, diagrams, newspapers, instruction books.
- **Recreational** — print used for leisure activities, e.g. novels, picture books, software programs.

Consider the following ideas.

Environmental

- *Label* objects in the environment, using whole sentences; this helps students to understand how words go together to make meaning. Make use of labelling on packages when appropriate, such as following directions in cooking activities.
- *Everyday print* in the environment can be referred to both inside and outside the classroom so that students can begin to understand the purpose of written language, and the way it works. This can be done by talking about everyday print, encouraging students to bring in examples, preparing charts of community signs, and taking students for walks around the community, pointing out and reading environmental print.
- *Charts* can be displayed where they are easily accessible. They may include lists of the students' or of members of the school community (with photographs next to the names), classroom helpers' charts, and alphabet and number charts.

Occupational

Centres or *corners* can be created and appropriate texts displayed so that students can use them in role playing situations; these could include catalogues and lists in the 'shop centre', letters and postcards in the 'post office centre'.

Informational

- *Word banks* and *word walls* contain words the students are currently learning or have recently learnt, such as common sight words, the teacher's name, and the names of the relevant town, city and state.
- *Calendars* and *planners* can be displayed and referred to on a daily basis. Holidays, special activities, and school and community events can be featured and discussed.

Recreational

- *Poems, songs, riddles* and *rhymes* that students have been working with can be written on charts and displayed so the students can either read them for pleasure or use them as a resource.

- *A reading/writing backpack* can be created for students to take home on a rotational basis. It could include literary or informational texts on different topics, suggested activities or discussion questions about the text or suggestions for parents, such as how to use the backpack and what strategies to try.

- *A writing table* is an area for personal-choice writing where students can experiment with writing in a non-threatening way. The provision of items such as coloured paper, pencils, envelopes, stamps and a letterbox may provide the stimulus and motivation to write. A display board placed in this area can be used to display students' completed work.

- A *reading corner* is a relaxed, informal area for independent reading. Cushions, comfortable seating, privacy and lighting can create an enticing setting and may encourage students to join a friend and share a book.

- *Learning centres* can be established, allowing students to explore print in a variety of settings. They should offer a range of texts, as well as developmentally appropriate tasks; the materials needed to complete the tasks should also be available. Consider using any of the following options.

A *reading centre*, featuring:
- a range of commercial and class-made books
- magazines
- book-promotional charts
- author information charts
- a list of new titles
- students' comments or drawings.

A *science table*, featuring:
- magazines
- information charts
- labels and captions
- suggestions and instructions for use of equipment
- posters, such as 'The Life Cycle of a Butterfly'.

A *writing centre*, featuring:
- instructions for using the computer
- alphabet cards
- suggestions for writing

– examples of text forms
– a range of commercial and class-made books
– a list of class names.

Interacting with Print

While it is important that the classroom has various examples of environmental print displayed, it is essential to model how to interact with and make use of these displays. This can be achieved in a range of ways.

- Take students on a print walk around the room so that they have the opportunity to 'read' and revisit charts they have made and words they have learnt, or to play games such as matching words or phrases.
- Model the use of the charts during Modelled, Shared and Guided Reading.
- Make the link to writing; for instance, say ' How do I spell Friday?', 'Look at the charts' or 'Where else might I find that word?'
- Model the use of charts during Modelled, Shared and Guided Writing.

Fostering Enjoyment of Reading

Fostering students' enjoyment of reading can be achieved in a number of ways.

- Read to them every day, introducing different text forms and authors.
- Provide time each day for students to be involved in independent reading sessions where the texts are self-selected and the pleasure of reading is experienced.
- Ensure that a wide selection of reading material is available in the classroom.
- Set up a listening post where students can listen to taped stories while following the text.
- Set up a computer to allow students to 'read' along with story CD-ROMs and software programs.
- Display students' favourite texts and allow time for them to explain why they are favourites.
- Share some of your favourite texts with students, explaining why they appeal to you.
- Encourage and organise visits to the school and town libraries so that students are exposed to a wide variety of reading material.
- Invite guest readers to visit; they could be family or community members who come on a regular basis and read to the whole class or a small group.
- Organise visits by authors to speak about their books.

• Develop a 'buddy reading' system with an older class at the school. (See *Reading Resource Book*, 2nd edn, Chapter 1: Use of Texts.)

Encouraging Risk-Taking

Experimental readers can be encouraged to become risk-takers if they are asked to:

• read a variety of texts;
• identify known words in a variety of contexts;
• use appropriate word-identification strategies to identify unknown words;
• use a variety of cues to comprehend;
• use a variety of strategies to comprehend;
• 'have a go' at reading and writing;
• talk about their reading strategies and the discoveries they have made;
• offer opinions about texts read or heard.

For further information about Environment and Attitude, see:
• *Linking Assessment, Teaching and Learning*, Chapter 5: Establishing a Positive Teaching and Learning Environment;
• *Reading Resource Book*, 2nd edn, Chapter 1: Use of Texts.

USE OF TEXTS

Major Teaching Emphases

- **Read and re-read a variety of texts both literary and informational, providing opportunities for students to do the same.**

- **Teach students to draw upon explicit information in the text to comprehend,** e.g. by sequencing events.

Teaching Notes

In this phase, students need to be exposed to and interact with a wide variety of texts. These could be:

- literary texts; e.g. songs, poems, rhymes, fairy tales and folk tales, traditional and modern stories;
- informational texts; e.g. simple reports, magazines and pictorial encyclopaedias;
- environmental print; e.g. messages, signs and advertising posters.

Experimental readers need opportunities to explore the relationship between words and illustrations, including those on CD-ROMs and in software programs.

The foci for helping Experimental readers in this substrand are organised under the following headings.

- Variety of Texts
- Responding to Texts

Variety of Texts

A selection of texts that have natural language, repetitive structure and supportive illustrations, and that deal with familiar experiences, can be read and re-read to Experimental readers. As well as listening to the teacher reading a variety of such texts, Experimental readers enjoy being given many opportunities to read and re-read them for themselves.

During Modelled Reading sessions, teachers can demonstrate many aspects of reading such as:

- how to select texts for different purposes; e.g. 'I want to find out some facts about spiders, so this book will be best. It has photographs and diagrams';
- how to navigate and manipulate text on screen;
- how to select texts that are related in some way, such as having the same topic and the same characters;

- the enjoyment that reading can bring;
- how to use expression to highlight a character;
- how to read fluently;
- how to select explicit information when retelling.

During Shared Reading sessions an enlarged copy of the text can be used so that students can, for example:
- use the pictures and the title to predict the storyline;
- join in with the familiar, repetitive sections;
- use expression to highlight a character;
- gain an overall understanding of the text.

Re-reading texts will help students become aware of the constancy of the message and provide them with examples of literary language.

Responding to Texts

In addition to reading and re-reading texts, Experimental readers will benefit from opportunities to respond to texts to show their understanding. There are many ways they can do this, such as:
- asking questions of the author or illustrator;
- retelling the story from the pictures;
- dramatising;
- constructing story maps; or
- drawing.

The focus in this phase will still be on identifying explicit information, but students can be encouraged to begin identifying implicit information.

Questioning students about their interpretation of a text is a natural way teachers may lead students to respond. There are many ways of organising and discussing types of questions; e.g. **Bloom's Taxonomy (Bloom 1956), Question–Answer Relationships (Raphael 1986), Three Level Guides (Herber 1970) or Open and Closed Questions.** Whichever questioning hierarchy is chosen, it is wise to include questions that require different levels of thinking and to help students, particularly EAL students, recognise the nature of each question.

Raphael (1986) categorises questions as Right There (Literal), Think and Search (Inferential), Author and You (Interpretive) and On Your Own (Critical/Evaluative), providing a useful framework for ensuring that different types of questions are used in the classroom.

Literal

Literal questions focus on what the author said. The answer is 'right there', explicitly stated in the text or pictures. Common literal questions begin with 'who', 'when', 'where' or 'what', and it is important that teachers follow them up with clarifying questions, such as 'What makes you say that?' or 'Can you show me/read the part in the book that says that?' so that students get the idea of substantiating answers by returning to the text.

Inferential

The answers to these questions can be found in the text but are not necessarily in the one place; they are the Think and Search questions. They are also sometimes the 'how' and 'why' questions, showing relationships such as cause and effect, compare and contrast, or sequence. The student has to 'put the answer together' from various sections or sentences in the text; for instance, 'What could have happened before/after/between . . .?, 'What does the author say that makes you think . . . ?', 'How are . . . and . . . alike?', 'Why did . . . get so angry when . . .?'

Interpretive

These are the Author and You questions. They require the student to base the answer on the text, but also to draw on previous personal experience to reach a reasonable answer. Examples are 'How are these texts similar?', 'From what the author has said, do you feel that . . . is a good idea?', 'If . . . changed, how would that affect . . .?' The answer must not be a wild guess, it must be probable in light of the text, not just possible from the reader's experience.

Critical/Evaluative

These questions go beyond the text, asking for students' own opinions or judgements. They are the On Your Own questions, as the answers are not to be found in the text at all, although it does provide a starting point for discussions about the underlying messages. After reading 'Cinderella', critical questions might be 'Are all stepmothers like the one in this book?', 'Why does the story end with Cinderella getting married?', 'Do you agree or disagree with . . .?'

For further information about the Use of Texts substrand, see *Reading Resource Book*, 2nd edn:
Chapter 1: Use of Texts
Chapter 4: Processes and Strategies.

Involving Students

1 Choral Reading

Refer to Chapter 4: Role Play Reading Phase, p. 59.

2 Read and Retell

Read and Retell (Browne & Cambourne 1987) is a simple activity that is flexible in its use and provides an opportunity for students to transform a text. Retelling requires readers to read or listen to a text, organise key information they have understood in it, then share their understanding with others in a retell. Retells can be created and shared orally, as a drawing, or through drama.

Traditional children's literature such as fables, myths and fairy tales, or songs, rhymes and picture books are all excellent texts for retelling.

Readers will benefit from creating different forms of retells.
• Oral to oral — students listen to a text read aloud by the teacher and retell it orally.
• Oral to drawing — students listen to a text read aloud by the teacher and retell by drawing.
• Oral to drama — students listen to a text read aloud by the teacher and retell through drama.
• Written to oral — students read a text and retell it orally.
• Written to drawing — students read a text and retell by drawing.

The following procedure can be adapted to suit the purpose, context, focus and the form of retell being used.

– Select a text and display the title.
– Read the text aloud to students.
– Allow them to hear or re-read the text as many times as is necessary.
– Provide time for them to prepare their retell (in any of the forms mentioned above).
– Select some students to share their retells.

Some ways to support readers in retelling are:
• using puppets as an aid for oral retells;
• using illustrations from a text;
• providing simple props;
• providing overhead transparencies for students to draw and retell.

3 Favourite Sentences

Selecting and sharing favourite sentences promotes critical thinking and provides an opportunity for students to revisit previously read texts. It is important that they have time to share their chosen sentences and the reasons for their choices.

– Direct students to identify favourite sentences from previously read or shared texts.
– Provide time for them to silently read and re-read the chosen sentences.
– Have them share the sentences in small groups or with the whole class.
– Record the sentences, display them, and use them for whole-class reading.

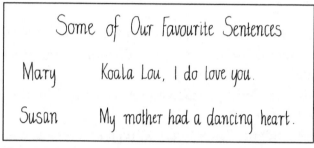

Figure 5.2

4 Story Prop Box

Story Prop Box is an independent activity that encourages readers to re-read a variety of familiar texts. A prop box consists of a familiar text and any props that will encourage the students to re-read, retell, dramatise, role play or perform the story; for example, after sharing 'Tough Boris', provide props such as a pirate hat, a treasure map, a sword, a violin case and a toy parrot. Taped versions of the text, if available, are also a useful addition to a prop box.

After sharing texts with the whole class, create prop boxes to accompany the ones they choose.

– Allocate students to work in small groups and to select a prop box.
– Allow time for them to discuss the text.
– Direct them to allocate roles and select props from the box.
– Allow time for them to create a role play, retell or dramatisation of the story.
– Invite them to perform for the whole class or another class, if appropriate.

Figure 5.3 A Story Prop Box

5 Get the Rhythm

Get the Rhythm is an opportunity for students to re-read a variety of texts for fun and enjoyment; Experimental readers identify the rhythms in a text and create music to accompany a shared reading. It is important to provide them with a range of musical resources such as percussion instruments, small electronic keyboards or student-made instruments. They may even begin to use clapping, tapping or stamping to produce the rhythm or the music. Warning: Be prepared for the noise!

– Provide students with a range of familiar texts from which to choose. Texts that contain rhyme and rhythm are essential.
– Allow time for them to re-read the chosen text, encouraging them to identify rhythms.
– Have them select one or more instruments to match the rhythm identified in the text.
– Provide opportunities for repeated readings incorporating the chosen musical accompaniment.
– Give them an opportunity to perform their group reading.

6 Story Maps

Story Maps are graphic representations of some or all elements of a literary text, showing the relationships between the elements. Whether they are used during or after reading, Story Maps represent a practical way for students to organise their thinking. They can vary greatly in structure according to the purpose of the activity, the students' phase of development and the nature of the text.

Readers benefit from creating a range of different maps.
• *Basic maps* — graphic representation of some of the main elements, such as the setting, characters, events, problem or resolution.
• *Chronological maps* — chronological representation of the sequence of events in a clockwise direction.

• *Geographical maps* — using setting as the central focus, illustrating how the story unfolds.

Creating Story Maps helps students to comprehend text by identifying explicit information.

– Read the text to students, or provide time for independent reading.
– Have them draw elements on cards or sticky notes. This allows the elements to be moved or the positions changed.
– Direct them to place the cards or notes to create a draft Story Map.
– Provide time for students to share and compare their draft maps, and to refine them as needed.
– Encourage them to use their Story Maps as a basis for retelling.

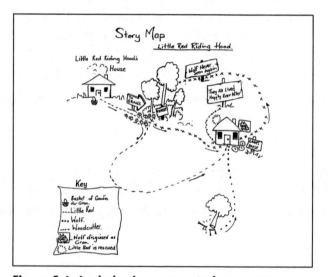

Figure 5.4 A whole-class generated story map

7 Wall Stories

Wall Stories are large representations (including text and illustrations) of the main events of a text either read or heard; they are an effective way of helping Experimental readers to focus on the meaning of words and pictures and to reconstruct a text they have heard or read.

It is appropriate for Experimental readers to work as a whole class or in small-group settings to create wall stories. Literary texts with simple storylines are a great source to use, and songs, poems, rhymes and language-experience activities can also provide a context for this activity.

– Read students a chosen text.
– Pair students to orally retell the text.
– Work with the students to elicit and record the main events of the text on a chart or on cards. (Alternatively, sequence prepared

cards that list the main events.) When students are unsure of information or disagree about a main event, model the process of returning to the text to clarify meaning.

– Organise students to work in small groups to illustrate the main events.
– Jointly sequence the cards and read the newly created text with students.
– Display the wall story, and refer to it frequently during classroom print walks.

8 Timelines

Timelines are a variation on regular sequencing activities, providing the additional dimension of the language used to describe the order of events in a text.

– Discuss timelines with students, indicating their purpose and explaining how to 'read' them. Illustrate the concept with a familiar time span, such as the school day.
– After reading a literary text, have students retell it by describing the main events.
– Have them put these events in order, using previously collected or drawn pictures.
– Draw a timeline and attach the pictures to it. Discuss the events, using language such as 'What happened before . . .?' and 'What happened after . . .?'

9 Same and Different

Same and Different can show the links and relationships between two or more texts. Experimental readers could work as a whole class and create Venn diagrams to compare information presented in two texts on the same topic, or to compare different text forms.

– As a class, brainstorm possible items of comparison; e.g. **information across texts or types of characters.**
– Encourage students to provide information from the texts on the selected item. Decide whether it is common to both texts or applicable only to one.
– List the information in the appropriate space on the Venn diagram.

10 Reading Riddles

Solving Who Am I? and What Am I? riddles encourages Experimental readers to return purposefully to a text to locate explicit information.

– After Shared Reading of a text, ask students to solve 'Who Am I?' or 'What Am I?' riddles that focus on the characters, objects, setting or events.

– Begin with broad, open clues and progressively add more specific clues, using those that focus on feelings, actions and speech as well as on attributes; for example:

– I am something beautiful that you can wear. I am made of unusual material.

– I was left on the steps of a palace after a ball.

– A prince carried me around on a cushion, looking for my owner.

– The ugly stepsisters could not fit their huge feet into me.

What Am I?

– Model how to use the clues and the text to solve the riddle.

– When students are familiar with creating the 'Who Am I?' and 'What Am I?' clues, guide them as a group to create their own riddles.

– Whole-class riddles could be created as part of Modelled and Shared Writing sessions.

CONTEXTUAL UNDERSTANDING

Major Teaching Emphases

■ **Provide opportunities for students to share and justify opinions and feelings about texts,** e.g. about characters, events, information.

■ **Discuss some of the decisions authors and illustrators make when creating texts,** e.g. what characters will look like.

■ **Draw attention to the ways people or characters are represented in texts, and discuss alternatives,** e.g. 'This giant is mean. How do we know this?'

Teaching Notes

Students in this phase benefit from the opportunity to discuss the content of texts and to express their opinions and feelings openly. Such discussions allow them to see that others may have different opinions that are equally valid, and encourage them to value the opinions of others. In this phase, the focus is on facilitating exploration of each student's thinking, while refraining from influencing opinions.

Experimental readers need support to develop the understanding that texts represent a view of the world that may or may not be similar to their own experiences. However, although analysis of a text is important, the overall enjoyment of it should remain the priority.

Modelled and Shared Reading sessions provide an opportunity to highlight and discuss the kind of decisions that authors and illustrators make.

The foci for helping Experimental readers to develop contextual understanding are organised under the following headings.
• Discussions about Texts
• Discussions about the Decisions Authors and Illustrators Make
• Discussions about the way People or Characters are Represented in Texts

Discussions about Texts

For students to understand texts, they need to make connections and comparisons between their own experiences and those presented in the text. This can be achieved in various ways.

- Assist students to make such connections; e.g. 'Has anything that happens in the story ever happened to you? Tell us about it.'
- Help them to compare events and people in texts with those in their own lives; e.g. 'My dad and mum both go to work, but in the book only dad went to work'.
- Support students to think beyond the literal level; e.g. 'Why do you think the troll lived under the bridge?'
- Encourage them to give reasons why a particular book is liked or disliked.
- Encourage them to give reasons why a certain text could be based on reality, or why it could not.

Discussions about the Decisions Authors and Illustrators Make

The choices authors and illustrators make can affect the interpretation of a text, and are often chosen for that reason. While not necessarily expressing things explicitly, both may use subtle ways to get their message across to the reader. The focus in this phase will be on discussing the way the illustrator has chosen to illustrate the text and the words the author has used to describe the people or characters, setting, facts or events.

Devices used by illustrators include:
- the use of light and shade;
- the size of one character relative to others;
- positioning on the page — for instance, the most important object is often in the centre foreground;
- the choice of medium, such as strong, bold colours.

Devices used by authors include:
- words to describe appearances, e.g. short, thin, blond;
- words to describe actions, e.g. raced, dawdled, slyly;
- words to describe emotions, e.g. excited, terrified, happy;
- humour and wit;
- repetition, e.g. 'He was a big, big man . . .'

Facilitate discussion by asking a variety of questions.
- What words did you hear in the text to describe . . .?
- How has the illustrator chosen to illustrate . . .? (mentioning size relative to other characters, or facial expressions).
- How do the illustrations support the text? (asking what the pictures tell you that the words don't).
- If you were drawing . . ., how would you have shown him?
- What would the author have needed to know to write this text?

- What does the author think people like to read about?
- What does the author think people already know about this topic?

Discussions about the Way People or Characters are Represented in Texts

In this phase, students benefit from the opportunity to discuss why and how authors and illustrators have chosen to represent people or characters in certain ways. Both literary and informational texts contain representations that can be questioned.

Facilitate discussion by asking a variety of questions.
- How has the author (or illustrator) represented people or characters? For example, in this text the nurses are female. Are nurses always female? How else could the author have represented the nurses?
- Do you know any real people who are like the characters in the text? Who are they? How are they the same? How are they different?
- Who is telling this story?
- Would you like to be anyone in the text? Who? Why?
- What message is the author giving?
- What does the author think about . . .? How do you know?
- How is a particular character — for example, Bob the Builder — portrayed from one text to another?
- How are similar characters represented across two texts? 'Let's look at the way princesses are represented.'
- How is information on a topic, such as spiders, the same or different in two texts?

> For further information about the Contextual Understanding substrand, see *Reading Resource Book*, 2nd edn, Chapter 2: Contextual Understanding.

Involving Students

1 Changing Places

Inviting students to choose which character to change places with enables Experimental readers to make connections to the characters or people in a text. In this activity, students are required to justify why they chose a particular character or person.

- After reading a text to students, invite them to choose anyone in it with whom they would like to change places.
- Invite them to share the names of the characters or people they choose, and give their reasons. Encourage them to return to the

text to justify their choices; e.g. 'I'd like to change places with Hush (Possum Magic) because she was invisible at the beginning of the story and I think it would be great to be invisible because I could sneak up on people and they wouldn't know. I don't think I'd like to be invisible forever, though'.

2 Goodies and Baddies Rating Scale

The Goodies and Baddies Rating Scale involves students in rating people or characters in a text, basing the judgement on both information in the text and personal experience. Readers can be introduced to some of the devices authors and illustrators use to influence the construction of meaning. When completing a rating scale, students can be encouraged to explore and share different interpretations of events and actions.

Readers would benefit from completing this activity as a whole class before working in small groups.

– Select two or three main characters from the text, such as Princess Elizabeth, the dragon or Prince Ronald.
– Ask students to rank the characters according to selected criteria; for example, the meanest, the kindest, the funniest or the smartest.
– Ask them to suggest one or two actions, events or illustrations in the text to justify their ranking of the character against the criterion; for instance, the dragon is the meanest because he burnt the castle.
– Record their suggestions on a class chart for future reference.
– Discuss other devices authors and illustrators use that may have escaped students' notice, such as the size of the characters relative to each other, or the colours used.

Goodies and Baddies Rating Scale		
Who was the ...?	Character ranking	We thought this because ...
Smartest	1. Elizabeth	She tricked the dragon.
	2. Dragon	He could fly around the world in twenty seconds.
	3. Ronald	He got taken away by the dragon and couldn't escape.

Figure 5.5

3 Catalogue Searches

Refer to Chapter 4: Role Play Reading Phase, p. 66.

4 Possible Predictions

Refer to Chapter 4: Role Play Reading Phase, p. 66.

5 Text Innovation

Text Innovation is the name given to the process of adapting an existing text. By completing innovation activities with a contextual understanding focus, students are encouraged to adapt characters, character traits or setting. They will also consider the impact of their changes on the storyline.

- Select a text for innovation.
- Read it to students several times.
- Select a feature that could be innovated upon. Innovations could involve:
  - changing the gender of one of the characters;
  - substituting new characters for those in the text; e.g. **how would the story change if Red Riding Hood met a bear at the grandmother's house?**;
  - changing characteristics; e.g. **instead of a mean wolf, have a kind wolf;**
  - changing the setting; e.g. **setting Possum Magic in another country.**
- Jointly innovate on the original text to create a new one (either oral or written). Discuss how any changes impact on the rest of the text: 'When we changed the wolf from being mean to being kind, the grandma didn't get eaten'.
- Encourage students to make comparisons between the original text and the new version, explaining which one they preferred, and why.
- Identify and discuss how the changes they made impacted on the text.
  - If the gender of a character changed, how was the language of the original text changed to suit?
  - If the gender of a character changed, was there any effect on the setting, the action or the events?
  - When characterisics were changed, how was the text changed?
  - What changes occurred when the setting was altered?
- If the text is written, invite students to illustrate the newly created one. It can be turned into a big book, a class book or a wall story.
- As a whole class, work with students to re-read the newly created text.

6 Same and Different

Same and Different focuses students' attention on similarities and differences in the information presented in two texts; those identified can be represented in the form of a Venn diagram. Experimental readers can compare how different authors have represented similar characters. In this phase, it is appropriate for students to compare characters from just two texts.

– Read two texts with similar characters, such as princesses.
– Select the characters to be compared; for example, Cinderella and the Paper Bag Princess.
– As a whole group, brainstorm and record things students remember about the characters in each text, such as character traits, actions and physical appearance.
– Examine the two lists to decide which things are common to both characters. These items should then be transferred to the intersecting space in the Venn diagram (see Figure 5.6).
– Transfer the remaining information in the lists to the appropriate space in the diagram.
– Provide time for students to discuss the similarities and differences in the characters.

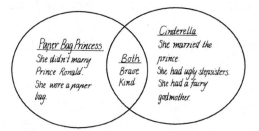

Figure 5.6

7 Like or Unlike?

Like or Unlike? is an activity that helps students to make connections and comparisons between what they know about the world in which they live and the way people or characters are represented in a text.

– Select a main character or person in a text; for example, Mrs Jones is Fred's stepmother.
– Before reading the text, invite students to share what they know about that type of person or thing in real life; for example, ask 'What do we know about stepmothers?'
– Record responses on a class chart.
– Ask students to draw their impression or idea of the character.
– Have them share their portraits with the whole class, discussing the characteristics they have included.

– Read the text to the class.

– Discuss how the character or person has been represented in the text. Record student responses on a class chart.

– Draw students' attention to any differences or similarities between what they know and how the characters or people may have been represented in the text.

– Provide opportunities for them to discuss how the author could change the way the character or person was represented, and the impact this would have on the text.

What We Know about Stepmothers	What the Book Says about Stepmothers
· Young and pretty	· Mean and ugly
· Intelligent	· Old
· Kind and helpful	· Jealous
· Wear nice clothes	· Nasty
	· Don't like children

Figure 5.7

8 Text Detective

Text Detective is an activity that requires students to consider the information provided in a title and in characters' names when making inferences. Completing this activity helps Experimental readers understand that authors and illustrators sometimes present a view of the world that may differ from their own.

– Before reading the text or showing the cover, read the title to the students.

– Have them discuss what they think the author, in choosing the title, wanted them to know about the text. Record responses.

– Introduce and write the name of each character on the board.

– Have students share inferences about each character, based on the title and the names. Record responses.

– Read the text to the students and record information about the characters.

– Have students make comparisons with the inferences they made.

– Discuss how much information the title and the characters' names had already given them before the text was read.

Text Detective				
Title	What we predict from the title	Characters	What we predict about each character	What the text said
John Brown Rose and the Midnight Cat by Jenny Wagner	It could be about a nocturnal cat It might be about a boy with a cat that comes out at midnight It could be about an old man and a cat that tricks him by coming out at midnight	John Brown Rose Midnight Cat	-a man - a boy - an old person -a girl dog - a bird - a little girl -a black and white cat - a cat that comes out at night	-he's a big dog -he loves Rose - he doesn't like the Midnight cat -she's an old lady - she likes cats and dogs -she's black and comes to live with Rose and John Brown.

Figure 5.8

9 Hidden Pictures

Hidden Pictures, like Text Detective, is an activity that allows students to decide how the characters or people in a text could be represented. Creating a drawing of characters or people before a text has been read or viewed helps Experimental readers to understand that authors and illustrators make decisions to present a view of the world, and that this may differ from their own.

- Read an unfamiliar text without showing students the illustrations.
- After reading, allocate students a character or person in the text. Ensure they have still not seen the illustrations.
- Ask them to draw the character or person.
- When the drawings have been completed, discuss:
  - what was heard in the text to help make decisions; e.g. 'It said he had big black heavy boots'.
  - what was inferred from the text to help make decisions; e.g. 'He hit the other man. I thought he was mean, so I drew him with a mean face'.
- Invite students to share their drawings.
- Provide time for them to compare their drawings with the text illustrations.
- Discuss similarities and differences, and speculate on why the author or illustrator made those choices.

CONVENTIONS

Major Teaching Emphases

■ **Continue to build students' sight vocabulary,** e.g. high-frequency words, personally significant words.

■ **Continue to build phonological awareness, graphophonic and word knowledge, such as:**
  – **segmenting words into sounds**
  – **linking letters with their regular sounds**
  – **recognising that letters can represent different sounds**
  – **recognising how word parts and words work.**

■ **Model the use of conventions of print,** e.g. question marks, exclamation marks.

■ **Build students' knowledge of different text forms,** e.g. purpose, structure and organisation.

Teaching Notes

Provide an environment rich in oral language that includes reading stories aloud, reciting poems and rhymes, singing songs and playing with language. It is important that the conventions of written language be introduced and practised in meaningful contexts. Modelled and Shared Reading and Writing provide a springboard for exploring many of the concepts and conventions of print. In this phase, continue to draw students' attention to the concepts and conventions of written language, such as the one-to-one match between spoken and written language.

The following suggestions are not intended to be prescriptive. Consider the needs of the students and the requirements of any curriculum or syllabus documents before making decisions about what to teach and when.

The foci for supporting Experimental readers to develop understandings about Conventions are organised under the following headings.
• Sight Vocabulary
• Phonological Awareness, Graphophonic Knowledge and Word Knowledge
• Concepts and Conventions of Print
• Knowledge about Text Forms

Sight Vocabulary

Sight vocabulary is the bank of words a reader is able to automatically decode, pronounce and understand in the contexts in which they are used. Such words are called 'sight words' because efficient readers need to instantly recognise them on sight to maintain the speed and fluency required to make sense of the author's message. Many of these words have irregular spellings, making them difficult to decode.

Fry et al. (1984) suggests that 100 words make up about half of all we read; they make up what is known as the high-frequency vocabulary. If students are to become fluent readers, they need to learn to recognise them quickly and easily.

In this phase, continue to build the sight vocabulary that students began to develop as Role Play readers. This could include:
- high-frequency words, such as words from the Dolch list (Dolch 1939), Basic Sight Vocabulary (Holdaway 1980), or Fry's 300 Instant Sight Words list (Fry et al. 1984);
- personally significant words, such as the student's address, and the names of the town or city, the school and other teachers.

Exploring and using these words in both reading and writing activities will help to reinforce their recognition and use. For some students, ongoing systematic instruction is essential to help them develop automaticity; for others, the repeated reading and writing of texts helps them develop the ability to immediately recognise a large number of words.

Phonological Awareness, Graphophonic Knowledge and Word Knowledge

Understandings to be developed in relation to phonological awareness include the following.
- Word awareness: spoken language is made up of words that represent objects, emotions and concepts.
- Syllable awareness: some words have a single syllable and some are multisyllabic.
- Phonemic awareness: words are made up of individual sounds, or phonemes.

Within phonological awareness is phonemic awareness (see *Reading Resource Book*, 2nd edn, Chapter 3). When developing phonemic awareness, the following progression may be considered.
- Isolating phonemes: alliteration, position (first, last), generating words with a given sound.

- Blending phonemes: putting sounds together to form words, using individual phonemes (p l ay) or onset and rime (pl ay).
- Segmenting phonemes: isolating sounds, hearing and counting sounds in words, producing sounds.
- Manipulating phonemes: adding, deleting or substituting sounds.

Graphophonic knowledge refers to a reader's knowledge of letters and combinations of letters and the sounds associated with them, including the following undestandings.

- A letter has a name, and represents a sound in a word. The focus in this phase is on the regular sound: This is the letter 'c', and in cat it sounds like /k/.
- A letter may represent different sounds: 'c' represents the sound /k/ in cat, but /s/ in city.

Word knowledge refers to a reader's knowledge of the meanings of words, and how they work.

Develop elements of word knowledge such as:

- plurals, e.g. **-s, -es;**
- past tense, e.g. **-ed;**
- compound words, e.g. **football;**
- contractions, e.g. **don't, can't, it's.**

Concepts and Conventions of Print

Continue to model and discuss the concepts and conventions taught in the Role Play phase. Introduce Experimental readers to:

- the use of punctuation marks, such as question marks and exclamation marks;
- the way punctuation marks affect meaning and expression, as in 'Come here!';
- the way sentences are structured — the describing word (adjective) comes before the naming word (noun). While correct terminology is important, the emphasis in this phase is on understanding.

Knowledge about Text Forms

Building students' knowledge about text forms will assist them to access information in texts. Analysing and discussing different forms will help them to understand the purpose, structure and organisation of texts.

Purpose

Texts are written for a purpose. The purpose may be to entertain, as in most literary texts, or to explain, describe or inquire, as in some informational texts.

Text Organisation

Text organisation refers to the layout. Experimental readers will benefit from understanding text-form frameworks; for instance, a letter may include a salutation, a retelling of events, and a close. It is also important for these readers to understand the function, terminology and use of organisational features such as:

- headings and subheadings;
- captions;
- diagrams and other visual aids (photographs, graphs, tables, cross-sections);
- paragraphs;
- bold or italicised words;
- illustrations;
- hyperlinks.

Text Structure

Text structure refers to the way ideas, feelings and information are linked in a text. These could include problem and solution; compare and contrast; cause and effect; listing — logical or chronological sequence, collection of details.

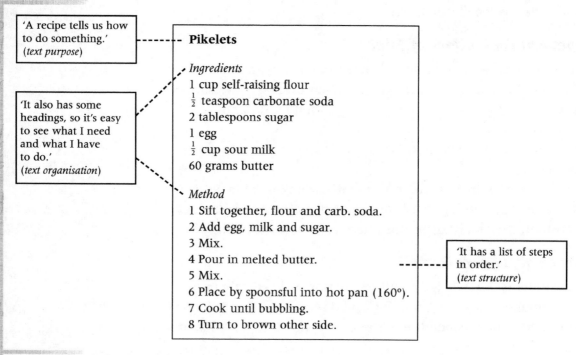

'A recipe tells us how to do something.' (*text purpose*)

'It also has some headings, so it's easy to see what I need and what I have to do.' (*text organisation*)

Pikelets

Ingredients
1 cup self-raising flour
$\frac{1}{2}$ teaspoon carbonate soda
2 tablespoons sugar
1 egg
$\frac{1}{2}$ cup sour milk
60 grams butter

Method
1 Sift together, flour and carb. soda.
2 Add egg, milk and sugar.
3 Mix.
4 Pour in melted butter.
5 Mix.
6 Place by spoonful into hot pan (160°).
7 Cook until bubbling.
8 Turn to brown other side.

'It has a list of steps in order.' (*text structure*)

Figure 5.9 Analysis of a Text Form

For further information about the Conventions substrand, see *Reading Resource Book*, 2nd edn, Chapter 3: Conventions.

Involving Students

1 Sight Vocabulary Activities

Modelled, Shared and Guided Reading and Writing provide excellent contexts for talking about words and supporting the development of students' sight vocabulary.

– Draw attention to high-frequency and personally significant words as they occur.
– Discuss these words; write them on a chart or the Word Wall.
– Provide each student with a copy of the text being read in which to find examples of specific words.
– Read the chart or display as part of a print walk.

There is a range of activities to support sight-vocabulary development.

Jumping over Puddles

Make 'puddles' from card and laminate; write sight words on them with erasable marking ink so that they may be used a number of times. Place them across the classroom floor and have the students jump over them, saying the words as they go.

Soap Boxes

Give students small containers into which they put cards bearing the five or six words they are learning. They can take these home to practise, as well as revisiting them in spare moments during the day. Encourage them to play games with their particular words.

Word Folders

Provide each student with a folder that has six pockets. Place up to six words in the first pocket. When a word can be identified, move it to the second pocket. Repeat this daily until each word has reached pocket six. After six successful identifications, remove the word and enter it in the student's permanent word bank. As words are removed from pocket six, continually add new words to pocket one.

2 Word Walls

A Word Wall is a designated space in the classroom devoted to displaying words. As words are discovered, introduced and discussed, Word Walls are constructed jointly with the students. Words can be sorted according to the current teaching focus; for Experimental readers students' names can provide a springboard for analysing many other words.

– Create the Word Wall jointly with the students. Begin by displaying enlarged letters of the alphabet (both upper and lower case).
– Add students' names one at a time, pointing out distinctive features such as letter patterns and the number of syllables.
– Add other words as they are discovered or introduced; for example, high-frequency words and days of the week (see Figure 5.10).
– Jointly work with students to sort the words in various ways; for example, according to beginning sounds or letter patterns.
– Read, refer to and use the words on the Word Wall during daily print walks, when modelling or during writing activities.

Ff	Gg		Hh	Ii
Francis	Greg	Gino	Harry	Italo
Fiona	Gary	giraffe	Heather	
fish	gate			
Friday	go			

Figure 5.10

3 Magic Words

Magic Words (Hoyt 2000) is an activity that provides an opportunity for students to identify sight words or to focus on parts of words, such as digraphs. The use of a familiar text projected onto a wall with an overhead projector is the context for Magic Words. Students use a piece of card and a 'little magic' to isolate selected letters or words from a whole text.

– Read and re-read a text with the whole class.
– Select a criterion for the magic words; for example, 'I am looking for a word with the sound /oo/ in it'.
– Demonstrate how to 'lift' words from the screen by using a piece of white card. Place the piece of card in front of the projected text on the wall or screen. Place the card on the selected word, ensuring it fits the word. Slowly move the card away from the screen, isolating the selected word. As if by magic, the word is now 'floating' on the white card.
– Have students examine the magic word to decide if it fits the criterion.
– Allow them time to take turns lifting words with identified criteria. They could find:
  – words in which a letter represents different sounds, such as in 'bed' and 'be';
  – words that start or finish with a particular letter;

– words that have a particular onset and rime, or the same number of syllables;

– identified punctuation marks.

4 Word Back Spied Her

Word Back Spied Her can be used for a wide range of purposes. It is an excellent open-ended activity to support the development of sight vocabulary and word knowledge. A number of words, based on student needs or interest, are printed on sticky labels. A label is then placed on each student's back and the student is challenged to identify the word by questioning others.

– Select the words to be used.

– Prepare a sticky label bearing one of the words for each student.

– Place a label on each student's back, ensuring that the word has not been seen.

– Provide each student with a complete list of the words.

– Discuss rules for questioning, such as these.

  – Questions need to be related to the features of the word; for example, 'Does my word start with 'a'? end with 's'? have two parts?'

  – Responses can only be 'yes' or 'no'.

  – A student can only ask another student one question before moving on.

  – A student who is unable to answer a question may say 'pass'.

– Teach students how to eliminate words from the list as they ask their questions.

– Direct them to move into designated groups as the words are determined; for example, one group could have all the words that begin with the letter 'a'.

It is critical that either during or at the end of the activity students are given the opportunity to reflect on and discuss the types of questions that were asked. This will help them to distinguish between useful and less useful questions to use in determining the words they have been given. Individualised lists can be created if necessary.

Figure 5.11

5 Word-Sorting Activities

Experimental readers can be involved in a range of word-sorting activities.

- *Beginning-or-final* letter sorts focus on the position of letters; for example, words that begin or end with the letter 't'.
- *Number-of-letters* sorts focus on the length of words.
- *Sound* sorts focus on the different sounds a single letter can represent; for example, sorting words containing 'g' according to the sounds it represents.
- *Letter-patterns* sorts focus on words that have or do not have a particular letter pattern; for example, words that have 'ea' and those that do not.
- *Number-of-syllables* sorts focus on grouping words according to whether they have one, two or more syllables.

For more information on word-sorting activities, refer to Chapter 4: Role Play Reading Phase, p. 74.

6 Text Innovation

Text Innovation in its purest form is the adoption of a language pattern used by an author. Texts that contain repetitive patterns can be copied to create innovations; they provide an opportunity for Experimental readers to work with high-frequency words in a meaningful context. Innovations may focus on substituting individual words, copying simple sentence patterns or copying the text structure. Students enjoy the challenge of creating text innovations, and these self-developed texts then provide a context for re-reading to practise the use of high-frequency words.

Innovation on Words

The T-Shirt Song (Rigby 1988)
I have a T-shirt. I have a T-shirt.
And I love it so.
I wear my T-shirt, I wear my T-shirt
Everywhere I go.

The _ _ Red Cap _ _ _ Song
I have a _ red cap _ _ _ _ _ _.
I have _ red cap _ _ _ _ _ _ _
And I love it so.
I wear my _ _ red cap _ _ _ _ _
I wear my _ red cap _ _ _ _ _
Everywhere I go.

Figure 5.12 Text Innovation framework for The T-shirt Song

Innovation on Repetitive Sentence Patterns

Brown Bear, by Bill Martin

Brown bear, brown bear, what do you see?
I see a white dog looking at me.

Red dog, red dog what do you hear?
I hear a cow mooing in my ear.

Innovation on Text Structure

Cumulative, repetitive texts such as *The Very Hungry Caterpillar* by
Eric Carle, *Rosie's Walk* by Pat Hutchins or *Possum Goes to School* by
Melanie Carter provide a framework for creating innovations based
on whole-text patterns. Changing the main character in a book is a
simple way for students to use the pattern of the text to create their
own version.

– Read the chosen text a number of times.
– As a whole class, change some aspects of the story but retain the
   original rhythm or rhyme. If necessary, the class could brainstorm
   a list of possible words from which to choose.
– Have students illustrate the new texts and encourage the reading
   of these during both shared and independent reading time.

7 Cloze Activities

Cloze activities encourage students to use context clues to predict
the missing parts of a text; they are easily prepared by deleting
words, parts of words or punctuation marks.

When working with students to complete cloze activities, it is
important to model how to gain the full benefit of context clues by
always reading to the end of a sentence before trying to 'cloze' it.
Also, it is beneficial for students to have the opportunity to discuss
answers and justifications, allowing them to hear about strategies
used by others, and alternative choices

The following list provides options for cloze activities.

Oral Cloze

When reading a familiar book to students, pause every so often and
have the students say the next word.

Punctuation Cloze

Use sections from a text the students are familiar with and have
read many times. Prepare a passage by deleting punctuation marks
so that students can fill the gaps. This activity can be adapted in a

shared book session by using removable stickers to cover key punctuation marks.

Word-Parts Cloze

Develop cloze activities from familiar texts by covering only parts of words, leaving graphophonic clues; for example, Mary st___ on a sharp rock. Encourage students to predict words by looking at the beginning letters.

Whole-Word Cloze

Prepare a passage by deleting any words that are chosen as a focus, such as high-frequency words, nouns or verbs; always leave the first sentence intact. Encourage students to think of a meaningful replacement for each deleted word. Provide scaffolding questions: What could the next word be? Does it make sense? If necessary, support students by providing a list of words from which to choose.

For directions on preparing cloze activities, see the section 'Cloze Procedures' in Chapter 3.

Figure 5.13

8 Sound Hunter

Participating in Sound Hunter helps students to make connections between letters and sounds; it is best introduced and practised in the context of a text. Texts such as books, charted songs and poems, modelled writing examples or written messages can provide contexts for Experimental readers to develop their graphophonic understandings by hunting for words.

– Choose a specific focus. For Experimental readers it could be:
  – any words with a particular letter, such as words that have the letter 'c' in them;

– any words with a particular sound, such as words that begin
  with an /s/ sound.
– Select a text that exhibits the chosen focus.
– Read the text for enjoyment.
– Revisit the text and encourage students to find and circle or
  underline examples of the chosen focus, such as all the words
  that have the letter 'c' in them.
– Discuss the words.
– If the chosen focus lends itself to this, ask the students to sort
  words into subgroups; this might be according to the sound the
  letter represents, such as in <u>c</u>at, <u>ch</u>op or <u>c</u>ity.
– Challenge students then to find as many other examples as they
  can from other resources provided.
– Create a chart of the words they find, leaving room to add more
  words to be added in later activities.
– Revisit, discuss and add to the chart on future occasions.

We are SUPER SOUND HUNTERS
We found these words with the letter 'c'

cat	chop	city
cold	cheese	cent
come	chocolate	

Figure 5.14

9 Secret Messages

Secret Messages is an activity that involves students in decoding.
The messages can be created using the sight vocabulary, word
knowledge and graphophonic understandings being introduced at
the time.

Experimental readers will find it easier to decipher messages that use
a combination of words and pictures. The type of clues provided in
one message may vary; however, it is appropriate to limit the
variation when students are first attempting the activity. Types of
clues might include:

• removing a consonant from the beginning or the end of a word —
  e.g. **take 'f' from 'fan'**;
• replacing a consonant at the beginning or the end of a word —
  e.g. **take 't' from 'take', add 'm' in its place**;
• removing a consonant or consonant cluster from a word and
  blending a new one in the same place — e.g. **take 'mp' off 'lamp',
  add 'st'**;

- finding a small word within a word — e.g. **find a three-letter word in 'sand'**;
- joining two words to form a compound word — e.g. **add 'ball' to 'foot'**;
- using an alphabet sequence for short words — e.g. **use the letter after 'h'**.

Modelling the process for solving Secret Messages is critical at this phase.

- Think of a simple sentence or message, such as 'Sit on the floor'.
- Write a series of clues that will enable students to decode the message.
- Ensure they have access to a copy of the alphabet.
- Work with them to jointly decode the message.
- Keep a copy of all activities to build up a permanent collection for future use.

Monday's Secret Message for Room 2

A B C D E F G H I J K L M N O P Q R S T U V W X Y Z

1 Take 'b' from 'bit' and add 's'.   (sit)
2 The letter after 'n' and the letter after 'm'.   (on)
3 The first word in this sentence .   (the)
4 Take 'd' from 'door' and put in 'fl'.   (floor)

Figure 5.15

10 What Comes Next?

What Comes Next? is an adaptation of what was known as the game Hangman. However, What Comes Next? requires students to guess the letters in the correct order rather than randomly.

As a daily activity for Experimental readers, What Comes Next? provides an excellent context for reinforcing and using any graphophonic or word understandings; for example:
- a word is made up of a series of letters in a sequence;
- letters together represent the specific sounds in a word;
- words have common letter patterns;
- prefixes can be added to the beginnings of words;
- suffixes can be added to the end of words.

- Choose a word from a familiar context that features the focus-letter sequence or word-study understanding. Draw lines representing each letter in the word.

– Provide a specific clue for the first letter; for example: The first
  letter is between 'r' and 't'. When students guess the correct letter,
  record it on the first line.
– Invite students to guess the remaining letters of the word.
– As they guess a letter, write any guesses that are incorrect but are
  possible sequences in a 'Could Be' column. Incorrect guesses that
  will not make possible sequences should be recorded in a
  'Couldn't Be' column as single letters (not modelling incorrect
  letter patterns). When students guess a letter that could not be
  right, a segment of a mouse outline is drawn.
– Continue this until the correct letters are given and recorded on
  the lines.
– The game ends if the drawing of the mouse is completed before
  the students complete the word.

As an extension, students can be challenged to find other words
linked to the patterns identified in the game word; for example,
if the chosen word is 'stop', groups could be challenged to find
words with 's', 'st' or 'op'.

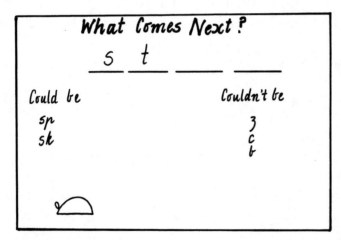

Figure 5.16

11 Elkonin Boxes

Refer to Chapter 4: Role Play Reading Phase, p. 79.

12 Building Words

Building Words is an activity that encourages Experimental readers
to create words by manipulating letters. Providing a variety of
stimulating resources will encourage them to experiment, developing
and practising their graphophonic understandings, phonological
awareness and word knowledge. Magnetic letters, letter tiles, foam
cut-outs or wooden blocks with letters can all be used for word-
building activities.

Challenge students to use their own ideas, or provide guidelines for the type of words they could build. These could include:
• words with the same first letter;
• words with the same final letter;
• words that contain a particular sound, such as /ee/ as in tree;
• two-, three- or four-letter words;
• words on a theme, such as colours, numbers or days of the week;
• words from a given set of letters;
• compound words;
• plural words.

13 Exploring Words

Exploring Words is an open-ended activity that provides students with the opportunity to work at their own level to create words.

– Provide students with one or more central focus letters, such as 'a'.
– Also provide a selection of letters and letter combinations that could be added to the central focus to create words.
– Provide guidelines about the creation of the words; for example:
  – each letter can only be used once in a word;
  – letters can be added both to the beginning and to the end of the central focus.
– Challenge students to create as many words as possible in a given time.
– Provide time to share the words and to reflect upon patterns in the lists.

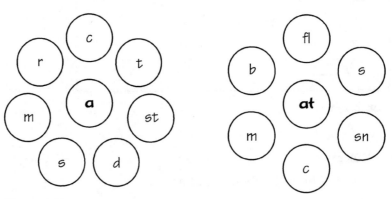

Figure 5.17

14 Change a Letter

Change a Letter involves students in creating new words by changing one letter at a time in a given word. This activity helps Experimental readers to focus on the regular sounds of letters and their position in words.

– Provide students with a three-letter base word, such as 'cut'.
– Challenge them to change one letter to make a new word, such as 'cot'. Initial, medial or final letters can be changed.
– Ask them to repeat this process with the new word.
– Challenge them to see how many new words they can create in a given time.
– Provide time to share words and to reflect upon patterns in those created.

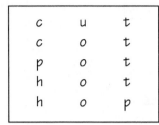

Figure 5.18

Once a bank of words has been created, they can be used for word-sorting activities using initial, medial or final letters.

15 Letter Poetry

Letter Poetry (Hoyt 2000) provides a structure for the creation of simple poems using words with a specified focus. It supports Experimental readers in further developing their graphophonic understandings. Creating whole-class poems is fun, and will provide Experimental readers with a clear framework for creating poems independently or in small groups.

– Select a focus, such as letter, onset or digraph.
– Have students brainstorm words that begin with the chosen focus.
– Record the words on sticky notes, blank cards or a whiteboard.
– Introduce a framework for creating a poem.
– Manipulate the brainstormed words, jointly selecting the best fit for each space in the framework.
– Read the poem several times, discussing the selected focus.
– Select a group of students to illustrate the poem. Display their work in the classroom.
– Create and collate further poems for other letters.
– Revisit the poems regularly.

___ ___ ___ is for ___ ___ ___.
a ___ ___ ___ and a ___ ___ ___.
A ___ ___ ___ a ___ ___ ___.
and the ___ ___ ___ on
the ___ ___ ___.

I like ___ ___ ___,
I like ___ ___ ___,
I like ___ ___ ___
but I don't like ___ ___ ___.

___ ___ ___ is for ___ ___ ___
who likes ___ ___ ___, ___ ___ ___
and ___ ___ ___.
___ ___ ___ doesn't like ___ ___ ___,
___ ___ ___ and ___ ___ ___.

A ___ ___ ___ is big.
A ___ ___ ___ is big.
A ___ ___ ___ is big,
but a ___ ___ ___ is small.

Figure 5.19 Letter Poetry frameworks

16 Sentence Reconstruction Activities

Sentence Reconstruction activities help students develop an understanding of the function of words and how they are combined to create sentences. They support students in identifying unknown words from the context. An understanding of the type of word that would be needed in a particular sentence provides an important clue when determining unknown words.

– Select a song, poem or rhyme to provide the context for the matching activity.
– Write the text, or parts of it, on sentence strips or word cards.
– Read the text several times, encouraging students to join in wherever possible.
– Ask students to reconstruct the text, or parts of it, using:
  – whole sentences on strips;
  – sentences that have been cut into phrases;
  – sentences that have been cut into individual words, including a card for punctuation marks.
– Re-read the entire text together, checking that it makes sense.
– Leave the word cards and sentence strips in an accessible area and encourage students to continue to reconstruct the text as they wish.

Figure 5.20

17 Punctuation Effects

Punctuation Effects provides students with an opportunity to practise reading sentences, varying expression according to the punctuation marks. It is essential for students to develop an understanding of the importance of punctuation, as it can alter the reading of even simply constructed sentences.

- Create cards showing punctuation marks and known sight words, including students' names.
- Jointly create simple sentences.
- Jointly read the sentences, using the punctuation marks as a guide to expression and volume.

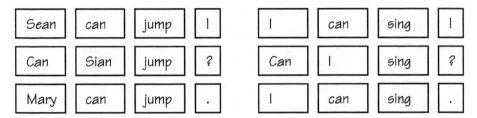

Sean	can	jump	!
Can	Sian	jump	?
Mary	can	jump	.

I	can	sing	!
Can	I	sing	?
I	can	sing	.

Figure 5.21

18 Vocab-o-Gram

Vocab-o-Gram involves students in using key words and knowledge of text form to make predictions about text content.

- Prior to sharing a text, provide students with a list of selected key words.
- Prepare a sorting framework that includes appropriate elements from the selected text.
  - A narrative-sorting framework might include elements such as setting, characters, problem and actions.
  - A sorting framework for a procedure might include elements such as goal, materials, steps and result.
- Invite students to categorise the key words using the sorting framework provided.
- Ask them then to use the sorted key words to make and share predictions about the text.
- Read the text together, noting similarities and differences in their predictions and the text.

Setting	Characters	Problem	Actions
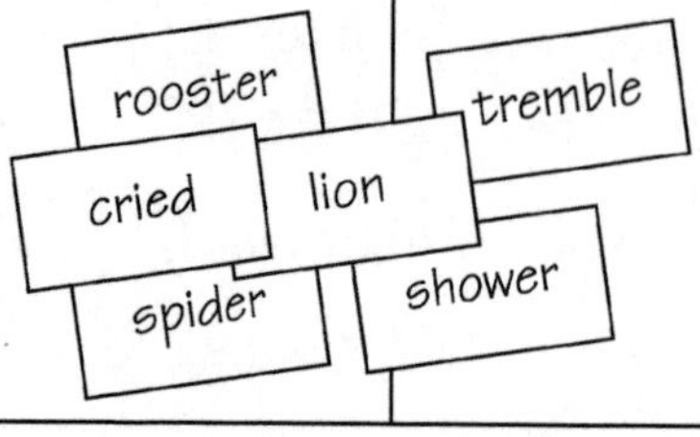 rooster tremble cried lion spider shower			

Figure 5.22 Sorting framework for a narrative text

19 Reading Plans

Reading Plans (Hoyt 2002) are a way of helping students to become aware of the organisation of different informational texts. The creation and use of these plans needs to be modelled. A new plan can be created and the purpose determined each time an informational text is shared.

– Provide a reading-plan framework.
– Introduce the text to the students.
– Discuss the purpose of the reading, and write it in the appropriate space in the framework.
– Invite the students to explore the text organisation to suggest how they might achieve the identified purpose.
– Record their suggestions on the plan framework.
– Work with them to complete the process.
– Provide time to evaluate the plan.

When new plans are created, point out that when the purpose for reading changes, then often the plan will change.

Our Reading Plan

• Our purpose for reading is to find out what spiders eat.

• We will begin by looking at the pictures.

• Then we will look at the headings.

• Next we will look for the word 'food' in the heading and read those sentences.

Figure 5.23 Whole-class generated Reading Plan.

20 Share and Compare

Share and Compare provides students with the opportunity to identify and compare the different features of literary and informational texts; they work in groups to sort a collection of texts into two categories — literary and informational. This interaction and conversation allows students to discuss and build on their knowledge of the features of different texts. They then brainstorm features of each category.

- Provide small groups with a collection of both literary and informational texts. These should be related to a particular topic or theme being studied across the curriculum, such as plants, animals or dinosaurs.
- Have students work together to classify the texts as literary or informational, discussing what influenced their choices.
- Ask them to explore the groups of texts more closely and to further analyse the features of each one. As a whole class, brainstorm and list specific features.
- Create a class chart, listing features of each category. The chart can be added to over time as students discover new similarities and differences between the two types of texts.

What We Discovered about Literary Texts	What We Discovered about Informational Texts
Tell a story	· Start with a contents page
Are not true	· Use real photographs
Have illustrations drawn by somebody	· Have lots of titles or headings
Start by telling us who, what, where, when	· Include graphs
Made us laugh	· Tell about real things
Have main characters	

Figure 5.24

21 Generic Games and Activities

The games and activities outlined in the Role Play Reading phase (see Chapter 4, pp. 86–93) can be used to continue the development of conventions of print, phonological awareness and graphophonic or word understandings in the Experimental Reading phase. The purpose in using each game or activity will be dependent on the chosen focus.

When using these activities, it is important to:
- keep them fun and informal;
- use settings that encourage interaction among students;

- embed them in the context of work that is already being done in the classroom;
- ensure that the students are fully familiar with the way to play the games.

The focus for these activities when used with Experimental readers could be:

- high-frequency words
- personally significant words
- sounds in words
- onset and rime
- single letters
- blends and diagraphs
- plurals
- rhyming words
- syllables.

Generic Games and Activities	CONVENTIONS										
					Phonological Awareness					
							Phonemic Awareness			
	Sight Vocabulary	Graphophonic Understandings	Concepts of Print	Conventions of Print	Word Awareness	Syllable Awareness	Rhyme	Phoneme Isolation	Phoneme Blending	Phoneme Segmentation	Phoneme Manipulation
I Spy . . .		•				•	•	•	•		
Bingo	•	•				•	•	•	•		
Snap	•	•					•	•			
Concentration	•	•					•	•			
Dominoes	•	•					•	•			
A Trip to the Moon						•	•	•			
I Say . . . You Say							•	•			
Play Ball		•	•	•	•	•	•	•			
Snap and Clap					•	•	•				
What Could It Be?		•				•	•	•		•	
Odd One Out	•					•	•	•		•	•
Mystery Bag						•	•	•		•	•
Hunting for Words	•	•			•	•	•				
Using Songs and Rhymes						•	•		•		
What Can You Show Us?	•	•	•	•	•	•	•				
Tic Tac Toe	•	•			•	•	•				

PROCESSES AND STRATEGIES

Major Teaching Emphases

- **Continue to build students' knowledge within the cues,** e.g. text organisation, vocabulary knowledge.

- **Consolidate known comprehension strategies and teach additional strategies,** e.g. self-questioning, predicting.

- **Teach word-identification strategies,** e.g. decoding using phonemes, onset and rime.

- **Continue to teach students how to locate, select and evaluate texts,** e.g. using alphabetical order, introducing browsing techniques.

- **Model self-reflection of strategies used in reading, and encourage students to do the same.**

Organisation of the Processes and Strategies Substrand

The organisation of Processes and Strategies differs in several ways from that of the other substrands.

Both the Teaching Notes and the Involving Students sections are located in Chapter 4 of the *Reading Resource Book*, 2nd edn.

The rationale for this difference in organisation is that reading processes and strategies are not hierarchical, and therefore not phase-specific. A variety of processes and strategies need to be introduced, developed and consolidated at *all* phases of development.

What varies from one phase to the next is the growth in:
- the number and integration of strategies;
- the awareness and monitoring of strategies;
- the efficiency in use and selection of strategies;
- the ability to articulate the use of the strategies;
- the awareness of how the use of strategies helps with making meaning;
- the ability to locate, select and evaluate texts.

Supporting Parents of Experimental Readers

General Description of Experimental Readers

Experimental readers often 'read' by using pictures or a memory of the storyline. They may identify some words in texts; however, they are more focused on getting across the meaning of a text rather than reading every word accurately.

Supporting Experimental Readers in the Home

Experimental readers will benefit from a range of experiences in the home setting. Ideas for providing appropriate experiences are available on Parent Cards located on the *First Steps* Reading CD-ROM.

Teachers can select appropriate cards for each Experimental reader from the Reading CD-ROM and copy them for parents to use at home. Also available on the CD-ROM is a parent-friendly version of the Reading Map of Development.

Parent Cards

1 General Description and How to Support Experimental Readers
2 Encouraging Reading
3 Reading to and with Your Child
4 Selecting Texts
5 Using Everyday Print
6 Reading and Writing Links
7 Developing Word Knowledge
8 Building a Love of Reading
9 Supporting Comprehension
10 Using Computers
11 Using the Library
12 Supporting Phonemic Awareness and Graphophonic Knowledge through Games

---

CHAPTER 6

Early Reading Phase

Figure 6.1

Global Statement

Early readers recognise a bank of frequently used words and use a small range of strategies to comprehend texts. These include short literary texts and structured informational texts that have familiar vocabulary and are supported by illustrations. Reading of unfamiliar texts is often slow and deliberate as they focus on exactly what is on the page, using sounding out as a primary word-identification strategy.

Early Reading Indicators

Use of Texts

◆ **Reads and demonstrates comprehension of texts by:**
  – **recalling key information explicit in a text**
  – **identifying the main idea explicit in a text**
  – **selecting events to retell a text, sometimes including unnecessary events or information**
  – **linking explicit ideas in a text,** e.g. comparing a character at different points in the text.

◆ **Locates and selects texts appropriate to purpose, interest and readability,** e.g. uses library systems, skims contents page.

• Compares texts, selected by the teacher, to determine the most appropriate.

• Attempts to decode a range of texts with less familiar content, structure or vocabulary, but does not always sustain comprehension.

• Discusses some information implicit in a text.

• Reads familiar texts fluently.

• Recognises the difference between literary and informational texts.

Contextual Understanding

◆ **Expresses and justifies personal responses to texts,** e.g. 'I didn't like . . . because . . .'.

◆ **Understands that authors and illustrators select information to suit a purpose and an audience.**

◆ **Recognises how characters, people and events are represented, and offers suggestions for alternatives.**

• Expresses personal views about the actions of a character and speculates on own behaviour, e.g. 'If I had been . . ., I would have . . .'.

• Discusses the author's purpose in writing a text.

• Recognises character traits providing substantiation from the text.

Conventions

◆ **Recognises a bank of frequently used words in different contexts,** e.g. high-frequency words, personally significant words.

◆ **Recognises all letters by name, and their regular sound.**

◆ **Explains how known text forms vary, by stating:**
  – **purpose,** e.g. procedures instruct
  – **some elements of organisation,** e.g. procedures have headings
  – **some elements of structure,** e.g. procedures list materials and steps.

• Uses knowledge of sentence structure and punctuation to aid comprehension.

• Explains the purpose of some simple organisational features of texts, e.g. headings, diagrams, chapters.

• Recognises the relationship signalled by simple conjunctions, e.g. the word 'because' signals that a reason is to follow.

• Recognises that one letter can represent different sounds, e.g. <u>a</u>n, <u>A</u>my, w<u>a</u>s.

• Recognises that one sound can be represented by different letters, e.g. b<u>ea</u>ch, tr<u>ee</u>, m<u>e</u>.

Processes and Strategies

◆ **Draws upon a small knowledge base to comprehend,** e.g. sight vocabulary, concept and text-structure knowledge.

◆ **Uses a small range of strategies to comprehend,** e.g. self-questioning, adjusting reading rate.

◆ **Determines unknown words by using word-identification strategies,** e.g. decoding using phonemes, onset and rime.

◆ **Focuses on decoding words accurately when reading an unfamiliar text, which may result in limited fluency, expression and loss of meaning.**

• Overrelies on decoding single phonemes for word identification.

• Sometimes self-corrects.

• Generates key words for a specific purpose from a text that may or may not be supported by pictures.

• Shows a growing understanding of the use of cues and strategies that is reflected in responses about the reading process, e.g. 'I slowed down when I came to a hard word'.

Major Teaching Emphases

Environment and Attitude
- Create a supportive classroom environment that nurtures a community of readers.
- Jointly construct, and frequently refer to, meaningful environmental print.
- Foster students' enjoyment of reading.
- Encourage students to take risks with confidence.
- Encourage students to select their own reading material according to interest or purpose.

Use of Texts
- Read and re-read a variety of texts, both literary and informational, providing opportunities for students to do the same.
- Teach students to identify explicit and implicit information.
- Teach students to make connections within texts using both explicit and implicit information, e.g. main idea and supporting detail, sequence of key events.

Contextual Understanding
- Encourage students to listen to the opinions and justifications of others, recognising different points of view and interpretations.
- Familiarise students with the devices that authors and illustrators use to influence construction of meaning, e.g. choice of language.
- Discuss how and why facts, characters, people or events are presented in a particular way by the author and illustrator.
- Discuss how texts are written for different purposes and audiences.

Conventions
- Continue to build students' sight vocabulary, e.g. topic words, signal words.
- Continue to build phonological awareness, graphophonic and word knowledge, such as:
  - recognising that a sound can be represented by different letters or letter combinations
  - recognising letter combinations, and the different sounds they represent
  - recognising how word parts and words work.
- Teach the use of conventions of print, e.g. commas, quotation marks.
- Continue to build students' knowledge of different text forms, e.g. purpose, structure, organisation and language features.

Processes and Strategies
- Continue to build students' knowledge within the cues, e.g. grammatical and cultural knowledge.
- Consolidate known comprehension strategies and teach additional strategies, e.g. skimming, scanning.
- Teach word-identification strategies, e.g. reading on, re-reading.
- Continue to teach students how to locate, select and evaluate texts, e.g. identifying different sources of information, checking publication dates.
- Model self-reflection of strategies used in reading, and encourage students to do the same.

Teaching and Learning Experiences

ENVIRONMENT AND ATTITUDE

Major Teaching Emphases

- Create a supportive classroom environment that nurtures a community of readers.

- Jointly construct, and frequently refer to, meaningful environmental print.

- Foster students' enjoyment of reading.

- Encourage students to take risks with confidence.

- Encourage students to select their own reading material according to interest or purpose.

Teaching Notes

Early readers require a safe, supportive classroom environment to help them continue to develop as confident readers. In order to see themselves as lifelong readers, Early readers benefit from an environment that allows them to feel confident to take risks, share texts with others, respond openly to texts, present diverse interpretations of texts and begin to question authors' messages. Such an environment also allows them the opportunity to work in a variety of flexible grouping arrangements. This type of classroom environment encourages students to see reading as an enjoyable experience and to view themselves as successful readers.

Exploring Print

Classroom print provides an excellent context for Early readers to continually learn about how letters, words, sentences and texts work; they benefit from opportunities to explore and interact with print in authentic, purposeful ways. A jointly constructed print-rich environment also helps them understand that print has a range of functions and can be referred to frequently over time. Print can be grouped according to four functions (Owocki 1999).

- **Environmental** — print that gives us information about the world, e.g. schedules, advertisements.
- **Occupational** — print associated with a job or profession, e.g. a chef's might be recipes, menus, food order lists.
- **Informational** — print for storing, retrieving and organising information, e.g. diagrams, encyclopaedias, newspapers, instruction books.
- **Recreational** — print for leisure activities, e.g. novels, magazines, comic books.

Consider the following ideas.

Environmental

- *Labels* of a functional nature can be created using full sentences; e.g. 'Shut down the computer after use'.
- *Captions* can be created for displays of work, using the students' language.
- *Classroom messages* can be posted outside the classroom door or on a message board and used as an independent reading activity before entering the classroom.
- *Name charts* can be created including the first and last names of students in the class and other significant people in the school community.

Occupational

Charts can be created to assist students with responsibilities in the classroom; for example, listing class or school rules, suggestions for students who finish work early, jobs for classroom helpers.

Informational

- *Word banks* can be created to record discoveries or develop vocabulary; for instance, Different Ways of Spelling the Sound /e/, as in 'eat', or Other Words for 'said'.
- *Alphabet charts* can be displayed prominently so that students are able to use them for class activities.
- *Word Walls* can provide a space for recording any new words students are learning or have recently learnt.
- *Charts* can be created and frequently used; examples are weatherwatch charts, class timetables, rosters, Days of the Week, the lunch order menu.

Recreational

- A *word study centre* can provide a stimulus for students to develop an interest in words and promote inquiry into how letters and words work. It can contain letter tiles and boards, pocket charts with word cards, word games or crossword puzzles.

- A *writing table* can give students an opportunity to consolidate, through writing, understandings they are gaining in reading. Items such as coloured paper, pencils or a computer may provide the stimulus and motivation to publish writing in a variety of ways. A display board located in this area can be used to share students' completed work.

- A *reading corner* can be a relaxed, informal area for independent reading. Cushions, comfortable seating, privacy and lighting can create an enticing setting and may encourage a student to join a friend and share a text. A wide range of texts should be made available in the reading corner; these may include dictionaries, atlases, posters, informational texts, magazines, newspapers, comics, class-made texts, interactive CD books, lists of suitable websites, and book and tape sets.

- *Songs*, *poems* and *chants* can be written on charts to provide authentic, enjoyable texts for students to read and re-read.

Interacting with Print

While it is important that the classroom has a variety of environmental print displayed, it is essential that students have ownership of the print, know how to interact with it, and make use of it for different purposes. This can be achieved in various ways.

- Provide opportunities for students to record literacy discoveries they are making.

- Take them on a print walk around the classroom so that they can read and revisit charts they have made, practise words they have learnt, or play games such as matching words or phrases.

- Model the use of charts during Modelled, Shared and Guided Reading.

- Model the use of charts during Modelled, Shared and Guided Writing; e.g. **'How do I work out this word? Look at the charts. Which one would be the best to use?'**

Fostering Enjoyment of Reading

Fostering students' enjoyment of reading can be achieved in many different ways.

- Provide a variety of quality reading materials.

- Create a comfortable physical environment that promotes independent reading.

- Allocate time each day for students to read independently, selecting their own reading materials.

- Read aloud to them regularly, modelling an enjoyment of reading.

- Provide multiple demonstrations of the reading strategies efficient readers use.
- Have a display of students' favourite books. Allow them time to explain their choices.
- Share your favourite books with them and explain why they appeal to you.
- Invite a variety of skilled readers, such as parents, older siblings or community members, to read aloud to the class.
- Ask other adults to share a favourite book from childhood and explain its personal significance.
- Provide opportunities for students to discuss with their peers what they have read or are reading.
- Accept and praise diverse interpretations of text, encouraging students to share and compare points of view.
- Provide ongoing, targeted feedback and encouragement.
- Encourage and organise visits to the school and local libraries.
- Organise visits by authors to speak about their books.
- Develop a 'buddy reading' system with another class in the school.
- Provide authentic reading experiences that are linked to students' interests and experiences, and have a clear purpose or focus.
- Create well-organised, consistent routines for reading experiences and the use of classroom reading materials.
- Involve students in Book Discussion Groups.

Encouraging Risk-Taking

Early readers can be encouraged to become risk-takers if asked to:
- use a variety of strategies to comprehend;
- use a variety of cues to comprehend;
- use a variety of word-solving strategies to identify unknown words;
- read for meaning — Early readers, who are very focused on the print, need to be reminded that reading is about making sense;
- discuss the message and issues in a text, exploring different perspectives and questioning the author's intent;
- 'have a go' at reading and writing;
- discuss their reading strategies and the discoveries they have made.

For further information about Environment and Attitude, see:
- *Linking Assessment, Teaching and Learning*, Chapter 5: Establishing a Positive Teaching and Learning Environment;
- *Reading Resource Book*, 2nd edn, Chapter 1: Use of Texts.

USE OF TEXTS

Major Teaching Emphases

- Read and re-read a variety of texts, both literary and informational, providing opportunities for students to do the same.

- Teach students to identify explicit and implicit information.

- Teach students to make connections within texts using both explicit and implicit information, e.g. main idea and supporting detail, sequence of key events.

Teaching Notes

Early readers benefit from the opportunity to read a range of texts for a variety of purposes. However, as they tend to focus intently on the printed word, they can often get a distorted view of what reading is all about.

The foci for helping Early readers in this substrand are organised under the following headings.
- Variety of Texts
- Identifying Explicit and Implicit Information
- Responding to Texts

Variety of Texts

It is important to ensure that Early readers have opportunities to read texts, both teacher-directed and self-selected, with varying degrees of difficulty. These might include:
- easy texts, e.g. those that been read previously;
- appropriate texts, e.g. those with limited new vocabulary, or about well-known topics;
- more challenging texts, e.g. texts often used in Guided Reading with teacher support.

Although there are many measures of text difficulty, the Rule of Thumb is a simple way to support Early readers when they are self-selecting. In using the Rule of Thumb, students select a text they wish to read and start on a page near the beginning. The page is read, and for each unknown word the student puts a finger down, in order, starting with the little one. If the thumb is put down before reaching the bottom of the page, the text may be too difficult at that time and the reader might like to select another one. Regardless of which measure is used, be aware that students may persist successfully with a difficult text if the content is appealing to them.

In Modelled, Shared and Guided Reading sessions teachers can demonstrate, for instance, how to:
- select texts for different purposes;
- use expression to add interest and enhance meaning;
- use punctuation to aid fluency;
- select explicit information;
- make predictions about the text using pictures, title, table of contents;
- identify the main idea to gain an overall understanding of the text;
- justify answers to questions, using supporting details.

Identifying Explicit and Implicit Information

Students in the Early Reading phase generally draw on information that is explicitly stated, but they are beginning to draw on information that is implied. Implicit information often requires readers to make predictions, connections or generalisations, or to draw conclusions from information that has been either directly or indirectly stated.

Understanding implied information in a text is largely dependent on a reader's prior knowledge (cues) and experience, and to build this knowledge and experience is a critical part of the teacher's role. Thinking aloud during Modelled and Shared reading sessions is an effective way of demonstrating how prior knowledge is accessed and used.

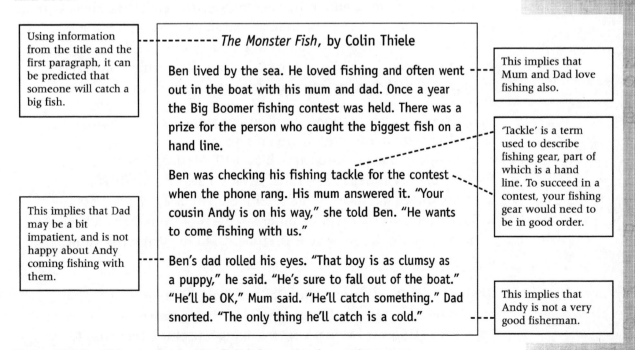

Figure 6.2 contents:

Using information from the title and the first paragraph, it can be predicted that someone will catch a big fish.

The Monster Fish, by Colin Thiele

Ben lived by the sea. He loved fishing and often went out in the boat with his mum and dad. Once a year the Big Boomer fishing contest was held. There was a prize for the person who caught the biggest fish on a hand line.

Ben was checking his fishing tackle for the contest when the phone rang. His mum answered it. "Your cousin Andy is on his way," she told Ben. "He wants to come fishing with us."

Ben's dad rolled his eyes. "That boy is as clumsy as a puppy," he said. "He's sure to fall out of the boat." "He'll be OK," Mum said. "He'll catch something." Dad snorted. "The only thing he'll catch is a cold."

This implies that Mum and Dad love fishing also.

'Tackle' is a term used to describe fishing gear, part of which is a hand line. To succeed in a contest, your fishing gear would need to be in good order.

This implies that Dad may be a bit impatient, and is not happy about Andy coming fishing with them.

This implies that Andy is not a very good fisherman.

Figure 6.2 Identifying and using implicit information in a written text

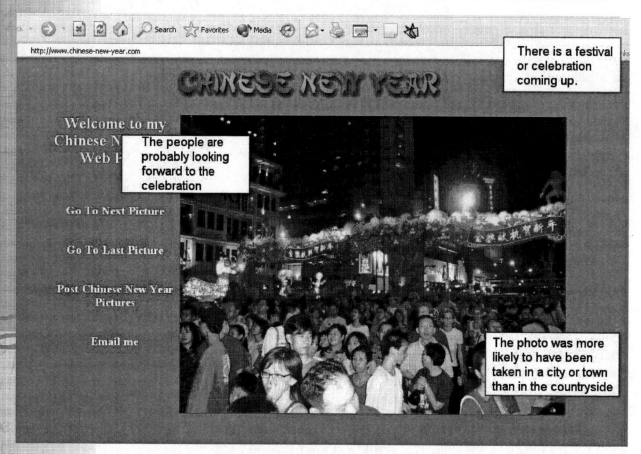

Figure 6.3 Identifying and using implicit information in a visual text

Responding to Texts

In addition to reading and re-reading texts, Early readers will benefit from opportunities to respond to texts and show their understanding. They can be encouraged to do this in a variety of ways, including written, oral and visual responses; in this way they achieve increased engagement and develop a deeper understanding of texts.

Teachers often ask questions to encourage students to respond to texts. There are many ways of organising and discussing types of questions, e.g. **Bloom's Taxonomy (Bloom 1956), Question–Answer Relationships (Raphael 1986), Three Level Guides (Herber 1970) or Open and Closed Questions.** Whichever hierarchy is used, it is wise to include questions that require different levels of thinking and begin to help students, particularly EAL students, to recognise the nature of each one.

Raphael (1986) categorises questions as Right There (Literal), Think and Search (Inferential), Author and You (Interpretive) and On Your Own (Critical/ Evaluative), providing a useful framework for ensuring that different types of questions are used in the classroom.

Literal

Literal questions focus on what the author said. The answer is 'right there' in the text or pictures. These questions require the students to recall information such as events, characters or main ideas. Common literal questions begin with 'who', 'when', 'where' or 'what', and it is important that teachers follow them up with clarifying questions, such as 'How did you know that? Can you show me where it is in the book?' so that students get the idea of substantiating answers by returning to the text.

Inferential

The answers to these questions can be found in the text but are not necessarily in the one place; they are the Think and Search questions. They are also sometimes the 'how' and 'why' questions, showing relationships such as cause and effect, sequence, or compare and contrast. The student has to 'put the answer together' from various sections or sentences in the text; for example, 'On the whole, this story is about . . .', 'What does the author want you to think/believe about . . .?' or 'Why do you think . . . behaved in that way?'

Interpretive

These are the Author and You questions. They require the student to base the answer on the text, but also to draw on previous personal experience to reach a reasonable answer. Examples are: 'From what you know about . . ., why did . . .?' or 'The author has said . . .. What does he mean by that?' The answer should not be a wild guess; it must be probable in light of the text, not just possible from the reader's experience.

Critical/Evaluative

These questions go beyond the text, asking for students' own opinions or judgements. They are the On Your Own questions, as the answers are not found in the text at all; the student answering the question does not need to have read the text, although it does provide a starting point for discussions about the underlying messages in the text. Questions might be 'I wonder why . . .?' or 'Was . . . the best solution to the problem?'.

For further information about the Use of Texts substrand, see *Reading Resource Book*, 2nd edn:
- Chapter 1: Use of Texts
- Chapter 4: Processes and Strategies.

Purposeful
Practice

Involving Students

1 Read and Retell

Refer to Chapter 5: Experimental Reading Phase, p. 107.

2 Readers' Theatre

Readers' Theatre is an activity that provides students with the opportunity to prepare simple scripts from familiar texts. It involves selecting an appealing piece of text, generally a literary one, then re-reading it together and making decisions about how it can be brought to life through performance reading. It is an ideal way to introduce students to a wide range of enjoyable texts and provides a meaningful context for repeated readings, which promotes the development of fluency and expression.

The many stages of Readers' Theatre engage readers in:
• searching to find appropriate texts;
• editorial reading to draft scripts;
• repeated reading to practise parts;
• reading aloud to perform.

Developing scripts from text could begin with short, familiar narratives or poems; these should have a range of characters, sufficient dialogue, and some action. Students will enjoy the challenge of finding texts that may make suitable scripts but they will require ongoing modelling and scaffolding during the process of creating them. Readers' Theatre usually involves no memorisation and only limited movement, costumes or props, although there is little harm in students introducing these elements with discretion.

– Read the text aloud to the students.
– Organise them in small groups. Mixed-ability groups can work well in this activity.
– Allocate character and narrator roles.
– Provide time for students to identify and highlight their own parts of the script. This may involve both deleting non-essential information and inserting extra dialogue to clarify meaning.
– Allow time for students to read the script aloud together and make any necessary changes.
– Provide assistance in adding minimal props, sound effects or movement to enhance the presentation.
– Provide an opportunity for students to present the reading to an audience.

3 Perfect Match

Perfect Match is a whole-class activity that provides students with the opportunity to re-read parts of texts. Finding specific parts of one text requires them to make meaningful connections. A range of texts can be used to cater for a variety of reading abilities.

– Select and copy three or four short pieces of different texts.
– Cut each text into meaningful chunks, ensuring that the total number of pieces is the same as the number of students participating.
– Give each student a chunk of text and provide sufficient time for all to silently read and re-read their allocated chunks.
– Encourage them to make annotations — for example, highlighting character names — to make it easier to find other chunks belonging to the same text.
– Have them move around the classroom searching for related chunks of texts. If a match is made, the two students continue looking as a pair.
– Provide time for students to sequence and re-read their chunks of text.

4 Buddy Bump Reading

Buddy Bump Reading (BBR) sessions are a powerful way of encouraging students to read and re-read; they also provide them with support, as they read together. Students choose a reading partner to work with, and the two work together for a set period, such as two weeks. Partners spend time discussing the selection of texts they may wish to share over that period. Texts may be brought from home, selected from the class library or chosen from those read to the whole class.

– Arrange for each pair to sit side by side to read their self-selected text.
– Invite them to begin by reading aloud together; for instance, reading the first paragraph.
– Direct them then to take turns to read aloud. Remind them of the previously agreed way of handing over the reading to the buddy, such as gently bumping, passing a marker or turning over a card. Each student can read up to a predetermined amount (such as half a page or two paragraphs), but is able to 'bump' to the partner at any stage.
– Encourage students to help each other out when necessary.

5 Favourite Passages

Selecting and sharing favourite passages promotes critical thinking and provides the opportunity to revisit texts previously read. It is important that students have time to share reasons for selecting particular pieces from a text; this will help them to hear a variety of choices and to further understand how authors create interest and construct meaning.

– Have students identify favourite passages from previously read or shared texts.
– Provide time for them to silently read and re-read the chosen passages.
– Have them share their passages in small groups or with the whole class.
– Record the passages to display and use for whole-class reading.

David

Leo had won an award for the first time in his life, and as he shook the principal's hand and blushed and said his thank-yous, he thought his heart would explode with happiness.

(*Every Living Thing*, by Cynthia Rylant)

Georgia

She raced outside and down to the shore.
Her heart was pounding as she reached the sea.
There enormous in the ocean, were the whales.
They leapt and jumped and spun across the Moon.
Their singing filled up the night.

(*Whale's Song*, by Dyan Sheldon and Gary Blythe)

Figure 6.4 Students' favourite passages

6 Get the Rhythm

Get the Rhythm is an opportunity for students to re-read a variety of texts for fun and enjoyment. In this activity, Early readers identify the rhythms in a text and create music to accompany a shared reading. It is important to provide them with a range of musical resources such as percussion instruments, small electronic keyboards or student-made instruments. They may even begin to use clapping, tapping or stamping to produce the rhythm or to create the music. Warning: Be prepared for the noise!

– Provide students with a range of familiar texts from which to choose. Texts that contain rhyme and rhythm are essential.

- Allow time for them to re-read the chosen text, encouraging them to identify rhythms.
- Have them select one or more instruments to match the rhythm identified in the text.
- Provide opportunities for repeated readings, incorporating the chosen musical accompaniment.
- Give them an opportunity to perform their group reading.

7 Record a Text

Allowing students to make their own recordings of texts encourages Early readers to re-read them. They can work in small groups to create recordings, but it is important that selected texts are familiar and are within their reading abilities. They will need to practise many times prior to recording the text.

- Organise students in small groups. Have each group select a text.
- Provide time for them to read the text.
- Encourage them to discuss it, to assist with fluency, expression and interpretation.
- Have them allocate a section of the text to each reader in the group.
- Provide time for them to practise reading the text.
- Organise them to record text on an audiotape. Make the tape and text available for home reading, at the listening post, or for independent reading time.

8 Find a Heading

Early readers enjoy the challenge of reading simple newspaper articles or articles from students' favourite magazines; these texts can become a rich source for discussions about the concept of a main idea and supporting details. In Find a Heading, students skim an article to determine the main idea and match it to a relevant title. A collection of pieces of text with titles removed could be added to continuously and could form the basis of an independent activity for students.

- Select a range of short texts that are of interest to students.
- Remove the titles.
- Arrange students in pairs or small groups. Have them skim the texts and match each one to its title.
- Ask them to discuss and create alternative headings for selected texts.
- Provide an opportunity for them to share new headings and justifications.

| Your sense of smell starts to fade as soon as you're born. By the time you are 20, you will have lost almost a quarter of your sense of smell. By the time you are 80, you will have lost three quarters! | Smell-testers test smells using a special machine called an olfactometer (ol-fac-tom-eter). The olfactometer sucks smells into a bag inside a drum — a bit like a vacuum cleaner. |

| TESTING SMELLS | FADING SENSE OF SMELL | FAKE NOSES |

Figure 6.5

9 Readingo

Readingo is a reading-incentive scheme that encourages Early readers to explore a wide variety of texts. A grid is filled with examples of different texts, or types of texts. As the student reads each text, the square is coloured to indicate the reader's response to it; for instance, red for brilliant, blue for good, green for okay or yellow for awful.

There are two types of Readingo grids: closed and open. A closed grid is created when specific titles are listed; for example, columns or rows might list particular texts from different learning areas. Closed grids enable the teacher to exercise more influence over the students' reading; however, they require consideration of reader ability and text difficulty.

An open grid lists the type of text rather than specific titles (see Figure 6.6). By providing extra space on the grids for titles and dates, the Readingo sheet can be used as a partial record of personal reading habits.

To complete the activity, students:
- choose one of the texts on the grid;
- read it;
- colour the square;
- take the text to a reading conference;
- explain what was felt about the text;
- ask the conference partner to initial the coloured square;
- choose another text from the grid to continue on the path horizontally, vertically or diagonally.

An incentive of some kind may be provided once students have completed a Readingo path.

READINGO				
A story that is written with lots of rhyme	A recipe that you actually use to cook something	Something written about your favourite sport	A text by your favourite author	A story with repetitive text
A different version of your favourite fairy tale	An instruction booklet for a favourite game	A piece of factual text about an Australian animal	Something of interest from a website	A text by a local author
A newspaper article	A comic	A section of a CD-ROM	A catalogue from a toy store	A book set in a place you would like to visit
A review of a movie you have seen	A collection of poetry	An advertisement that attracted your attention	A hobby or leisure magazine	A diagram explaining how to make or do something
A menu from a restaurant	A joke book	A book with chapters	A collection of cereal packets	A software instruction booklet

Figure 6.6 An open Readingo grid

10 Favourite Texts

Favourite Texts gives students the opportunity to read and re-read favourite texts, giving opinions and justifications and making recommendations for other class members. Texts that are short-listed for awards can also be used for this activity.

- Select a range of texts from the school or local library, or ask students to bring some from home.
- Discuss and make a list of features, such as illustrations, plot, characters, diagrams, headings or glossary.
- Have students read or re-read their texts and use the list of features to make judgements about them.
- Direct students to complete recommendation cards.
- Display texts and recommendations for all class members to see.
- Arrange play-offs in which, following a period for reading excerpts, students vote on which of two books is the funniest, scariest or most exciting.

Favourite Texts

Text _Stone Soup_____ Author _Monica Hughes_

Illustrations	poor	good	(very good)
Plot	poor	(good)	very good
Characters	(poor)	good	very good
Setting	poor	(good)	very good
	poor	good	very good
	poor	good	very good

Recommendation

OK (Good) Fantastic
It was interesting how the soldier fooled all the
people and got what he wanted.

Figure 6.7 A favourite literary text

Favourite Texts

Text _Animal Shelters_____ Author _Faye Bolton and Esther Cullen_

Diagrams	poor	good	(very good)
Glossary	(poor)	good	very good
Information	poor	good	(very good)
Index	poor	(good)	very good
Sub-headings	poor	good	(very good)
Contents page	poor	(good)	very good

Recommendation

OK Good (Fantastic)
Lots of information ð about different types
of shelters. A glossary would have helped.

Figure 6.8 A favourite informational text

11 Character Webs

Creating Character Webs provides an opportunity for students to examine relationships between characters and to make connections between character traits and events. Character Webs encourage them to return to text and use explicit and/or implicit information to justify their choices.

Students will benefit from working in small groups or with a partner to create Character Webs.

– Have students list all characters in a story on sticky notes. The name of the main character (or characters) is placed in the centre of a page; the others are placed around the central figure according to the closeness of the relationship between them.
– Have students use arrows, key words, pictures or jottings to represent the interrelationships.
– When students disagree about the nature of the main character's relationships, encourage them to return to the text to justify their jottings.

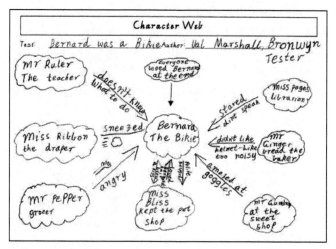

Figure 6.9

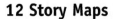

12 Story Maps

Refer to Chapter 5: Experimental Reading Phase, p. 109.

13 Meet and Greet

This activity provides an opportunity for students to use and make connections between explicit and implicit information. Meet and Greet involves Early readers in deciding who they would like to meet in a text, and why.

– After reading a text, ask students to select a character (if it is a literary text) or person (if it is informational) they would choose to meet and greet, and to justify the choice.
– Have them list some questions they would like to ask the character or person.
– Provide an opportunity for them to put their questions to the class. Other students may volunteer to answer questions from the character or person's perspective, using the text as a basis for their replies.

14 Facts and Falsehoods

Facts and Falsehoods can be used to categorise items and clarify concepts. In this activity, students create a series of statements of which all but one are factual. The challenge is for another student to determine which one is the falsehood, and why. Texts related to whole-class, cross-curriculum topics work best for this activity.

– Ask students each to read about a particular topic and list facts they find. If the task is to be completed orally, three or four statements are sufficient; if the list is to be read, up to 10 items would be possible. Generally, the greater the number, the greater will be the difficulty of the task for the person who must identify the falsehood.
– Have students write one falsehood to be included in the list.
– Provide opportunities for each student to challenge another to find the falsehood.

The essence of a fair challenge requires teacher modelling, as some students will misinterpret the aim of the activity and will attempt to trick the reader rather than create a fitting task. Facts need to fall somewhere within student experience, and falsehoods need to be substantially different.

For example, a falsehood that reads 'Jupiter has a diameter of 128 400 kilometres' (Jupiter actually has a diameter of 142 800 kilometres) would be considered an unfair challenge because very few people would recall that level of detail.

Facts and Falsehoods	
Statements	Text: _Dolphins_
Dolphins, Porpoises and whales are called cetaceans.	Fact/Falsehood
A dolphin don't have bones.	fact/Falsehood
Dolphins communicate with each other.	Fact/Falsehood
Dolphins are different from Porpoises.	Fact/Falsehood
Dolphins only live in the ocean	fact/Falsehood

Figure 6.10

15 Who Said . . .?

Who Said . . .? encourages students to infer character actions and behaviour in a text, using implicit information.

– Have a group of students read a common text that has several characters or participants.
– Direct them to individually select a character and write on a slip of paper something that character might typically say. This should not be a direct quote.
– Toss the slips of paper into a container and ask each student to draw one out, read the statement aloud, and declare who in the story would say something like that. The choice should be substantiated with reference to the story.
– If there is any disagreement, ask the writer of the statement to refer to the parts of the text that were used.

16 Celebrity Heads

Celebrity Heads requires students to draw on explicit and implicit information as they guess the name of a character or person in a text. During the activity a small number of students are each allocated a character or person and are required to ask a series of questions to determine who it is. Restricting responses to 'Yes' and 'No' encourages questioners to listen critically, remember information supplied and build on questions already asked.

– After reading several texts, make headbands each featuring the name of a different character or person.
– Select students to wear the headbands (sight unseen).
– Make a list of the characters or people as an aid for these students to create effective questions.

– Have them then take turns to ask the class questions to try and determine the identity of the characters. A 'Yes' response from the class allows the questioner another turn. A 'No' response passes the questioning to the next student.

– Conclude the questioning when one character or person is successfully identified.

Figure 6.11

17 What's the Message?

Readers benefit from the opportunity to begin exploring implied messages in texts. What's the Message? promotes this type of discussion. Students are provided with a list of statements and are asked to identify those they believe the author or illustrator meant to convey. They justify their responses by identifying how, where or when the author or illustrator gave the message.

– Create statements that relate to the topic or message in a selected text. Ensure that some are messages presented by the author or illustrator and some are not.

– Have students indicate which statements reflect messages in the text, and justify their answers by referring to the text or illustrations.

What's the Message?		

Text: *The Paper Bag Princess*   Author *Robert Munsch*

Statements	Message Given? (Yes / No)	Justification
1. Elizabeth loved Ronald very much.	Yes	she worked so hard to rescue him
2. Princesses think they should wear beautiful clothes all the time.	No	This princess was happy to wear a paper bag.
3. Dragons are clever.	Yes	Although they can do lots of things, they are tricked easily.
4. It's what you are, not what you look like, that counts.	no	Ronald looked nice but he wasn't a nice person. Elizabeth wore a dirty paper bag but she was kind

Figure 6.12

CONTEXTUAL UNDERSTANDING

Major Teaching Emphases

- **Encourage students to listen to the opinions and justifications of others, recognising different points of view and interpretations.**

- **Familiarise students with the devices that authors and illustrators use to influence construction of meaning,** e.g. choice of language.

- **Discuss how and why facts, characters, people or events are presented in a particular way by the author and illustrator.**

- **Discuss how texts are written for different purposes and audiences.**

Teaching Notes

Early readers often 'believe everything they read' and will require support to develop an awareness that all texts have a purpose and an intended audience. This will help them to understand that authors try to shape the reader's interpretation of the meaning of both literary and informational texts.

Modelled, Shared and Guided Reading sessions can incorporate an introductory discussion about the purpose and audience of a text. In these sessions, teachers can assist Early readers to become aware of how their prior knowledge influences their interpretation of a text, and to recognise different points of view. Students benefit from being given many opportunities to participate in discussions that allow them to share their opinions and justifications of text interpretation.

The foci for helping Early readers to develop contextual understanding are organised under the following headings.
- Discussions about Texts
- Discussions about the Devices Authors and Illustrators Use
- Discussions about the Way Facts, People, Characters or Events are Represented in Texts

Discussions about Texts

It is important for Early readers to continue to make connections and comparisons between their own experiences and those presented in a text. The focus in this phase will be on listening to and valuing different points of view and different interpretations. This can be achieved in a range of ways.

- Encourage students to discuss and make connections between personal experiences and the text; e.g. 'Have you ever been in a similar situation? What did you do?'
- Have them compare events and characters in texts with their own lives and themselves.
- Ask questions or set tasks that encourage them to think beyond the literal level; e.g. 'What would you have done if . . .?'
- Support them in accepting different points of view and interpretations; e.g. 'That's interesting. Rami thinks . . ., but Sally thinks . . .'.
- Encourage them to speculate whether or not the author is portraying real events and people; e.g. 'From your experience, do you think this could have happened?'
- Have students identify the author's and illustrator's points of view and discuss alternatives; e.g. 'What does the author/illustrator want you to think about . . .? How do you know this? What do you think about . . .?'
- Encourage them to speculate about the intended audience; e.g. 'For whom do you think this was written? What does the author think this audience would be interested in? What does the author think this audience already knows about this topic or experience?'.
- Have students speculate about the purpose of the text; e.g. 'Why do you think the author has written this text?'

Discussions about the Devices Authors and Illustrators Use

It is important to provide opportunities for ongoing conversations about devices authors and illustrators have chosen to influence the reader's interpretation of a text. Discussions about these choices and the possible reasons for them will give Early readers a deeper understanding of the impact the choices may have on their own interpretations of text.

Devices used by illustrators include:
- choice of colour;
- amount of detail included;
- size of characters, tables or diagrams relative to others;
- medium, e.g. collage, etching, watercolours;
- composition of the page, e.g. placement of photographs or drawings;
- artistic style, e.g. a cartoon style rather than realistic style.

Devices used by authors include:
- choice of language, e.g. descriptive, emotive;
- inclusion/omission of details;

- print size;
- font selection;
- foreshadowing — giving a hint of things to come, e.g. **The door creaked and groaned as it was pushed open;**
- irony, wit, humour.

Facilitate discussion by asking a variety of questions.
- How do the illustrations support or add to the text? e.g. **what do the graphs, tables or diagrams tell you that the words don't?**
- How do the illustrations detract from the text? e.g. **incorrect positioning, lack of detail, or size.**
- How does the illustrator show the importance of different aspects of the text? e.g. **the size of photographs.**
- Why do you think the illustrator has chosen to draw the characters in a certain way? e.g. **in cartoon form or closely resembling reality.**
- What words has the author used to represent the characters, people, events or facts? e.g. **'a sleeping giant' used to describe a volcano.**
- Why do you think the author has used certain words to describe the characters, people, events or facts?

Discussions about the Way Facts, People, Characters or Events are Represented in Texts

Early readers are beginning to understand that reading involves not only making sense of a text, but also analysing and questioning why and how authors represent groups in particular ways. Providing students with the opportunity to consider what they know about specific groups and to make comparisons between their world view and that presented by authors and illustrators is of great importance. Both informational and literary texts will provide opportunities for these discussions.

Facilitate discussion by asking a variety of questions.
- How has the author (or illustrator) represented events, facts, people or characters, such as wolves?
- Is this accurate? For example, are wolves always like that?
- Is this a fair representation?
- Do you know any real people who are like the characters or people in the text? Who are they? How are they the same? How are they different?
- Have you experienced a real event similar to any in the text? How was it the same or different?
- Would you like to be anyone in the text? Who? Why?
- Who is telling the story?
- What does the author or illustrator say about . . .?

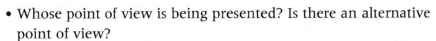

- Whose point of view is being presented? Is there an alternative point of view?
- What expertise or authority does the author have to be writing about . . .?
- Do you know anything about this topic that the author has not included in the text? Why do you think it may have been left out?
- What does the author or illustrator think is the most important point to make? How do you know? How is this done?
- How is the same character, such as Harry Potter, portrayed in a series of texts?
- How have similar characters, such as clever children, been portrayed across several texts?
- How is information on a particular topic the same or different across several texts?

> For further information about the Contextual Understanding substrand, See *Reading Resource Book*, 2nd edn, Chapter 2: Contextual Understanding.

Involving Students

1 Reading Response Journals

A Reading Response Journal provides a place for students to record their personal expectations, reactions and reflections about texts before, during and after reading. Keeping a Response Journal provides opportunities for Early readers to develop their own opinions and interpretations of a text.

- Explain the purpose and use of a Reading Response Journal.
- As students read independently, have them consider and make notes about:
  - questions of the text they want or expect to be answered;
  - predictions they make about what might happen;
  - confirmation of predictions;
  - puzzles, confusions or unanticipated outcomes;
  - questions they want to discuss with others;
  - connections they are making;
  - opinions and justifications.
- Provide opportunities for students to share their journal entries with peers or in teacher–student conferences.
- Invite them to re-read their journal entries periodically. Have them discuss and/or record what they have learnt about text interpretation, and their use of cues and strategies.

<u>Reading Response Journal Questions</u>

What are some similarities or differences between the character in the text and yourself?

Has anything similar to what happens in the text happened to you? Explain.

What do you think will happen next? What makes you think that?

What is the problem the main character must solve?

Which is your favourite scene? Describe or draw it.

What is unclear or puzzling about the story?

Why did _____ behave in that way?

Does this text remind you of any books you have read or movies you have seen?

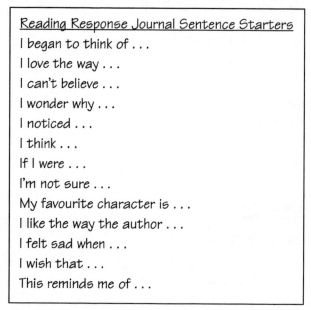

<u>Reading Response Journal Sentence Starters</u>
I began to think of . . .
I love the way . . .
I can't believe . . .
I wonder why . . .
I noticed . . .
I think . . .
If I were . . .
I'm not sure . . .
My favourite character is . . .
I like the way the author . . .
I felt sad when . . .
I wish that . . .
This reminds me of . . .

Figure 6.13

2 Stop, Think, Feel, Share

Stop, Think, Feel, Share works best as a whole-class activity as it allows all students to share personal interpretations of actions, behaviours or events presented in a text. Readers are encouraged to consider a range of perspectives. Texts with several characters, a strong plot, and elements of conflict are most suitable for this activity.

It is critical that students are allowed time to consider their own responses to the text before they are asked to share in a small group or across the whole class.

– Ask students to predict the content of the text from author, title, key words or phrases.
– Invite several to share their predictions with the class.
– Arrange students in small groups. Read the first section of the text, to set the scene. Stop, and encourage students to compare their personal predictions with the actual text so far.

- Allocate a character to each small group and have them continue listening to the text from the perspective of that character.
- At a selected point, stop reading and ask the students to think about what their character might be feeling at that point. Have them share their feelings in their group before asking a spokesperson for the group to share with the whole class.
- Continue reading the text, inviting students to 'become' the character.
- At further selected points, stop reading and have the students share what the character might be feeling. It is important at this and subsequent stops that students be asked to imagine themselves as the character. When reporting back, the spokesperson should speak in the first person: 'I'm feeling . . . because . . .'.
- Conclude the activity with the groups predicting what their characters may be doing in ten years time. Responses should be justified from the text.

3 Character Self-Portrait

Creating a Character Self-portrait provides Early readers with an opportunity to combine information in the text with prior knowledge. While completing the profile, students discuss inferences and opinions about characters, and listen to the points of view and interpretations of others.

- Jointly construct a Character Self-portrait framework consisting of appropriate sentence stems related to the text. It is important to vary the framework for different texts.
- Arrange students in pairs or small groups. Allocate a character from the text, or have students select one.
- Have students discuss the character, referring to the sentence stems on the framework.
- Direct each group or pair to complete the sentences in the framework, ensuring that they refer to the text.
- Invite selected students to share their completed self-portraits with the whole class, justifying their responses.

Character Self-Portrait
Text _Wombat Stew_
Author _M. Vaughan_
My character is _the dingo_
I am _A very clever dingo_
I live _In the bush in a cave_
I eat _big fat juicy wombats!_
I have _a pot, a bbb of mud, a lots of feathers a few fleas, bts of bugs and a wombat for my stew!_
I like _the bush and animals around me_
I dislike _the animals tricking me_
I wish _I could eat the fat wombat_

Figure 6.14

4 Four Corners

Four Corners is a small-group activity that provides an opportunity to discuss and share different points of view and different interpretations of a text. It involves four students reading a common text, recording thoughts as they read, then sharing their interpretations.

Each group of four is given a large sheet of chart paper. This provides each student with a 'corner' in which to jot, sketch or write words or phrases that come to mind during the individual reading.

– Organise students in groups of four.
– Have them silently read the text.
– Encourage them to periodically stop reading to record their connections, questions and thoughts in their corners.
– Once they have completed the individual reading, direct them to use the Four Corners chart as a stimulus for conversation about the text.

Figure 6.15

5 Possible Predictions

Refer to Chapter 7: Transitional Reading Phase, p. 223.

6 Dear Diary

In the activity Dear Diary, students think and write about what it would be like to be a particular character or person in a text. This encourages Early readers to raise and answer questions about how characters, people or events have been presented. The creation of diary entries involves students in making inferences and judgements, and helps to build a deeper understanding of the actions and behaviour of the character or person in question.

– Select a familiar text and allocate characters or people to small groups.
– Allocate an event in the text to each group.
– Have each group discuss what the character or person they have been given would be thinking and feeling at that point in the text.
– Have students, individually or in pairs, create a diary entry that recounts the event from the character or person's perspective.

> Monday
>
> What a day! I woke up this morning feeling cramped and stiff from sleeping in the cupbord yet again.

> 21 July 1969
>
> Today is a very exciting day for me. I'll be the first person to walk on the moon.

Figure 6.16 Dear Diary entries

7 Describe the Character

Describe the Character provides an opportunity to consider characters, identify traits and develop associated vocabulary. This activity helps Early readers, who sometimes have difficulty describing and analysing characters because of their limited vocabulary associated with character traits.

CHARACTER TRAITS	Singenpoo	Mother	Major Mac	Scott	JUSTIFICATION
courageous	X				Singenpoo outwitted Major Mac
funny		X			
loyal				X	
selfish			X		
demanding			X		
responsible		X			
self-confident	X				
considerate				X	

Describe the Character
Text: Singenpoo Strikes Again   Author: Paul Jennings

Figure 6.17

– Brainstorm and record a list of character traits with the students.
– Discuss and clarify each one as it is recorded. Add any further traits associated with the characters being studied.
– Work with the students to randomly select and list character traits from the brainstorm list. Record these on the grid.
– Have students read the selected text.
– Direct them to list the main characters on the grid.
– Provide time for them to work together to complete the grid, identifying words that best describe each character's traits.
– Have them justify their choices by citing examples from the text. Record these on the grid.

8 Despicability Rating

Completing a Despicability Rating involves students in combining information both from the text and from personal experience to rank characters according to the level of despicability. In doing this, they can be introduced to the devices authors and illustrators use to influence the construction of meaning, and they can be encouraged to explore and share different interpretations of events and actions in a text.

– Select three characters or people in a text.
– Have students individually rank the characters or people from most despicable to least despicable.
– Direct them to search for and record evidence in the text to justify their ranking of each character or person.
– Invite several students to share and compare their rankings and justifications with the whole class.

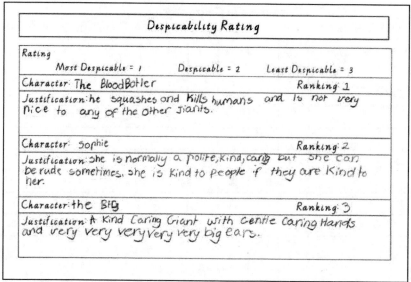

Figure 6.18

9 Author Study

Refer to Chapter 7: Transitional Reading Phase, p. 227.

10 Picture the Author

Picture the Author asks students to think about the author of a text being studied. They are asked to explore background information, and to think how this background may have influenced the author's choices.

– After reading a text, have students gather information about the author. They can use the jacket of the text, the Internet, author reviews or biographies to consider any of the following questions.
  – Is the author male or female?
  – When was the text written? Was the author young, middle-aged or elderly?
  – Where did the author live when writing it?
  – Does the author have expertise in this topic? How do you know?
  – What other texts has this author written?
– Allow time for students to discuss how finding out about the author has helped them to understand choices made in the text.

11 Text Innovation

Refer to Chapter 7: Transitional Reading Phase, p. 226.

12 Like or Unlike?

Refer to Chapter 7: Transitional Reading Phase, p. 229.

13 Same and Different

Same and Different focuses students' attention on similarities and differences in the information presented in two or more texts; those identified can be represented in the form of a Venn diagram. Early readers can compare how different authors have represented similar characters. To begin, it is appropriate for students to compare characters from just two texts; as they become familiar with the process, characters from more than two can be compared.

– Invite students to read two texts with similar characters, such as Australian animals.
– Select the characters to be compared; for example, Hush and Koala Lou.
– Have students work with partners or in small groups to record things they remember about each one, such as character traits, actions and physical appearance.
– Ask them to examine the two lists to decide which things are common to both characters, then transfer this information to the intersecting space on a Venn diagram.

– Direct them to transfer the remaining information in the lists to the appropriate space on the diagram.
– Provide time for them to discuss the similarities and differences in the characters.

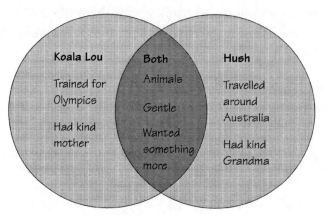

Figure 6.19 A class-generated diagram

14 Character Profile Study

Conducting a Character Profile Study involves students in describing and discussing features of characters in literary texts. The aim is to draw conclusions about the representation of 'good' and 'bad' characters; discussion could centre on features such as the physical appearance, clothing, speech or actions of the characters. Encourage students to speculate about the choices made by the author and illustrator.

– Provide each student with a Character Profile Study chart (Figure 6.20).
– Have them read a text individually.
– Invite them to make notes on the chart as they read, describing the features. They should also record whether a character is represented as good or bad.
– Have the whole class use their charts to discuss what they noticed about the way the good and bad characters were represented.
– Following the generation of a number of profiles, have students examine the features that seem to be common among representations of 'good' and 'bad' characters; for example, by comparing the profiles of foxes in fables, Early readers will notice that most are represented as bad characters that are sly and cunning.
– Generate a class chart listing features of 'good' and 'bad' characters. Add to the chart as new information is discovered.

CHARACTER PROFILE STUDY					
Character's Name	Appearance	Clothing	Actions	Speech	'Good' or 'Bad' Character?

Figure 6.20

As a variation, comparisons can be made between different groups — such as young and old, wealthy and poor, male and female — to determine how authors represent these groups.

15 Advertisement Searches

Advertisement Searches provide Early readers with the opportunity to explore the decisions authors and illustrators make to influence a reader's construction of meaning. The focus of this activity is to look at the decisions made in advertising products.

- Provide students with a collection of advertisements or advertising catalogues focusing on selling a particular type of product, such as toys, clothing or food.
- Have them skim through the advertisements and discuss the products for sale.
- Involve them in a discussion of how the products are presented. Discuss both explicit and implied information, and how both influence the reader. Discussion questions could include the following.
  - Who does the author think will buy the product?
  - How does the author catch your attention?
  - What words has the author used to try to persuade you? What pictures or images have been used? What can be inferred from these images?
  - What else has the author done to try to persuade you to buy the product? e.g. **is there a choice of words to make the product seem fun, cool or healthy?**
  - How has the author chosen to represent the people in this advertisement? Why do you think this is done?
- Jointly create a class list of the devices used to try to influence readers' construction of meaning and persuade them to buy particular products; examples could be happy people, bright colours or catchy slogans.

16 Comparison Chart

Completing a Comparison Chart allows students to become familiar with the devices authors and illustrators use to influence the construction of meaning or to suit different audiences and purposes. Early readers benefit from examining different versions of the same text (different versions of The Three Little Pigs) or texts on one topic written from different points of view.

- After sharing a text, have students record the characters, setting and main events on the Comparison Chart format.
- Have them consider and discuss questions such as these.
  - From whose point of view — the narrator or a particular character — is the text is written? How do you know this?
  - From what other point of view could the text be written?
  - What changes would need to be made to the text to reflect a different point of view?
- Provide students with a different version of the same text. Repeat the recording and discussions as with the original one.
- Summarise the information contained in the chart, noting similarities and differences between the two texts. Discuss what changes were made in the different versions or when the point of view was changed.

Comparison Chart				
TEXT / AUTHOR	CHARACTERS/ PEOPLE	SETTING	EVENTS	POINT OF VIEW
The three little Pigs by ….	3 Pigs wolf mother pig men selling bricks, straw, sticks	houses of the Pigs in the country	Pigs built their own houses. Wolf went to the Pigs houses. The wolf blew 2 houses down. Wolf went looking for dinner. The Wolf blew houses down. Pigs end up at the house made of brick.	
Jon Scieszka	3 Pigs The wolf the wolf's Grand mother	houses of pigs	The wolf was looking for Suger to make his grand mother's cake. He blew two houses down because he had a cold and kept sneezing. He ended up in jail	Wolf's

Figure 6.21

CONVENTIONS

Major Teaching Emphases

- **Continue to build students' sight vocabulary,** e.g. topic words, signal words.

- **Continue to build phonological awareness, graphophonic and word knowledge, such as:**
  - recognising that a sound can be represented by different letters or letter combinations
  - recognising letter combinations, and the different sounds they represent
  - recognising how word parts and words work.

- **Teach the use of conventions of print,** e.g. commas, quotation marks.

- **Continue to build students' knowledge of different text forms,** e.g. purpose, structure, organisation and language features.

Teaching Notes

For Early readers, there is a need to continue building upon the sight vocabulary, phonological awareness, and graphophonic and word understandings that have been developed in previous phases. It is important that these be introduced and practised in meaningful contexts during Modelled, Shared and Guided Reading and Writing. When selecting a teaching focus, it is important to consider both what the students already know and the requirements of the curriculum.

The foci for supporting Early readers to develop understandings about conventions are organised under the following headings.
- Sight Vocabulary
- Phonological Awareness, Graphophonic Knowledge and Word Knowledge
- Conventions of Print
- Knowledge about Text Forms

Sight Vocabulary

Sight vocabulary is the bank of words a reader is able to automatically decode, pronounce and understand in the contexts in which they are used. These words are called 'sight words' because effective readers need to recognise them instantly on sight in order to maintain the speed and fluency required to make sense of the author's message. Many of these words have irregular spellings, making them difficult to decode.

Fry et al. (1984) suggest that 100 words make up about half of all we read; they make up what is known as the high-frequency vocabulary. If students are to become fluent readers, they need to learn to recognise them quickly and easily.

Sight vocabulary for Early readers can include any of the following.
- High-frequency words; e.g. **those that occur frequently in all written language.**
- Topic or theme words; e.g. **those related to current studies.**
- Personally significant words; e.g. **interest words.**

Attention can be drawn to these words as they occur in print. They can be discussed, written on a chart or cards, and displayed where they can be easily accessed — for example, on the Word Wall. For some students, systematic instruction is essential to help them develop automaticity; for others, the repeated reading of texts is enough for them to develop the ability to immediately recognise a large number of words.

Phonological Awareness, Graphophonic Knowledge and Word Knowledge

For Early readers it is vitally important to continue to consolidate phonological awareness, but most important also to place an emphasis on the development of their graphophonic and word knowledge. These understandings are important to help them identify unknown words when reading, and also to assist them when writing.

Understandings to be consolidated in relation to phonological awareness include:
- syllable awareness — that some words have a single syllable and some are multisyllabic;
- phonemic awareness — that words are made up of individual sounds, or phonemes.

Graphophonic knowledge refers to a reader's knowledge of letters and combinations of letters and the sounds associated with them. Develop graphophonic knowledge such as that:
- a sound can be represented by different letters or letter combinations, such as /i/ in hide, find, high, pie, my;
- one letter combination may represent different sounds, such as 'ea' in pear, hear, pearl, heart.

Word knowledge refers to a reader's knowledge of words, their meanings and how they work. Develop elements of word knowledge such as:

- prefixes and suffixes, e.g. **ing, ed, un, dis**;
- plurals, e.g. **ladies, fish**;
- synonyms and antonyms;
- homophones, e.g. **their, there**;
- contractions.

Conventions of Print

Early readers need to understand:

- the use of punctuation, e.g. **commas, question marks, exclamation marks and quotation marks**;
- the effects of punctuation on expression, meaning and fluency, as in Go! Go?;
- elements of grammar, such as pronouns, verbs and adjectives.

Knowledge about Text Forms

Analysing and discussing different text forms will help Early readers understand the purpose, organisation, structure and language features of different forms, and how that knowledge can affect the way a text is read. Modelled, Shared and Guided Reading sessions provide an opportunity to discuss these conventions in the context of authentic texts.

Purpose

Texts are written to achieve a purpose. The purpose may be to describe, as in a report, or to persuade, as in an advertisement.

Text Organisation

Text organisation refers to the layout. Early readers will benefit from understanding text-form frameworks; for instance, a scientific report may include a classification, a description and a summarising comment. It is also important for these readers to understand the function, terminology and use of organisational features such as:

- headings and subheadings
- captions
- diagrams and other visual aids (photographs, graphs, tables, cross-sections)
- tables of contents
- indexes
- glossaries
- paragraphs
- bold or italic print
- illustrations

- hyperlinks
- Internet site maps.

Text Structure

Text structure refers to the way ideas, feelings and information are linked in a text. These could include:
- problem and solution;
- compare and contrast;
- cause and effect;
- listing: logical or chronological sequence, collection of details.

Having an understanding of these patterns can assist Early readers to comprehend text.

Language Features

Language features refers to the type of vocabulary and grammar used. Each text form has specific features appropriate to that form. These include:
- tense, e.g. **past or present**;
- choice of words, e.g. **adjectives, verbs, linking words**;
- style, e.g. **colloquial or formal.**

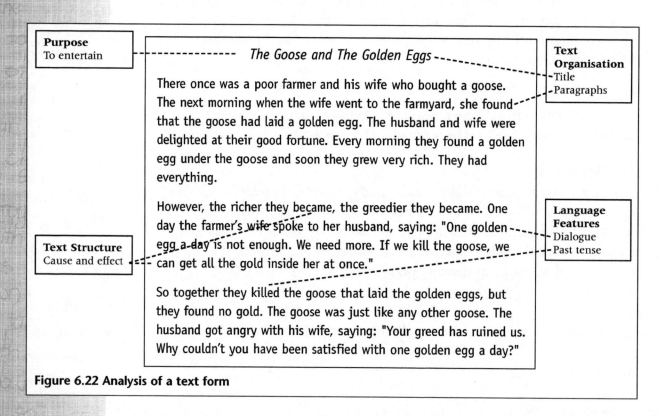

Purpose
To entertain

The Goose and The Golden Eggs

Text Organisation
- Title
- Paragraphs

There once was a poor farmer and his wife who bought a goose. The next morning when the wife went to the farmyard, she found that the goose had laid a golden egg. The husband and wife were delighted at their good fortune. Every morning they found a golden egg under the goose and soon they grew very rich. They had everything.

However, the richer they became, the greedier they became. One day the farmer's wife spoke to her husband, saying: "One golden egg a day is not enough. We need more. If we kill the goose, we can get all the gold inside her at once."

Language Features
- Dialogue
- Past tense

Text Structure
Cause and effect

So together they killed the goose that laid the golden eggs, but they found no gold. The goose was just like any other goose. The husband got angry with his wife, saying: "Your greed has ruined us. Why couldn't you have been satisfied with one golden egg a day?"

Figure 6.22 Analysis of a text form

For further information about the Conventions substrand, see *Reading Resource Book*, 2nd edn, Chapter 3: Conventions.

Involving Students

1 Semantic Association

Semantic Association is designed to extend students' vocabulary. It is an activity in which they brainstorm words associated with a topic, such as celebrations. Where necessary, additional words can be provided to introduce new vocabulary. The initial brainstorming activity can then be extended into a Semantic Association activity by inviting students to group and categorise the words into familiar subtopics.

Once readers have participated in numerous whole-class brainstorming and Semantic Association activities, opportunities to work in pairs or small groups can be provided.

– Ask students to work together to list all the words they can think of related to a given theme or topic.
– Provide additional words to introduce essential new vocabulary.
– Ensure that they discuss the meaning of any words unfamiliar to some.
– Provide time for them to group and categorise the words.
– Direct them to attach a label to each category.
– Invite pairs or groups to share their words and categories.
– Encourage use of the new vocabulary in writing activities.

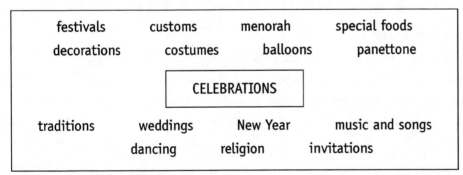

Figure 6.23 A class brainstorm chart

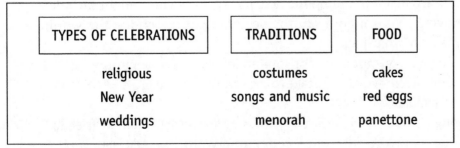

Figure 6.24 Sorting and labelling categories

2 Word Walls

A Word Wall is a designated space in the classroom devoted to displaying words. Words can be sorted according to the current teaching focus. Word Walls could consist of:
- sight-vocabulary words;
- words illustrating particular graphophonic understandings;
- words from other learning areas;
- words being studied, such as contractions, compound words, plurals, synonyms and antonyms.

As words are discovered, introduced and discussed, Word Walls are constructed jointly with the students.

- Begin by displaying enlarged letters of the alphabet (both upper and lower case).
- Add words as they are discovered or introduced, discussing distinctive features, e.g. **letter patterns and the number of syllables.**
- Jointly work with students to sort words in various ways; e.g. **according to sound patterns, letter patterns, number of syllables, parts of speech, names or compound words.**
- Read, refer to and use the words on the Word Wall during daily print walks, when modelling, or during writing activities.

3 Word Back Spied Her

Refer to Chapter 5: Experimental Reading Phase, p. 127.

4 Secret Messages

Secret Messages is an activity that involves students in decoding. The messages can be created using the sight vocabulary, word knowledge and graphophonic understandings currently being introduced.

Early readers will enjoy deciphering messages that use a combination of clues. The types of clues provided in one message may vary; however, it is appropriate to limit the variation when students are first attempting the activity. Types of clues might include:
- removing a consonant from the beginning or the end of the word; e.g. **take' h' from 'hand';**
- replacing a consonant or consonant cluster at the beginning or the end of the word; e.g. **take 'b' from 'bit' and add 's', take 'fl' from 'floor' and add 'd';**
- finding a small word within a word; e.g. **find a small word in 'friend';**
- joining two words to form a compound word; e.g. **add 'sun' ' to 'shine';**

- using an alphabet sequence for short words; e.g. **add the letter after 'n' to the letter before 'g'**;
- adding and deleting prefixes or suffixes; e.g. **add 'un' to 'happy'**.

Modelling the processes for solving the messages is important.
- Think of a meaningful sentence or message; e.g. **'Look in the surprise box for something funny'**.
- Write a series of clues that will enable students to decode the message.
- Ensure they have access to a copy of the alphabet.
- Provide time for them to 'crack' or decode the message. They could record it in a 'spy pad'.
- Keep a copy of all activities to build up a permanent collection for future use.

Monday's Secret Message for Room 6

A B C D E F G H I J K L M N O P Q R S T U V W X Y Z

1 Take 'b 'from 'book' and put in 'L'.	(Look)
2 Add the letter after 'h' to the letter after 'm'.	(in)
3 Take mo_ _ _r out of 'mother'.	(the)
4 Add 'rise' to 'surp'.	(surprise)
5 A word that rhymes with 'fox' but starts with b.	(box)
6 A small word in 'before', beginning with 'f'.	(for)
7 some + thing = _ _ _ _ _ _ _ _ _.	(something)
8 Take 's' from 'sunny' and add 'f'.	(funny)

Figure 6.25

5 Word-Sorting Activities

Using Word-sorting activities helps develop students' ability to identify and categorise words according to selected criteria. The activities provide an excellent opportunity for readers to interact with sight words, and to further develop their graphophonic and word understandings in a problem-solving context.

Word-sorting activities can be organised in a range of ways.
- *Closed sorts* use criteria chosen by the teacher.
- *Open sorts* require the students to choose the criteria.
- *Guess my sort* involves an individual, a group or the teacher sorting the words. Another group deduces the criteria.

Word-sorting activities can be completed using individual word cards provided in envelopes, words on overhead transparencies and an overhead projector, pocket charts and word cards, or even physical sorting activities.

Readers can be involved in a range of sorting activities.
- *Letter-patterns sorts* focus attention on the different letter patterns that can represent the same sound, e.g. b<u>ea</u>ch, t<u>ee</u>th, th<u>ie</u>f, funn<u>y</u>.
- *Sound sorts* focus attention on the different sounds represented by the same group of letters, e.g. 'ear' in h<u>ear</u>d, p<u>ear</u>, cl<u>ear</u>.
- *Type-of-word sorts* focus attention on different types of words, e.g. contractions, compound words, words with prefixes or suffixes.
- *Word-meaning sorts* focus attention on meanings; e.g. all the words that describe what you could find under water and all those that do not, all the words that have a similar meaning to 'said' and all those that do not.
- *Number-of-syllables sorts* focus attention on the number of syllables in a word.

Physical word-sorting involves students in moving around the classroom holding word cards.

– Provide students each with a word written on a large card.
– Instruct them to move around the room looking for other students' words that will fit with theirs in some way, so they can form a group.
– At the conclusion of the whole-class sort, ask students to stay in the groups they formed. Each group is then asked to hold up their cards and explain why they are together. Alternatively, ask other class members to guess the sorting criterion.

Figure 6.26 Students move in a physical word-sorting activity

6 Exploring Words

Exploring Words is an open-ended activity that provides students with an opportunity to work at their own level to create words. Early readers enjoy the challenge of creating as many words as possible from a given central letter sequence and a range of other letters.

– Provide students with a central focus letter pattern; e.g. 'ee'.
– Also provide a selection of other letters or letter combinations that could be added to this to create words.
– Establish guidelines for the creation of words; e.g. **letters or letter combinations can only be used once in a word, but letter combinations can be added to either the beginning or the end of the central letter pattern.**
– Challenge students to combine the central letter pattern with other letters to create as many words as possible in a given time.
– Allow time for them to share and reflect upon the words created.

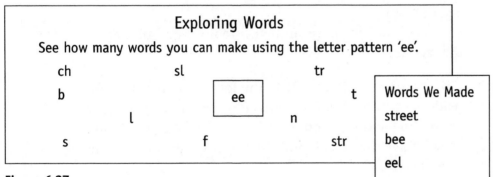

Exploring Words

See how many words you can make using the letter pattern 'ee'.

ch	sl	tr
b	ee	t
l	n	
s	f	str

Words We Made
street
bee
eel

Figure 6.27

7 Change a Letter

Change a Letter involves students in creating new words by changing one letter at a time in a given word. This activity helps Early readers to focus on the letters in a word and the sounds they make.

– Provide students with a four-letter word, e.g. **'stop'**.
– Challenge them to change one letter to make a new word; e.g. **'step'**. Initial, medial or final letters can be changed.
– Ask students to repeat this process with the new word.
– Challenge them to see how many new words they can create in a given time.
– Provide time to share words and to reflect upon patterns in those created.

Students enjoy challenging a partner to continue to create new words on a shared list. Once a bank of words has been created, they can be used for word-sorting activities.

8 Making Words

Making Words (Cunningham 2000) supports the development of graphophonic and word knowledge, specifically helping students to focus on letters in the words. Making Words involves using letters to make words.

Prior to introducing the activity, the following steps need to be completed.
- Select a word from a current classroom context; for example, 'scratch'. This will be the secret word.
- Make a list of smaller words that can be made from the letters of this one, such as cart, rat, chart, crash, at, art and tar.
- Choose about fifteen words from this list. They could include words:
  - with a particular letter pattern to be emphasised, e.g. 'ar';
  - of varying length;
  - that can be made with the same letters in different places, e.g. **cats, scat;**
  - that most students have in their listening vocabularies;
  - that are plural.

Once the preparation is complete, the following steps apply.
- Provide each student with an envelope or tub containing each letter of the focus word on a card; e.g. 'a' 'c' 'c' 's' 't' 'h' 'r' for 'scratch'. Have the vowels and consonants copied onto different-coloured cards.
- Direct students to make specified words one at a time. Select words from the list previously created. Ensure each one is recorded on a card.
- Start with two- or three-letter words and work up to longer ones; e.g. **'Take two letters to make the word 'at'. Add another letter to make 'art'. Change 'art' into 'tar'.**
- Continue directing students to make words, discussing key features of each one.
- Challenge students to use all the letters to discover the secret word.
- Use the words created to discuss patterns, e.g. 'ar', within them and to generate new words, such as cart, dart and chart.

9 What Comes Next?

What Comes Next? is an adaptation of what was known as the game Hangman. However, What Comes Next? requires students to guess the letters in the correct order rather than randomly.

As a daily activity for Early readers, What Comes Next? can provide an excellent context for reinforcing common letter sequences and word understandings being introduced; for example:

- letters together represent the specific sounds in a word;
- prefixes can be added to the beginning of words;
- suffixes can be added to the end of words;
- endings can be added to make a word plural;
- past tense can be represented by 'ed' or 't'.

To play the game, use the following procedure.

– Choose a word from a familiar context that features the focus-letter sequence or word-study understanding. Draw lines representing each letter in the word.

– Provide a specific clue for the first letter; e.g. **the first letter is a consonant in the second half of the alphabet.** When students guess the correct letter, record it on the first line.

– Invite students to guess the remaining letters of the word.

– As they guess a letter, write any guesses that are incorrect but possible sequences in a 'Could Be' column. Incorrect guesses that will not make letter sequences should be recorded in a 'Couldn't Be' column as single letters (not modelling incorrect letter patterns). When students guess a letter that could not be right, a segment of a mouse outline is drawn.

– Continue this until the correct letters are given and recorded on the lines.

– The game ends if the drawing of the mouse is completed before the students complete the word.

As an extension, students can be challenged to find other words linked to the letter patterns identified in the game word; e.g. **if the chosen word is 'straight', groups could be challenged to find words with 'str,' 'ai' or 'ght'.**

Once Early readers are familiar with the game, encourage them to play What Comes Next? with a partner.

Figure 6.28

10 Sound Hunter

Participating in Sound Hunter helps students to make connections between letters and sounds in words. They can become sound hunters in any context where they are involved with meaningful print. Texts such as books, charted songs and poems, magazines, modelled writing examples or written messages can provide contexts for Early readers to develop their graphophonic and word understandings by hunting for words.

– Choose a specific focus. For Early readers it could be:
  – any word with a particular letter pattern, e.g. **words with 'er'**;
  – any word with a particular sound, e.g. **words that have an /ee/ sound.**
– Choose texts that exhibit the chosen focus.
– Read the text for enjoyment.
– Revisit the text and encourage students to find and circle or underline words with the chosen focus, e.g. **all the words that have an /ee/ sound.** The words could then be written on pieces of card.
– Discuss the words.
– Ask students to sort them into subgroups; e.g. **according to letter patterns that represent the /ee/ sound.**
– Create a chart of the words, listing groups into which they have been sorted. Leave room for more words to be added to the chart.
– Students may then be formed into groups and challenged to find other words from a selected subgroup; they might find them in specific texts, on class charts or on the word wall.
– Revisit, discuss and add to the chart on future occasions.

11 Cloze Activities

Refer to Chapter 5: Experimental Reading Phase, p. 129.

12 Text Innovation

Text Innovation is the name given to the process of adapting an existing text. Texts that contain repetitive patterns can be copied to create innovations; they provide an opportunity for Early readers to work with a variety of words in a meaningful context. Innovations may focus on substituting individual words, copying simple sentence patterns or copying the text structure. Students enjoy the challenge of creating text innovations, and these self-developed texts then provide a context for re-reading.

Innovation on Words

> **I Know an Old Lady**
>
> I know an old lady who swallowed a _pie_ .
> I don't know why p
> she swallowed a _Pie_ .
> I think she'll _cry_ .

Figure 6.29

Innovation on Repetitive Sentence Patterns

Alligator Pie, by Dennis Lee

Alligator pie, alligator pie,
If I don't get some I think I'm gonna die.
Give away the green grass, give away the sky,
But don't give away my alligator pie.

> Alligator _Cake_
>
> Alligator _cake_ , Alligator _cake_ ,
> If I don' get some I think I'm goin' _break_
> Give away the _french fries_ give away the _shake_ .
> But don't give away my _Alligator Cake_ .

Figure 6.30

Innovation on Text Structure

Cumulative, repetitive texts such as *Give a Mouse a Cookie* by Laura Joffe Numeoff, *Possum Magic* by Mem Fox or *Wombat Stew* by Marcia Vaughan provide a framework for creating innovations based on whole-text patterns. Changing the main character in a book is a simple way for students to use the pattern of the text to create their own version.

– Read the chosen text a number of times.
– As a whole class or in small groups, change some aspects of the text but retain the original rhythm or rhyme. If necessary, the class could brainstorm a list of possible words as an aid for students having difficulty.
– Have students then work in small groups or with partners to create their own innovations on the text provided.
– Have them illustrate the new texts, and encourage the reading of these during both shared and independent reading time.

13 Punctuation Effects

Refer to Chapter 5: Experimental Reading Phase, p. 137.

14 Sentence Manipulation Activities

Manipulating sentences, phrases and words helps Early readers to focus on their sight vocabulary, knowledge of language features, sentence structure and conventions of print. Sentence manipulation activities can be created using vocabulary from Shared Reading texts, Language Experience sentences, Modelled Writing samples, students' own writing or cross-curriculum texts. A range of these activities suitable for use with Early readers include the following.

Sequencing Sentences
A series of sentences are taken from a familiar text and written on individual word or phrase cards. Students work to sequence them in an order that makes sense.

Sentence Making
Familiar words are written on individual cards. Students are encouraged to use them to create basic sentences.

Sentence Expansion
A series of basic sentences are created and written on individual cards. Students are then provided with additional adjectives, adverbs and phrases with which to extend the sentences.

Sentence Transformation
A series of repetitive sentences are created and written on individual word cards. Students then transform the sentences by changing one word at a time. It is important that they substitute parts of speech correctly; e.g. **a noun for a noun, a verb for a verb.**

15 Graphic Overlays

Graphic Overlays provide students with an opportunity to build their knowledge of text organisation. It is sometimes difficult for Early readers to follow texts that include pictures, diagrams, tables, graphs, text and photographs. Some informational texts are arranged in columns or have print placed beside unrelated graphics, and this may hinder comprehension.

The creation of a Graphic Overlay prior to reading provides students with a clear visual outline of how and where information is located in the text.

– Provide students with non-permanent markers and transparent overlays, e.g. **overheads, plastic sheeting or tracing paper.**

– Have them place transparent sheeting over each page of text in order to create a visual representation of the layout of the page.

– Direct them to draw boxes to represent chunks of text, diagrams, headings, labels or photographs and to label each box, describing what it represents, e.g. **text, subheading, photograph or caption.**

– Provide opportunities for them to use the graphic overlays to explain the layout of their text to a partner.

– Direct students to use the overlays to identify the parts of the text that may help to achieve the reading purpose.

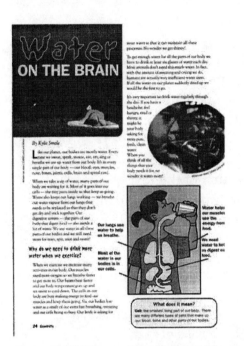

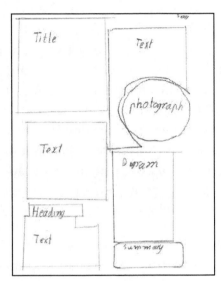

Figure 6.32 A student's prepared graphic overlay

Figure 6.31 Text page to be used for overlay
Source: CSIRO, published in *Scientriffic* Magazine, 2001

16 Reading Plans

Reading Plans (Hoyt 2002) are a way of helping students to become aware of the organisation of different informational texts. The creation and use of these plans initially need to be modelled. With ongoing modelling readers will be able to begin to create their own plans and determine the purpose each time a new informational text is read.

– Provide a reading-plan framework.

– Introduce the text to students.

– Discuss the purpose of the reading, and write it in the appropriate space in the framework.

– Encourage students to explore the text organisation to suggest how they might achieve the identified purpose.

– Invite them to record their responses.

```
                      Our Reading Plan
• Our purpose for reading is  to find out how volcanoes erupt.

• We will begin by  looking at the table of contents.

• Then we will  look at the headings.

• Next we will  look for the word 'erupt' in the heading and
  look to see if there is a drawing.
```

Figure 6.32 A class-generated reading plan

17 Connect the Text

Connect the Text is an activity that allows students to build on their knowledge of text organisation and explore how parts of a text work together. In some texts it is difficult to see how items of information in different parts of the text are related, so it is important that Early readers develop understandings such as these.

- Illustrations usually have captions.
- Illustrations are usually linked to a section of the text.
- Subheadings are usually linked in some way to the text that follows.
- Tables and graphs usually illustrate something explained in the text.

Follow this procedure to complete the activity.

- Copy selected pages of an informational text for students to use individually or in small groups.
- Cut the text into its component pieces, e.g. **headings, subheadings, illustrations, photographs, and meaningful chunks of text.**
- Provide each student or group with an envelope containing the cut pieces of text. This becomes the 'jigsaw package'.
- Allow time for students to reconstruct the text, using organisational features such as the headings and subheadings as a starting point.
- When this is done, provide them with copies of the original text and invite them to compare their arrangement of the information with that of the original.

It is important for Early readers to have multiple opportunities to participate in Connect the Text activities, using a wide variety of text forms.

18 Vocab-o-Gram

Refer to Chapter 5: Experimental Reading Phase, p. 137.

19 Share and Compare

Share and Compare provides students with the opportunity to identify and compare the features of different texts. They work in groups to sort a collection of texts into categories, then brainstorm features of each category. The interaction and conversation allows them to discuss and build on their knowledge of the structure, organisation and language features of different texts.

– Provide small groups with a collection of different texts, e.g. **reports and procedures.** The texts should be related to a particular topic or theme being studied across the curriculum, e.g. **magnets, explorers or fairy tales.**

– Have students work together to sort the texts into categories. Discuss what influenced their choices.

– Ask them to explore the groups of texts more closely and to further analyse the features of each one. They can be encouraged to focus on features such as the following.

  – The organisation of the texts; e.g. **'This report has lots of photographs of the animals'.**

  – The language features of the text; e.g. **'These reports all use lots of words that describe the animals'.**

  – The text structure; e.g. **'All these reports describe the animals by listing facts'.**

– Invite students to share with the whole class what they discovered.

– Create a class chart, listing features of the texts that could be generalised to each form (see below). The chart can be added to over time as students discover new features.

Things We Discovered about Procedures

Purpose: to tell you how to do something

1 The title or first paragraph gives you information about what you're going to do, e.g. Making a Deep-Water Diver

2 Have a list of materials

3 Have a numbered sequence of steps

4 Have pictures/photos for some of the steps

Things We Discovered about Reports

Purpose: to tell you about something

1 The title tells you what the topic is, e.g. *What is Water?*

2 Each paragraph tells you something about the topic

3 Have pictures or diagrams

4 Has words specific to the topic, e.g. *liquid, gas, solid, ice, evaporation*

---

20 Generic Games and Activities

The games and activities outlined in the Role Play Reading phase (see Chapter 4, pp. 86–93) can be used to continue the development of conventions of print, phonological awareness and graphophonic or word understandings in the Early Reading phase. The purpose in using each game or activity will be dependent on the chosen focus.

When using these activities, it is important to:
- keep them fun and informal;
- use settings that encourage interaction among students;
- embed them in the context of work that is already being done in the classroom;
- ensure that the students are fully familiar with the way to play the games.

The focus for these activities when used with Early readers could be:
- high-frequency words;
- topic words;
- personally significant words;
- sounds in words;
- onset and rime;
- letter patterns;
- punctuation marks such as commas, question marks, direct-speech marks;
- prefixes and suffixes;
- compound words;
- plurals;
- contractions;
- synonyms and antonyms;
- homophones (different spelling, same pronunciation, e.g. 'bare' and 'bear');
- homonyms (same spelling, different pronunciation, e.g. 'tear').

PROCESSES AND STRATEGIES

Major Teaching Emphases

- **Continue to build students' knowledge within the cues,** e.g. grammatical and cultural knowledge.

- **Consolidate known comprehension strategies and teach additional strategies,** e.g. skimming, scanning.

- **Teach word-identification strategies,** e.g. reading on, re-reading.

- **Continue to teach students how to locate, select and evaluate texts,** e.g. identifying different sources of information, checking publication dates.

- **Model self-reflection of strategies used in reading, and encourage students to do the same.**

Organisation of the Processes and Strategies Substrand

The organisation of the Processes and Strategies substrand differs in several ways from that of the other substrands. Both the Teaching Notes and the Involving Students sections are located in Chapter 4 of the *Reading Resource Book*, 2nd edn.

The rationale for this difference in organisation is that reading processes and strategies are not hierarchical, and therefore not phase-specific. A variety of processes and strategies need to be introduced, developed and consolidated at all phases of development.

What varies from one phase to the next is the growth in:
- the number and integration of strategies;
- the awareness and monitoring of strategies;
- the efficiency in use and selection of strategies;
- the ability to articulate the use of the strategies;
- the awareness of how the use of strategies helps with making meaning;
- the ability to locate, select and evaluate texts.

Supporting Parents of Early Readers

GENERAL DESCRIPTION OF EARLY READERS

Early readers confidently read familiar texts, but when meeting new texts they may read slowly and deliberately as they focus on the printed word, trying to read exactly what is on the page. Early readers express and justify their own reactions to texts they have read or listened to.

Supporting Early Readers in the Home

Early readers will benefit from a range of experiences in the home setting. Ideas for providing appropriate experiences are available on Parent Cards located on the *First Steps* Reading CD-ROM. Teachers can select appropriate cards for each Early reader from the Reading CD-ROM and copy them for parents to use at home. Also available on the CD-ROM is a parent-friendly version of the Reading Map of Development.

Parent Cards

1. General Description and How to Support Early Readers
2. Encouraging Reading
3. Reading to and with Your Child
4. Selecting Texts
5. Using Everyday Print
6. Reading and Writing Links
7. Developing Word and Text Knowledge

8. Supporting Oral Reading
9. Understanding How Texts are Read and Organised
10. Building a Love of Reading
11. Supporting Comprehension
12. Using Computers
13. Using the Library
14. Supporting Graphophonic and Word Knowledge through Games

CHAPTER 7

Transitional Reading Phase

Figure 7.1

Global Statement

In this phase, readers are beginning to integrate strategies to identify unknown words and to comprehend text. These strategies, combined with an increasing bank of sight words, enable readers to read texts such as novels, newspapers and websites with familiar content fluently and with expression. Transitional readers reflect on strategies used and are beginning to discuss their effectiveness.

Transitional Reading Indicators

Use of Texts

◆ **Reads and demonstrates comprehension of texts by:**
  – **identifying the main idea(s), citing supporting detail**
  – **selecting events from a text to suit a specific purpose**
  – **linking ideas, both explicit and implicit, in a text,** e.g. cause and effect.
◆ **Locates and selects texts appropriate to purpose and audience,** e.g. uses search engines, checks currency of information.
● Decodes texts with unfamiliar content, structure or vocabulary, but does not always sustain comprehension.
● Selects and connects explicit information for a specific purpose.

Contextual Understanding

◆ **Recognises own interpretation may differ from that of other readers or the author/s.**
◆ **Recognises devices that authors and illustrators use to influence construction of meaning,** e.g. visual clues, omissions.
◆ **Recognises that authors and illustrators attempt to position readers.**
◆ **Recognises how characters or people, facts and events are represented, and can speculate about the author's choices.**
● Compares aspects of texts, such as points of view and character traits.
● Discusses and justifies own interpretation of a text.
● Questions the credibility of events in literary texts and the validity and accuracy of informational texts, e.g. discerns fact from opinion in promotional material.

Conventions

◆ **Recognises an increasing bank of words in different contexts,** e.g. subject-specific words, less common words.
◆ **Explains how known text forms vary by using knowledge of:**
  – **purpose,** e.g. to persuade
  – **text structure,** e.g. problem and solution
  – **text organisation,** e.g. headings, subheadings, an index, glossary
  – **language features,** e.g. conjunctions.
● Uses knowledge of punctuation to enhance phrasing, intonation and comprehension.
● Identifies and explains the purpose of text organisational features, e.g. subheadings, paragraphs.
● Identifies how words and phrases are used to signal relationships, e.g. the phrase 'on the other hand' signals that a different point of view is to follow.
● Recognises that the same letter combinations can represent different sounds, e.g. rough, cough, dough, plough.
● Recognises less common sound–symbol correspondences, e.g. ocean, suspicion.

Processes and Strategies

◆ **Draws upon an increasing knowledge base to comprehend,** e.g. text structure and organisation, grammar, vocabulary.
◆ **Uses an increasing range of strategies to comprehend,** e.g. creating images, determining importance.
◆ **Determines unknown words by using word-identification strategies,** e.g. reading on, re-reading.
● Generates appropriate key words from a text for a specific purpose.
● Is aware of and talks about the use of cues and strategies.

Major Teaching Emphases

Environment and Attitude
- Create a supportive classroom environment that nurtures a community of readers.
- Jointly construct, and frequently refer to, meaningful environmental print.
- Foster students' enjoyment of reading.
- Encourage students to take risks with confidence.
- Encourage students to select their own reading material according to interest or purpose.

Use of Texts
- Provide opportunities for students to read a wide range of texts.
- Continue to teach students to analyse texts, identifying explicit and implicit information.
- Continue to teach students to make connections within texts, using both explicit and implicit information.
- Model how concept knowledge and understandings can be shaped and reshaped using information from a variety of texts.

Contextual Understanding
- Discuss how readers may react to and interpret texts differently, depending on their knowledge, experience or perspective.
- Discuss how authors and illustrators have used devices to target specific audiences, e.g. quoting statistics.

- Provide opportunities for students to challenge the author's world view.

Conventions
- Continue to build students' sight vocabulary, e.g. less common words, subject-specific words.
- Continue to build students' graphophonic and word knowledge, such as:
  - recognising less common sound–symbol relationships
  - recognising letter combinations, and the different sounds they represent
  - recognising how word parts and words work.
- Jointly analyse texts where combinations and adaptations of text structure and text organisation have been used.
- Teach students to identify the role of language features in a variety of texts.

Processes and Strategies
- Continue to build students' knowledge within the cues, e.g. orthographic, world knowledge.
- Consolidate known comprehension strategies and teach additional strategies, e.g. synthesising, paraphrasing.
- Consolidate word-identification strategies.
- Continue to teach students how to locate, select and evaluate texts, e.g. conducting Internet searches, recognising bias.
- Model self-reflection of strategies used in reading, and encourage students to do the same.

Teaching and Learning Experiences

ENVIRONMENT AND ATTITUDE

Major Teaching Emphases

- Create a supportive classroom environment that nurtures a community of readers.

- Jointly construct, and frequently refer to, meaningful environmental print.

- Foster students' enjoyment of reading.

- Encourage students to take risks with confidence.

- Encourage students to select their own reading material according to interest or purpose.

Teaching Notes

A classroom environment designed for Transitional readers reflects elements of support and challenge. Embedded in both the climate and the physical setting of the classroom is support for risk-taking, questioning and alternative interpretations of text. Texts of varying difficulty challenge students to engage in independent reading for different purposes. Discussions and activities that are open-ended encourage many different responses to texts. Involving Transitional readers in these experiences will assist them to see reading as enjoyable and purposeful.

Exploring Print

Creating a print-rich environment is still important for Transitional readers. The type of print available in the classroom will reflect a diversity of purposes. A jointly constructed print-rich environment also helps students understand that print has a range of functions and can be referred to frequently over time. Meaningful print for Transitional readers could reflect the following functions of print (Owocki 1999).

- **Environmental** — print that gives information about the world, e.g. schedules, rosters, labels and captions for class work, messages on a class message board.

- **Occupational** — print associated with a job or profession, e.g. a fashion designer's could include patterns, order forms, instruction manuals, catalogues.
- **Informational** — print for storing, retrieving and organising information, e.g. a grid recording the loan of class reading books, a timetable indicating allocation of computer time, a tree diagram outlining the classification of a species of animal.
- **Recreational** — print for leisure activities, e.g. news displays, magazines, newspapers, instructions for games.

At this phase it is still important to draw students' attention to print, and to model how to use it effectively.

The diverse range of print can be used to demonstrate the many different ways readers access texts, according to their context and purpose; for example, scanning a calendar is done by using month, date and day reference points, while scanning a dictionary involves the use of guidewords at the top of each page. Although many of these skills are often demonstrated in instructional reading sessions, it is frequent and purposeful practice that helps students consolidate and apply their understandings to new contexts.

Fostering Enjoyment of Reading

It is important for Transitional readers to see reading as a purposeful and worthwhile activity. Some who can read often choose not to do so, yet they can be encouraged to interact with a variety of texts for different purposes.

In the classroom reading environment, teachers can introduce a wide variety of literary and informational texts, including:
- science fiction, fantasy, realistic fiction, reports, explanations and recipes;
- procedural texts — for example, instructions to use equipment such as the computer, or copies of school evacuation plans;
- popular texts such as magazines, topical articles and song lyrics;
- different versions of one story or event — for example, different printed versions or versions from different media;
- local and provincial newspapers;
- easily accessible reference material, such as telephone books, street directories, atlases, dictionaries, thesauri, Internet, and CD-ROMs.

The enjoyment of reading can be fostered in many ways.
- Provide many opportunities for students to be involved in focused conversations about reading. This may happen in an informal way when they discuss their reading with a peer or in Book Discussion Groups, which provide for a more formalised opportunity to talk

about texts and suggest a supportive structure (see *Reading Resource Book*, 2nd edn, Chapter 1: Use of Texts).

- Provide opportunities every day for students to be read to by a skilled reader modelling good reading strategies and exposing them to different genres. While this reader is usually the class teacher, there is no reason why others could not be involved, such as parents, older siblings or community members.
- Provide an opportunity for students to write to a celebrity of their choice asking about the text he or she is currently reading or about a favourite childhood book. Knowing that people they admire find reading to be worthwhile often helps Transitional readers to maintain a positive attitude to reading.
- Organise daily, independent silent reading of self-selected texts.
- Provide comfortable, quiet spaces for independent reading.
- Share your favourite books with students, explaining their appeal.
- Accept and praise diverse interpretations of text, encouraging students to share and compare points of view.
- Provide ongoing, targeted feedback and encouragement.
- Encourage and organise visits to the school and local libraries.
- Organise visits by authors to speak about their books.
- Develop a 'buddy reading' system with another class in the school.
- Provide authentic reading experiences that are linked to students' interests and experiences, and have a clear purpose or focus.
- Create well-organised, consistent routines for reading experiences and the use of classroom reading materials.

Encouraging Risk-Taking

Transitional readers can become risk-takers if asked to:
- extend the variety of texts they read;
- use a variety of strategies to maintain and monitor comprehension;
- use a variety of cues to comprehend text;
- question the author's message and explore issues from different perspectives;
- use a multistrategy approach to understand unknown words;
- investigate word meanings and extend their vocabulary;
- discuss their reading strategies.

For further information about Environment and Attitude, see:
- *Linking Assessment, Teaching and Learning*, Chapter 5: Establishing a Positive Teaching and Learning Environment;
- *Reading Resource Book*, 2nd edn, Chapter 1: Use of Texts.

USE OF TEXTS

Major Teaching Emphases

■ Provide opportunities for students to read a wide range of texts.

■ Continue to teach students to analyse texts, identifying explicit and implicit information.

■ Continue to teach students to make connections within texts, using both explicit and implicit information.

■ Model how concept knowledge and understandings can be shaped and reshaped using information from a variety of texts.

Teaching Notes

Readers in this phase may derive enjoyment and consolidate their skills and strategies by reading a series of texts that have similar content, author or structure. This allows them to begin building connections between texts and to develop consistent reading habits. However, if one type of text dominates a student's independent reading to the exclusion of all others, it is possible that the student may not become familiar with the structure, features and vocabulary of a wider range of texts.

There are many ways teachers can interest students in broadening their repertoire of texts.

• Provide them with a text and regularly ask about milestones, such as 'Have you got to the part where he . . .?.

• Read an extract from a text, but do not reveal the title or the author, creating a sense of mystery and challenge.

• Read the first page (or a set number of pages) of four texts and have students vote on which one to continue reading.

• Display results of text-popularity contests, both in and beyond the classroom.

• Arrange displays based on frequently changing themes, genres or style.

• Invite other students, parents, siblings or community members to talk about their favourite texts.

The foci for helping Transitional readers in this substrand are organised under the following headings.
- Variety of Texts
- Responding to Texts

Variety of Texts

Transitional readers benefit from opportunities to read texts of varying degrees of difficulty, both teacher-directed and self-selected. These might include:
- easy texts, e.g. those that have been read previously;
- appropriate texts, e.g. those with limited new vocabulary or about well-known topics;
- more challenging texts, e.g. texts used in Guided Reading with teacher support.

Although there are many measures of text difficulty, the Rule of Thumb is a simple way to support Transitional readers as they self-select. In using the Rule of Thumb, students select a text they wish to read and start on a page near the beginning. The page is read, and for each unknown word the student puts a finger down, in order, starting with the little one. If the thumb is placed down before reaching the bottom of the page, the text may be too difficult at that time and the reader might like to select another one. Regardless of which measure is used, be aware that students may persist successfully with a difficult text if the content is appealing to them.

Reading-incentive schemes that focus on extrinsic rewards can also be helpful, but need to be investigated to ensure that positive reading habits are sustained and that the focus remains on reading for meaning and enjoyment rather than on receiving the incentive.

In Modelled, Shared and Guided Reading sessions, teachers can demonstrate how to:
- select texts for different purposes;
- make connections and generalisations;
- draw conclusions from explicit and implicit information;
- make predictions about the text using the pictures, title and table of contents;
- identify the main idea to gain an overall understanding;
- justify answers to questions, using supporting details;
- use information from different sources to shape knowledge.

Responding to Texts

Transitional readers can be encouraged to respond to texts in a variety of ways. The responses can be written, oral or visual. Instruction in question–answer relationships can help them develop the strategic thinking skills necessary to make distinctions about information that is explicit in the text and that which is implicit. Students in this phase draw on both types.

Information that is implied requires the reader to draw on knowledge outside the text to make connections or associations. It often requires readers to make predictions, draw conclusions or make generalisations from information that has been either directly or indirectly stated. The focus in this phase is on helping readers to make connections between explicit and implicit information; for example, identifying cause and effect.

Recording information and thoughts about a text before, during and after the act of reading will help students realise that reading is constantly reshaping knowledge. For example, opinions shared about a text may change when information about the author's background comes to light.

Answering questions is another way students can respond to texts. There are many ways of organising and discussing types of questions e.g. Bloom's Taxonomy (Bloom 1956), Question–Answer Relationships (Raphael 1986), Three Level Guides (Herber 1970) or Open and Closed Questions. Whichever hierarchy is chosen, it is wise to include questions that require different levels of thinking.

Raphael (1986) categorises questions as Right There (Literal), Think and Search (Inferential), Author and You (Interpretive) and On Your Own (Critical/Evaluative), providing a useful framework for ensuring that different types of questions are used in the classroom.

Literal
Literal questions focus on what the author said. The answer is 'right there' in the text or pictures. Common literal questions begin with 'who', 'when', 'where' or 'what', and it is important that teachers follow them up with clarifying questions such as 'Can you read out the part where it says that? Where is that in the text?' so that students get the idea of substantiating answers by returning to the text.

Inferential

The answers to these questions can be found in the text but are not necessarily in the one place; they show relationships such as cause and effect, sequence, or compare and contrast. They are also sometimes the 'how' and 'why' questions; the student has to 'put the answer together' from various sections or sentences in the text; for example, 'How is . . . similar to or different from . . .? 'What is the author trying to tell us here?', 'Was . . . an effective solution to the problem?'.

Interpretive

These are the Author and You questions. They require the student to base the answer on the text, but also to draw on previous personal experience to reach a reasonable answer. The answer must not be a wild guess; it must be probable, not just possible. Examples are: 'From the evidence presented by the author, is it a good idea to . . .?', 'Based on what you have read so far, what do you think will happen when . . .?'.

Critical/Evaluative

These questions go beyond the text, asking for students' own opinions or judgements. They are the On Your Own questions, as the answers are not found in the text at all. The reader can answer the question without having read the text, although it does provide a starting point for discussions about the underlying messages or themes. Questions might be 'How would you feel if . . .?', 'What is your opinion of . . .?','What makes you feel that way?'.

For further information about the Use of Texts substrand, see *Reading Resource Book*, 2nd edn:
• Chapter 1: Use of Texts
• Chapter 4: Processes and Strategies.

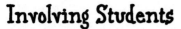

Involving Students

1 2C2D (Collect, Compare, Display, Discuss)

2C2D refers to collecting, comparing, displaying and discussing either specific text types or parts of texts for the purpose of analysis. Apart from entire texts, students can collect:

- beginnings
- endings
- plot fragments
- settings
- character descriptions
- dialogue
- authors
- devices that authors use, e.g. similes, metaphors.

Collecting

Collecting is inspired by a personal interest; e.g. 'I enjoyed the story that was set in Africa, so I asked the librarian if there were any other books or stories that took place in Africa'. Collecting allows comparisons to be made between a variety of texts, such as books, movies, songs, poems, CD-ROMs and Internet sites.

Comparing

Comparing can simply be a mental process, or be represented by a table, a diagram, an oral presentation or a written text; e.g. 'I couldn't help but notice that these two stories depicted the wilderness of Africa as really beautiful and enchanting, but this one focused more on how harsh the living conditions are . . .'. An innovative way of encouraging students to make comparisons is to provide a question to promote inquiry: 'What do the stories x, y and z have in common? They all have . . .'.

Displaying

Displaying representations of compared texts and text parts provides:

- models, e.g. 'You've now read three books all by the same author. What about constructing a table to compare them, just as I did on that large sheet of paper?';
- ongoing referencing opportunities, e.g. 'The documentary that was on last night had the sort of scenery described in the three books I compared in my 2C2D chart'.
- inspiration, e.g. 'Abdul has now read a fourth story set in Africa, so he is going to add to my chart'.

Discussing

Discussing focuses on similarities and differences, including how and why a text is crafted in a particular way; e.g. 'I suppose the final story was written from the point of view of the indigenous inhabitants of the country. It probably reflects how tough it is to live in that environment, rather than how exotic certain parts of the country look through the eyes of a tourist'.

- Direct students to collect examples of texts or parts of texts over a given time. Each needs to contain a chosen criterion, such as dialogue.
- Allow time for them to individually make comparisons between the chosen pieces.
- Have students represent their comparisons. Display their representations.
- Provide time for them to discuss similarities and differences in texts.

2 Readers' Theatre

Refer to Chapter 6: Early Reading Phase, p. 154.

3 Read and Retell

Read and Retell (Browne & Cambourne 1987) is a simple activity that is flexible in its use and provides an opportunity for students to transform a text. Retelling requires students to read or listen to a text, organise key information in it they have understood, then prepare to share and compare their retell with others. Retells at the Transitional reading phase can be created and shared orally, in writing, as a drawing, or through drama.

Retelling provides an excellent context for students to analyse text and identify both explicit and implicit information in it. Transitional readers can be involved in retelling both literary and informational texts.

Students will benefit from creating different forms of retells.
- Written to written retells — students read a text and retell it in writing.
- Written to oral retells — students read a text and retell it orally.
- Written to drawing retells — students read a text and retell it by drawing.
- Written to drama retells — students read a text and retell it through drama.
- Diagram to oral or written retells — students read a diagram and retell it in writing or orally.
- Drama to written retells — students view a dramatic presentation and retell it in writing.

The following procedure can be adapted to suit the purpose, context, focus and form of retell being used.

– Select a text and display the title.
– Ask students to predict the plot and the vocabulary that may be used. Share their predictions in small groups.
– Direct students to read the text.
– Allow them to re-read it as many times as is necessary.
– Provide time for them to prepare their retells (in any of the forms previously mentioned).
– Have them share their retells with a partner, a small group or the whole class.
– Provide time for them to discuss and compare the retells.

4 Simply the Best

In Simply the Best, students collect pieces of text — or whole texts — that constitute the best examples to meet a given criterion, such as the best setting, factual description, dialogue or excitement build-up. They justify why they like the chosen pieces and vote on the overall best from the class or group collection.

– Support students each to collect, from their reading, the single best example from a text to meet a selected criterion. If they have difficulty finding examples, suggestions can be made.
– Allow time for them to set the context of the chosen pieces; for example, a summary of the story to that point.
– Have them read their nominations aloud, with appropriate expression, tone and volume. Each should be followed with an explanation of why it is considered an award-winning piece of writing.
– Have students vote on which example is the best. The 'finder' of the winning nomination receives due credit for discovering it.
– Jointly discuss and record the features of the nominated texts, such as fresh, accurate adjectives, variation in sentence length and believable lines.
– Encourage students to refer to the list of features when writing their own texts.

5 Readingo

Readingo is a reading-incentive scheme that encourages students to read a wide variety of texts. A grid is filled with examples of different texts, or text types. As the student reads each example, the square is coloured to indicate the reader's response to it; for instance, red for brilliant, blue for good, green for okay or yellow for awful.

There are two types of Readingo grids: closed and open. A closed grid is created when specific titles are listed; for example, columns or rows might list particular texts from different learning areas. Closed grids enable the teacher to exercise more influence over the students' reading; however, they require consideration of reader ability and text difficulty.

An open grid lists the type of text rather than specific titles (see Figure 7.2). By providing extra space on the grid for titles and dates, the Readingo sheet can be used as a partial record of personal reading habits.

To complete the activity, students:
– choose one of the texts on the grid;
– read it;
– colour the square;
– take the text to a reading conference;
– explain what was felt about the book;
– ask the conference partner to initial the coloured square;
– choose another text from the grid to continue on the path horizontally, vertically or diagonally.

An incentive of some kind may be provided once students have completed a Readingo path.

READINGO				
A magazine article about a celebrity	A recipe that you actually use to cook a meal	A mystery novel	A story written by an author you have read before	A biography
A Letters to the Editor column	A software instruction booklet	A science fiction novel	A series of websites	A book by a local author
A feature newspaper article	A comic	A romance novel	An encyclopaedia entry (for research)	A book set in a country you would like to visit
A review of a movie you have seen	A collection of poetry	A historical fiction novel	A hobby or leisure magazine	A book that is the first in a series
A classified advertisement section	A joke book	An adventure novel	A collection of cereal packets	A section of a CD-ROM

Figure 7.2 An open Readingo grid

6 Transformations

Transformations involve students in changing text information into a different genre, form, mode, medium or format. Examples of transformations include:

- a fairy tale rewritten as a news article;
- a novel re-created as a board game;
- a short story represented as a comic strip;
- a poem represented as a performance.

Transformations require the student comprehending the original text to create a new text. They can vary greatly in their degree of difficulty according to text content and text form, and degree of compatibility between the original and the new form. Although a fairy tale may be familiar to a student, the structure and organisation of a newspaper article may not. Similarly, a student may have played many board games but rarely considered how one might be constructed.

Students attempting transformations require significant support in understanding and manipulating the two text forms. Teachers can best support them with extensive modelling, sharing and guiding.

7 Facts and Falsehoods

Facts and Falsehoods can be used to categorise items and clarify concepts. In this activity, students create a series of statements of which all but one are factual. The challenge is for another student to determine which one is the falsehood, and why. Texts related to whole-class, cross-curriculum topics work best for this activity.

Note that this activity changes in orientation according to how the reading is done. For example, students can read texts about individual areas of interest and create Facts and Falsehoods for their peers; classmates can investigate these using sources such as the Internet and reference material. This is a good test of the classmates' general knowledge. Alternatively, all students can read the same text and create Facts and Falsehoods for each other; this is more a test of comprehension for all students.

- Ask students each to read about a particular topic and list facts found in the text. If the task is to be completed orally, three or four statements are sufficient; if the list is to be read, up to ten items would be possible. Generally, the greater the number, the greater will be the difficulty of the task for the person who must identify the falsehood.

- Have students write one falsehood to be included in the list.
- Provide opportunities for each student to challenge another to find the falsehood.

The essence of a fair challenge requires teacher modelling, as some students will misinterpret the aim of the activity and will attempt to trick the reader rather than create a fitting task. Facts need to fall somewhere within student experience, and falsehoods need to be substantially different. For example, a falsehood that reads 'Jupiter has a diameter of 128 400 kilometres' (Jupiter actually has a diameter of 142 800 kilometres) would be considered an unfair challenge because very few people would recall that level of detail.

An adaptation of Facts and Falsehoods involves the odd one out being the fact and the remainder being falsehoods. However, participating in this activity requires a stronger knowledge of the topic to make decisions about the statements.

Facts and Falsehoods	
Statements	Text: Heinemann Outcomes: Science 2
The moon is always the same distance from earth.	fact/**falsehood**
There were many superstitions about eclipses in ancient times.	**fact**/falsehood
Tides are caused by the force of gravity from the earth and moon.	fact/**falsehood**
Humans would need specialised equipment to live on the moon.	**fact**/falsehood
Jupiter is located in the Milky Way galaxy.	**fact**/falsehood
The universe began with a gigantic explosion of gas and matter.	**fact**/falsehood
	fact/falsehood
	fact/falsehood
	fact/falsehood

Figure 7.3

8 Extend a Heading

Owing to the nature of the text form, newspaper headings often omit adjectives and adverbs. In Extend a Heading, students read and find the main idea of a newspaper article that has a heading consisting of at least one noun and one verb; for example, Dog Attacks Man.

- Provide students with a number of newspaper articles with short headings. Allow time for groups of four to select an article and read it.
- Have students individually brainstorm adjectives and/or adverbs that would be suitable to extend the heading. Each student

creates an extended heading; for instance, Savage Dog Attacks Elderly Man.

– Organise students in pairs to combine their ideas and reach consensus. Discussion need not be lengthy, but should be based upon literal and inferential information in the text that supports a particular adjective or adverb being chosen.

– Once pairs have agreed on the extended heading, re-form the group of four. Encourage this group to again reach consensus. Students may find themselves debating the relative meanings of a number of synonyms in an effort to choose the most appropriate adjectives and adverbs.

– Display the articles and the newly created headings.

9 Who Said . . .?

Refer to Chapter 6: Early Reading Phase, p. 162.

10 Story Maps

Story Maps are graphic representations of some or all elements of a literary text, showing the relationships between the elements. Whether they are used before, during or after reading, Story Maps represent a practical way for students to organise their thinking. They can vary greatly in structure according to the purpose of the activity, the students' phase of development and the nature of the text.

Transitional readers will benefit from creating a variety of maps.
- **Chronological maps** — chronological representation of the sequence of events in a clockwise direction.
- **Geographical maps** — using setting as the central focus, illustrating how the story unfolds.
- **Relationship maps** — created as above, but also including lines that indicate relationships such as cause and effect, compare and contrast.

Creating Story Maps at the Transitional phase assists students to identify both explicit and implicit information in a text.

– Read text to students, or provide time for independent reading.
– Have students draw elements on cards or sticky notes (this allows the elements to be moved or the positions changed).
– Direct them to place the cards or notes to create a draft story map.
– Provide them with time to share and compare their draft maps with others, and to refine the drafts as needed.
– Encourage them to use their Story Maps as a basis for retelling.

11 DIRDS

DIRDS is an activity that assists students to look at characters from several perspectives, drawing upon implicit and explicit information in the text. Students are asked to see how characters are described (D), illustrated (I) and responded to (R) by others, as well as what they do (D) and say (S). They are then asked to draw inferences from the information in the text. Information and inferences can be recorded, and shared with others.

D — Described

How does the author describe the character? What does that description say about the character? For example, 'Her blouse had bits of breakfast all over it — toast crumbs and tea stains and splotches of dried egg-yolk' would indicate a character with unhygienic traits.

I — Illustrated

How has the illustrator represented the character? If the text is not illustrated, have students draw what they think the character would look like from the words of the author.

R — Responded to by others

How do other characters react to this one? For example, shying away from the character indicates fear; being absorbed in what the character says may indicate respect.

D — Do

What do the characters do that give clues about their distinguishing traits and qualities? A character that taps a foot may be seen as impatient, while one who pushes or shoves others may be seen as aggressive.

S — Say

What does the character actually say that gives clues about those traits? A character who yells may be seen as unfriendly, while a character who sneers may be seen as contemptuous.

As a variation, the activity can be used to get a picture of a character at different points in the text. If two characters have been considered, this can be the basis for making comparisons.

DIRDS

Text: The Great Mouse Plot by Roald Dahl

Character/Party Mrs Pratchett	Inferences Made
Described Small, skinny old hag filthy, mean black fingernails disgusting old woman small malignant pig eyes vinegary voice	She was poor and didn't eat very much
Illustrated No illustrations	
Responded to By Others hated loathed had it in for her	Because she was so disliked the children were always thinking of plans to get back at her
Do never smiled never welcoming cackled shrieked put the sweets in newspaper instead of paper bags	She had a mean and nasty streak. She despised in others what was true for her.
Say "Keep your thieving fingers off" "Boys is hideous and orrible" "...the nasty dirty little pigs"	She didn't like children especially boys and thought they were all out to rip her off.

Figure 7.4

12 The Drammies

The Drammies is an activity in which readers determine an award that is appropriate for a particular character or person. Completing this activity encourages readers to summarise the contribution of a character or person to the text by drawing on explicit and implicit information to make judgements.

- After reading a text, direct students to select a character or person in it and determine an appropriate award; for example, Charlotte, in Charlotte's Web, might win an award for creativity because she spun words in her web.
- Ensure that students provide justification for their nominations by referring to events or actions in the text.
- Allow time for them to record their nominations and their reasons, and create the award.
- Provide time for them to share their work, and display awards with the text.

13 Dear Abby

Dear Abby is a partner activity in which students take on the role of either a character or an adviser to share or solve a problem occurring in the text. Participating in this activity encourages students to infer actions and behaviours, and to 'read between the lines' if asked to provide advice. Transitional readers should have the opportunity to be involved with characters in literary texts or people from informational texts.

- Arrange students in pairs. In each pair, one student is allocated a character or person from the text; the other is to become the adviser (Abby).
- Allow time for students to begin reading the selected text. Direct them to stop reading at a point where there is a problem or issue for a character or person.
- Allow time for the student being the character or person to seek advice from Abby. The student taking the role of Abby then responds, offering advice on what the other should do.
- Have students continue reading to a point where another problem or issue arises, and repeat the above process.
- If the whole class have read the same text, have students share requests and responses, and the way they relate to the original text.

14 Let's Consider

Let's Consider (Wilson 2003) encourages students to document how their attitudes, knowledge and understandings are shaped and reshaped when collecting information from various texts. By providing them with a variety of sentence starters, they are directed to reflect how attitudes, knowledge and understandings are affected by what is read.

- Encourage students to gather a range of texts on a particular topic.
- Allow time for them to read the texts.
- Direct them to use the framework provided (see Figure 7.5) to record their reflections.

Let's Consider	
Topic:	
I never knew that . . .	I've changed my mind about . . .
The most important thing I'll remember is . . .	I'm still wondering about . . .

Figure 7.5

15 Celebrity Heads

Refer to Chapter 6: Early Reading Phase, p. 162.

16 What's the Message?

Refer to Chapter 6: Early Reading Phase, p. 163.

17 Text Rating Scale

A Text Rating Scale invites students to make judgements about the qualities of a whole text. By completing such a scale, Transitional readers have the opportunity to assess the qualities of the text and justify that assessment in a discussion with peers.

- Have the whole class generate a list of words to describe the qualities of texts. Discuss each word and its opposite, and record these on a class chart. This chart becomes a resource for students when completing Text Rating Scales (see Figure 7.6).
- Select a text to be read by all students.

- Have them create their scales by recording the nominated qualities on the framework provided (see Figure 7.7).
- Have each student individually rate the whole text according to the nominated qualities.
- Direct them to record their justifications on the framework provided.
- Invite some to share their ratings and justifications.

Our Class Words to Describe Texts	
LITERARY TEXTS	**INFORMATIONAL TEXTS**
exciting_____boring	accurate_____inaccurate
believable_____far-fetched	comprehensive_____sketchy
humorous_____lacking in humour	balanced_____biased
suspenseful_____predictable	interesting_____boring
engaging_____slow	well organised_____poorly organised
sequential_____confusing	
clear_____confusing	clear_____confusing

Figure 7.6

Figure 7.7

CONTEXTUAL UNDERSTANDING

Major Teaching Emphases

- **Discuss how readers may react to and interpret texts differently, depending on their knowledge, experience or perspective.**

- **Discuss how authors and illustrators have used devices to target specific audiences,** e.g. quoting statistics.

- **Provide opportunities for students to challenge the author's world view.**

Teaching Notes

Among the possible misconceptions Transitional readers may have about the reading process is the notion that texts convey a single meaning that is comprehended in the same way by all readers. It is critical that readers in this phase become aware that one text may be reacted to, responded to and interpreted differently, according to the reader's prior knowledge and experience.

Teachers can welcome more than one interpretation of a text, encouraging students to provide evidence to support their thinking. Transitional readers benefit from opportunities to discuss and challenge the view presented by an author.

The foci for helping Transitional readers to develop contextual understanding are organised under the following headings.
- Discussions about Texts
- Discussions about the Devices Authors and Illustrators Use
- Discussions about the Author's World View

Discussions about Texts

While it is important for Transitional readers to continue to make connections and comparisons between their own experiences and those presented in texts, the focus in this phase will be on discussing how and why readers may react differently to the same text.

This can be achieved in a range of ways.
- Encourage students to make connections and comparisons between the text and their prior knowledge; for example:
  - 'What do you know about . . .?'
  - 'Have you ever been in this situation? How did you react?'

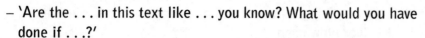

- 'Are the . . . in this text like . . . you know? What would you have done if . . .?'
- 'Do you think . . . was right to . . .?'
- 'From what you know about . . ., could what the author is saying be true? Why? Why not?'

- Support students in identifying and justifying their points of view; for example:
  - 'What is your opinion of this text?'
  - 'What are your reasons for feeling that way?'
  - 'Do you agree with the author or not?'
- Support students in discussing how and why texts are interpreted differently; for example, **'That's interesting. Luke thinks . . . Why might Luke have interpreted the text in that way?'**
- Assist students to identify the author's point of view; for example:
  - 'What does the author think about . . .? How do you know that?'
  - 'What message does the author give about . . .? Do you agree or disagree with that? Why?'
- Encourage students to discuss texts from different perspectives or points of view; for example:
  - 'The author has said . . .. Which groups might agree with that? Which groups might disagree? Why?'
  - 'If you were a . . ., what would you think of . . .?'
  - 'If you wanted to . . ., what information would you include that the author hasn't? What would you omit?'

Discussions about Devices Authors and Illustrators Use

Although most Transitional readers are aware that a text is constructed for a particular audience, they require opportunities to explore how the author and illustrator achieve this. Discussions can focus on the purpose of the text and the devices authors use to target particular audiences. Discussing the reasons for these choices and their effectiveness will give Transitional readers a deeper understanding of how these impact on readers' interpretation of texts.

Devices used by illustrators include:

- choice of colours;
- amount of detail;
- size of characters, tables or diagrams relative to others;
- composition of the page, e.g. **placement of visuals;**
- artistic style, e.g. **abstract representation rather than realism.**

Devices used by authors include:

- choice of language, e.g. **descriptive, emotive;**
- inclusion or omission of details;

- foreshadowing — giving a hint of things to come, e.g. **As she sat in silence, the door blew open;**
- irony, wit, humour;
- flashback — interrupting the text to show something that happened earlier;
- understatement — downplaying the gravity of a situation, e.g. **'It's nothing,' said Josie as she clutched her broken arm to her chest;**
- symbolism — objects used to represent other things, e.g. **He wore a flowing black cloak and a black hat pulled down to cover his face;**
- opinions disguised as facts, e.g. **It has been widely reported that . . .;**
- quoted statistics, e.g. **80% of mothers prefer . . .;**
- selected evidence and proof;
- print size;
- font selection.

Devices used by an author to position readers can be deconstructed and analysed within the context of the text. Deconstructing texts in this way assists students to become aware that an author's message can be challenged, resisted or rejected.

Discussions about the Author's World View

Transitional readers need many opportunities to discuss and challenge authors' points of view.

Facilitate discussion by asking a variety of questions.
- How has the author represented characters or people, facts or events?
- What does the author want the reader to feel or think about the characters or people, facts or events?
- What is the author's purpose in writing this text?
- Who is to be the audience? What has the author done to appeal to this audience?
- What expertise or authority does the author have for writing about this topic?
- Why has the author chosen to use the words . . . to describe this character or person?
- What does the author not want the reader to know? Why do you think that might be?
- From whose point of view is the author writing? Why do you think this was done?
- From what other point of view could the text have been written? How would it change?
- What do you know about the author's background?
- How could the author's background affect the way the text has been written?

- What has the illustrator done to let you know that this character or person is . . .?
- What do the pictures, diagrams or maps tell? Do they give the same meaning as the words?
- Who is funding the website or research? How might it have influenced the information being reported?

For further information about the Contextual Understanding substrand, see *Reading Resource Book*, 2nd edn, Chapter 2: Contextual Understanding.

Involving Students

1 Stop, Think, Feel, Share

Refer to Chapter 6: Early Reading Phase, p. 168.

2 Four Corners

Refer to Chapter 6: Early Reading Phase, p. 170.

3 Feelings Guide

Creating a Feelings Guide encourages the generation and use of a range of 'feeling' words. Completing the guide helps Transitional readers to express their feelings about and reactions to a text.

- Have students brainstorm a list of words to describe feelings that readers might have towards a character, person, event, issue, topic or text.
- As a class, discuss and clarify the meaning of each word.
- Record words on a Feelings Guide chart (see Figure 7.8).
- Add to the chart as new words are discovered.
- Use the Feelings Guide to support class discussions about texts, encouraging students to explain their feelings either with reference to the text or by making connections to personal experience; e.g. 'Ryan, how were you feeling about the author's description of how settlement occurred?' 'I'm feeling confused and a bit curious because the book says that settlers staked claim to plots of land, but I'm wondering who that land belonged to before they came'.
- Highlight the similarities and differences in the ways readers feel about the same piece of text; e.g. 'Well, this is interesting. Ryan is feeling confused and curious about who owned the land before the settlers arrived, whereas Rana is feeling sorry for the settlers because of the hardship they had to endure'.

OUR CLASS FEELINGS GUIDE		
delighted	embarrassed	cheated
appreciative	astonished	terrified
eager	flustered	betrayed
elated	discouraged	miserable
satisfied	confused	disappointed
contented	anxious	annoyed
curious	ashamed	irritated
disturbed		

Figure 7.8

4 Interviews

This is an activity that involves students' role playing an interview with a character or person in a text.

One student takes the role of the person or character being interviewed, while another asks the questions. Participating in this activity encourages Transitional readers to consider reasons for a character or person's actions and begin to interpret behaviours presented in a text.

Students role playing the interviewee respond orally to the questions asked; they are required to make inferences, draw conclusions and make connections, presenting their own interpretation of the text being considered.

Students conducting the interviews need to create questions that will elicit the reasons for choices made in the text. It is important to model the types of questions that will help students to focus on finding details about the person's or character's actions, feelings and behaviours; they can be of a speculative nature, requiring the interviewee to think beyond the actual events presented in the text. Students would benefit from watching and analysing several real-life interviews prior to attempting this activity, and discussing the types of questions and answers that contribute to an informative, entertaining interview.

- Organise students in pairs. Have each pair select a character or person from a common text read.
- Direct them to negotiate who will be the character or person and who will be the interviewer.
- Pairs then work together to develop appropriate questions.
- Provide time for them to conduct their interviews.

- Invite some to share their interviews with the whole class.
- At the conclusion of each shared interview, invite students to discuss which parts of the text influenced the questions and answers.

5 Change the Point of View

Change the Point of View provides readers with the opportunity to discuss a text, identify the point of view from which it is written and consider how it would change if written from a different one.

This activity helps readers to discuss a text from more than one point of view, stimulating ideas about alternative actions, behaviours and events that could have occurred. Following the group discussions, students can create oral, written or visual reconstructions of text or excerpts from a different point of view.

- After students read a text, discuss from whose point of view it is written. Ask students to identify sections that led them to their conclusions.
- Discuss with them whose point of view is not presented.
- Arrange them in small groups and have them discuss a particular event from a different point of view; for example, that of another character, or a group not represented in the text.
- Ask them then to create a reconstruction of that event from the point of view chosen.
- Invite several groups to share their reconstructions, explaining aspects that needed modification.

6 Possible Predictions

Making Possible Predictions assists readers to focus on how and why texts may be interpreted differently by different people. By making comparisons between personal predictions and the text, and listening to justifications for these predictions, students begin to realise that prior knowledge plays an important part in constructing meaning. This activity also provides an opportunity for readers to discuss the decisions authors make and to speculate about possible alternatives.

- Have students read a text, stopping at a preselected point; this should either be at a significant 'crossroad', or offer a variety of options as to what might happen next.
- Invite students to think about what they have read so far and to make a prediction of what actions, events and/or outcomes might happen next. Encourage them to supply reasons for their predictions.
- Invite them to record their predictions on cards or sticky notes.

– Collect predictions and group similar ones. As a whole class, discuss the reasons for the different types. Encourage students to refer to the text and/or to prior knowledge when stating their reasons.
– Have students continue to read, stopping at the next preselected point to discuss and make further predictions. At appropriate points in the text have them compare their predictions with the author's choices and speculate about the possible reasons for those decisions.

7 Headlines

Headlines requires students to make predictions about the content of the text that follows a headline. Participating in this activity helps Transitional readers to develop an understanding of how prior knowledge impacts on interpretation of texts.

– Collect examples of headlines and their associated articles from newspapers, magazines and advertising material. Headlines that may be interpreted differently are essential for this activity.
– Have students work in pairs. Randomly distribute the headline of an article to each pair.
– Have each student predict the content of the article by writing key words or phrases.
– Direct them to compare their key words and phrases, and explain the reasoning behind their choices. Encourage them to discuss which words in the headline may have led them to give different interpretations.
– Have them read the article and compare it with their predictions.

Headline

> **LIONS FEELING THE HEAT**

Student predictions

Student 1	**Student 2**
• Long dry summer, extreme temperatures	• Football team is not winning any games
• African lions suffering	• Lots of players have injuries
• Lack of food available	

Figure 7.9

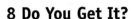

8 Do You Get It?

When participating in Do You Get It?, students collect a series of favourite cartoons or comic strips that they understand and find amusing. By sharing a cartoon and asking the question 'Do you get it?', Transitional readers develop an understanding of how readers' prior knowledge impacts on their interpretation of texts. As cartoons and comic strips rely heavily on inference, more prior knowledge is required to comprehend meaning than is necessary with most texts.

– Have students work in pairs. The initiating student presents a favourite cartoon or comic strip to the partner, asking 'Do you get it?' The reader responds either positively, giving an explanation such as 'I get it. She's tricking him into . . .', or negatively, saying 'I don't get it'.
– If the response is positive, have the first student consider whether the explanation matches his or her interpretation of the humour in the piece and, if not, supply that interpretation.
– If the response is negative, have the first student explain the joke by supplying information that allows the reader to understand the humorous meaning.
– Invite all students to participate in a class discussion, focusing on what prior knowledge helped to make the cartoons meaningful.

9 Despicability Rating

Completing a Despicability Rating involves students in combining information both from the text and from personal experience to rank characters or people according to level of despicability. In doing this, they can be introduced to the devices authors and illustrators use to influence the construction of meaning, and they can be encouraged to explore and share different interpretations of events and actions in a text.

– Select three characters or people in a text.
– Have students individually rank those characters or people from most despicable to least despicable.
– Direct them to search for and record evidence in the text to justify their ranking of each character or person.
– Invite several students to share and compare their rankings and justifications with the whole class.

10 Spot the Devices

Refer to Chapter 8: Proficient Reading Phase, p. 278.

11 What's Missing?

Refer to Chapter 8: Proficient Reading Phase, p. 280.

12 Text Innovation

Text Innovation is the name given to the process of adapting an existing text. By completing Text Innovation activities with a contextual understanding focus, students are encouraged to adapt characters, character traits, or the setting. They will also consider the impact of their changes on the storyline and the devices used by authors and illustrators.

- Select a text for innovation.
- Have students read it several times.
- Select features that could be innovated upon. Innovations could involve:
  - changing the gender of one of the characters;
  - substituting new characters for those in the text;
  - changing characteristics (for instance, instead of a mischievous child, have a well-behaved child);
  - changing the setting such as from a rural area to a city;
  - changing the time from the original period to a past, present or future one;
  - changing the dialogue between characters;
  - changing the sociocultural group, age, occupation, values or beliefs of the main character.
- Organise students in small groups.
- Have them create the new text.
- Invite several groups to read their innovations to the whole class.
- Have students compare the original text with the new versions, explaining which they prefer and justifying the choice.
- Identify and discuss how the changes made impacted on the text.
  - If the sociocultural group of a character changed, how was the language changed to suit?
  - If the age of a character changed, was there any effect on the action or the events?
  - When a character's occupation was changed, how was the text changed?
  - What changes occurred when the setting or time of the text was altered?
- If the text is written, invite students to illustrate the newly created one. It can be turned into a big book, a class book or a wall story.

13 Author Study

The Author Study activity provides opportunities for readers to examine a number of texts written by the same author — or illustrated by the same illustrator — to make generalisations about the devices used in those texts to target specific audiences across a number of texts.

– After sharing a text, discuss different aspects of it. For literary texts, students could examine the language, style, theme or target audience; for informational texts they could examine the word choice, selection of details, or point of view presented.

– As more texts by the same author or illustrator are analysed, record students' observations. Use the cumulative chart for making comparisons and generalisations about the style and the devices used.

Author Study				
Author: Paul Jennings				
TEXTS	LANGUAGE	STYLE	THEME	TARGET AUDIENCE
Singenpoo Strikes Again	Colloquial Language - casual speech	• Use of humour • Elements of 'naughtiness' and 'grossness'	• Good wins over evil • Quirky happenings	Teenagers and younger children (Grade 5-7)
The Paw Thing	Colloquial Language - casual speech	• Use of humour • Elements of 'grossness'	• Quirky happenings • Good wins over evil	Teenagers and Grades 4-7
Sneeze'n Coffin from Quirky Tails	Colloquial Language - casual speech	• Use of humour • Elements of 'grossness' • Exaggeration	• Quirky happenings	Teenagers

Figure 7.10

14 Picture the Author

Picture the Author asks students to think about the author of a text being studied. They are asked to explore background information, and how this may have influenced the author's choices.

– After reading a text, have students gather information about the author. They can use the jacket of the text, the Internet, author reviews or biographies to consider any of the following questions.
  – Is the author male or female?

– Was the author young, middle-aged or elderly when the text was written?

– When was the text written?

– Where did the author live when writing it?

– Does the author have expertise in this topic? How do you know?

– What other texts has this author written?

- Allow time for students to discuss how finding out about the author has helped them to understand and challenge the choices made in the text.

15 Deconstructing a Character

Deconstructing a Character provides opportunities for Transitional readers to collect and record information from texts, analysing the way the author or illustrator has represented the characters. The information can be recorded on a chart and used to either analyse characters from one text or compare characters from several.

- Have students read a text.
- Invite them to choose the characters to be deconstructed and record their names on the framework provided (see Figure 7.11).
- Have them work individually to retrieve information from the text about each character. Key words and phrases should be recorded on the framework.
- Organise students in small groups to share the information that has been collected.
- Encourage them to discuss how the characters have been constructed. Focus questions could include the following.
  – How are the . . . portrayed in this text?
  – Are all . . . like this? Do you know any . . . who are not like this?
  – Is it fair to portray . . .. in this way?
  – Why might the author have chosen to portray one character in this way? How else could the character have been portrayed?
  – How did this character respond to situations? What other response could there have been?
  – What are some of the words to describe other characters and their actions?
  – Would it have mattered if the main character had been of the opposite gender, from a different culture or had a disability?

Deconstructing a Character				
TEXT:	AUTHOR:		ILLUSTRATOR	
CHARACTER, GENDER	AGE, CULTURAL GROUP	APPEARANCE	CLOTHING	ACTIONS / FEELINGS

Figure 7.11

16 Like or Unlike?

Like or Unlike? is an activity that encourages readers to begin to challenge the world view presented by an author. It helps them to make connections and comparisons between what they know about the world in which they live and the way characters or people are represented in a text.

– Select a main character or person in a text and identify his or her role; for example, Lui is a teenage girl.
– Before reading the text, invite students to share what they know about real-life people who fall into the same category.
– Record responses on a class chart.
– Have students read the text.
– Provide time to discuss how the character or person has been represented. Record students' views on a class chart.
– Draw students' attention to any differences or similarities between what they know and how the character or person may have been represented in the text.
– Provide opportunities for them to discuss how the author could have changed the role of the character, and the impact this would have had on the text.

17 Reading Response Journals

Refer to Chapter 8: Proficient Reading Phase, p. 273.

CONVENTIONS

Major Teaching Emphases

- **Continue to build students' sight vocabulary,** e.g. less common words, subject-specific words.

- **Continue to build students' graphophonic and word knowledge, such as:**
  - recognising less common sound–symbol relationships
  - recognising letter combinations, and the different sounds they represent
  - recognising how word parts and words work.

- **Jointly analyse texts where combinations and adaptations of text structure and text organisation have been used.**

- **Teach students to identify the role of language features in a variety of texts.**

Teaching Notes

Transitional readers are able to decode many words; however, they continue to benefit from ongoing support and explicit instruction. They have already been exposed to many literary and informational texts, but they are now being exposed to a variety of more complex texts in learning areas across the curriculum and may require support in reading these new genres and text forms.

Modelled, Shared and Guided Reading sessions provide ideal procedures for teaching conventions, as attention can be drawn to them as they occur.

The foci for supporting Transitional readers in developing further understandings about conventions are organised under the following headings.
- Sight Vocabulary
- Graphophonic Knowledge and Word Knowledge
- Knowledge about Text Forms

Sight Vocabulary

Sight vocabulary is the bank of words a reader is able to automatically decode, pronounce and understand in the contexts in which they are used. Such words are called 'sight words' because effective readers need to recognise them instantly on sight to maintain the speed and fluency required to make sense of the author's message. Many of these words have irregular spellings, making them difficult to decode.

Transitional readers will be exposed to an increasing bank of words as they encounter a wider variety of texts; however, while they have become efficient at decoding and pronouncing many words, some do not understand the meaning of all they can decode. Since it is not possible to teach students all the words they will need to understand, it is appropriate to invest time in teaching them how to learn new vocabulary independently. This may involve helping them to analyse words by looking at their component phonemes and morphemes, using the context, or considering the grammatical function a word serves.

Sight vocabulary for Transitional readers will often include subject-specific words from all learning areas.
- English, e.g. **idioms, bias, homophones.**
- Mathematics, e.g. **diameter, circumference, mass, volume, length, area, multiple, hexagon.**
- Science, e.g. **mammal, osmosis, sedimentary, experiment, classify.**
- Health and Physical Education, e.g. **circulation, cholesterol, digestion, harassment, consequences.**
- Technology, e.g. **hydraulic, manufacture, design.**
- Society and Environment, e.g. **environment, politics, resources, investigate.**

Graphophonic Knowledge and Word Knowledge

Graphophonic knowledge refers to a reader's knowledge of letters and combinations of letters and the sounds associated with them. When selecting the graphophonic understandings to introduce to these readers, it is important to consider both what they already know and the requirements of the curriculum.

Word knowledge refers to a reader's knowledge of words, their meanings and how they work. As students are exposed to a wider variety of texts, they will encounter words with less common letter patterns and sound–symbol relationships, and it is helpful for them to begin to collect evidence to support and challenge their growing understandings. For instance, they may investigate and collect words from other languages, words with common bases or words containing the same letter patterns that represent different sounds. Not only will activities such as these support students' reading development, they will support writing and spelling development as well.

Displays of student learning can be added to as required.

Knowledge about Text Forms

Students will benefit from reading different examples of a particular text form, making comparisons with other forms and identifying the defining features. Teacher questioning is very important in drawing attention to the features of a form. Students' comments can be recorded and used to draw up a set of guidelines when reading or writing a particular form.

Continuing to provide opportunities for students to analyse and discuss different text forms will help to consolidate understandings about the purpose, organisation, structure and language features of a wide range of texts. Modelled, Shared and Guided Reading sessions provide an opportunity to discuss these conventions in the context of authentic texts, and can also include a focus on texts that 'break the rules' to achieve a specific purpose and enhance impact. For example, a literary text may be used to persuade, or a procedural text to entertain.

When deconstructing texts with Transitional readers, the following provide a focus.

Purpose

Texts are written to achieve a purpose. The purpose may be to entertain, as in a limerick, or to argue a point of view, as in an exposition.

Text Organisation

Text organisation refers to the layout. Transitional readers will benefit from understanding text-form frameworks; for example, a narrative may include orientation, conflict and resolution. It is also important for these readers to understand the function, terminology and use of organisational features such as:
- headings and subheadings
- captions
- diagrams and other visual aids (photographs, graphs, tables, cross-sections)
- tables of contents
- indexes
- glossaries
- paragraphs
- bold or italic print
- illustrations
- hyperlinks
- Internet site maps.

Text Structure

Text structure refers to the way ideas, feelings and information are linked in a text. These could include:

- problem and solution;
- compare and contrast;
- cause and effect;
- listing: logical or chronological sequence, collection of details.

Having an understanding of these patterns can assist Transitional readers to comprehend text.

Language Features

The term 'language features' refers to the type of vocabulary and grammar used. Each text form has specific features that are appropriate to that form. These include:

- tense, e.g. **past or present**;
- word choice, e.g. **adjectives, verbs, signal words**;
- style, e.g. **colloquial or formal**.

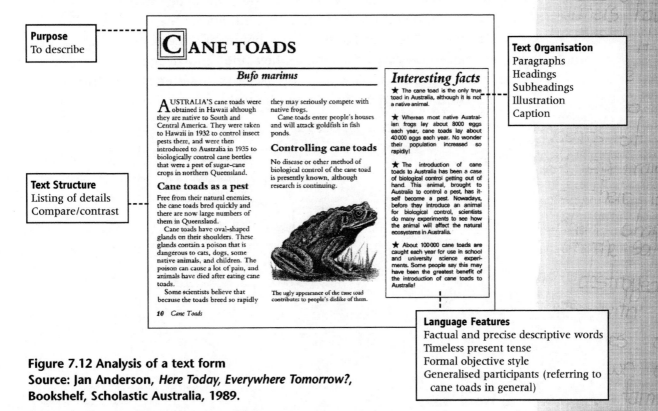

Purpose
To describe

CANE TOADS

Bufo marinus

AUSTRALIA'S cane toads were obtained in Hawaii although they are native to South and Central America. They were taken to Hawaii in 1932 to control insect pests there, and were then introduced to Australia in 1935 to biologically control cane beetles that were a pest of sugar-cane crops in northern Queensland.

Cane toads as a pest

Free from their natural enemies, the cane toads bred quickly and there are now large numbers of them in Queensland.

Cane toads have oval-shaped glands on their shoulders. These glands contain a poison that is dangerous to cats, dogs, some native animals, and children. The poison can cause a lot of pain, and animals have died after eating cane toads.

Some scientists believe that because the toads breed so rapidly

they may seriously compete with native frogs.

Cane toads enter people's houses and will attack goldfish in fish ponds.

Controlling cane toads

No disease or other method of biological control of the cane toad is presently known, although research is continuing.

The ugly appearance of the cane toad contributes to people's dislike of them.

10 *Cane Toads*

Interesting facts

★ The cane toad is the only true toad in Australia, although it is not a native animal.

★ Whereas most native Australian frogs lay about 8000 eggs each year, cane toads lay about 40 000 eggs each year. No wonder their population increased so rapidly!

★ The introduction of cane toads to Australia has been a case of biological control getting out of hand. This animal, brought to Australia to control a pest, has itself become a pest. Nowadays, before they introduce an animal for biological control, scientists do many experiments to see how the animal will affect the natural ecosystems in Australia.

★ About 100 000 cane toads are caught each year for use in school and university science experiments. Some people say this may have been the greatest benefit of the introduction of cane toads to Australia!

Text Organisation
Paragraphs
Headings
Subheadings
Illustration
Caption

Text Structure
Listing of details
Compare/contrast

Language Features
Factual and precise descriptive words
Timeless present tense
Formal objective style
Generalised participants (referring to cane toads in general)

Figure 7.12 Analysis of a text form
Source: Jan Anderson, *Here Today, Everywhere Tomorrow?*, Bookshelf, Scholastic Australia, 1989.

For further information about the Conventions substrand, see *Reading Resource Book*, 2nd edn, Chapter 3: Conventions.

Involving Students

1 Word Cline

Word Cline is an activity that helps build students' sight vocabulary as it encourages them to discuss connotations and nuances of meaning. Students arrange words that are similar in meaning to show a graduating intensity according to a given criterion.

- After students have read a common text, select a key word, such as 'friend'. It is important to be able to generate at least four synonyms for the key word.
- Have students generate synonyms (or words that are closely related) for the key word; for example, acquaintance, amigo, buddy, colleague, ally, partner or mate.
- Invite them to arrange the words in rising intensity against a criterion, such as distant to close relationship.
- Organise them in small groups to discuss the words and reach a consensus about the order in which they are to be placed.
- Have them reflect on the factors that influenced the choice of placement. They need to be aware that readers' perceptions of meanings will vary according to their prior knowledge.
- As a whole class, discuss how the use of the different words from the Word Cline would impact on the text.

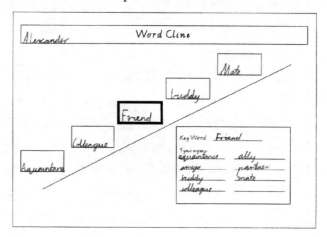

Figure 7.13

2 Word Walls

Refer to Chapter 6: Early Reading Phase, p. 182.

3 Concept/Definition Maps

Concept/Definition Maps (Schwartz & Raphael 1985) have students explore new vocabulary by focusing attention on key components to create a definition.

234

– Select a focus word.
– Have students construct a concept/definition map by answering the following questions about this word.
– What is it? (Which broader category does it belong to?)
– What is it like? (What are its properties or characteristics?)
– What are some examples? (Illustrations of the concept.)
– Students record and share this information (see Figure 7.14).
– Provide time for them to create a definition for the focus word.

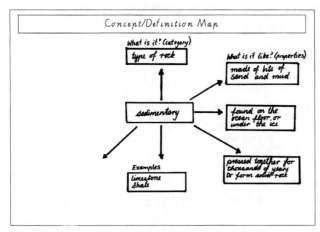

Figure 7.14

4 Semantic Association

Refer to Chapter 6: Early Reading Phase, p. 181.

5 Crosswords

Crosswords are made up of a series of intersecting words of which some letters are common; the words are indicated by clues. While there are software packages available for the creation of crosswords, students benefit from working together to manually complete the process; this helps to consolidate vocabulary and word understandings.

It is important to model the creation of clues, which could include:
• simple definitions — a person in a story;
• cloze activity — a TV show, The _____ Life of Us;
• stating a relationship — nephew and _____;
• offering a synonym or antonym — not happy.

Creating or completing crosswords requires Transitional readers to focus on defining features of words as well as investigating both the structure and meaning of key words.

– Arrange students in pairs.
– Provide each pair with two crossword grids, 15 squares by 15 squares.

– Have them select thematic words, subject-specific words or words from discrete sections of a text and arrange them on one of the grids, ensuring that some of the letters intersect.
– Direct them to number the first letter of each word in the grid.
– Have them then transfer these numbers onto the same squares in the blank grid and shade the squares that will not contain a letter when the crossword is complete.
– Ask students to create a clue for each of their selected words.
– Students then swap clues and blank grids with another pair, who will complete the crossword

6 Odd Word

Odd Word is used to categorise items, clarify concepts and alert students to patterns. When a small series of items is presented and all but one share a common attribute, the challenge is to determine which one is odd, and why.

– Have students prepare for Odd Word by collecting key words on a particular topic that share a common attribute. An 'odd word' is then added to the collection that is related but does not share the common attribute of the others; for example, the words could be stalactites, stalagmites, caves, waterfalls, mountains.
– Each student gives the selected key words to a partner. It is the partner's task to identify the classification and the odd word, stating reasons for the choice; for instance, in the above example 'waterfalls' is the odd word because the others are rock formations.

7 Secret Messages

Secret Messages is an activity that involves students in decoding. The messages can be created using sight vocabulary, word knowledge and graphophonic understandings currently being introduced or consolidated.

Transitional readers will enjoy deciphering messages that use a combination of clues. The types of clues used might include:
• removing prefixes or suffixes from words, e.g. **take the prefix from 'disrepair'**;
• adding prefixes or suffixes to words, e.g. **add the prefix 'pro' to the word 'active'**;
• combining syllables from different words, e.g. **add the first syllable of 'monkey' to the third syllable of 'Saturday'**;
• replacing letters from the beginning or end of a word, e.g. **take 'de' from 'delete' and replace it with 'comp'**;
• finding a small word within a word, e.g. **find a four-letter word in 'friendship'**;

- creating compound words, e.g. add 'light' to 'house';
- using an alphabet sequence for short words, e.g. add the letter after 'l' to the first letter of the alphabet.

Modelling the process for solving the messages is important.

– Think of a meaningful sentence or message, such as 'Complete your project by Friday'.
– Write a series of clues that will enable students to decode the message.
– Ensure they have access to a copy of the alphabet.
– Provide time for them to 'crack' or decode the message. They could record it in their diaries.
– Keep a copy of all activities to build up a permanent collection for future use.

Once students are familiar with deciphering Secret Messages, challenge them to write some for the class.

8 What Comes Next?

What Comes Next? is an adaptation of what was known as the game Hangman. However, What Comes Next? requires students to guess the letters in the correct order rather than randomly.

As a daily activity for Transitional readers, What Comes Next? can provide an excellent context for introducing and reinforcing letter sequences, as well as word understandings such as these.
- Letters together represent the specific sounds in a word.
- Prefixes and suffixes can be added to words.
- An ending can be added to make a word plural.
- Past tense can be represented by 'ed' or 't'.
- Some words can be spelt the same and pronounced the same but have different meanings, such as 'table' and 'fair'.
- Some words are pronounced the same but are spelt differently and have different meanings, such as 'bear' and 'bare', 'there' and 'their'.
- Some words are spelt the same but are pronounced differently and have different meanings, such as 'tear' and 'minute'.

To complete the activity, follow this procedure.
– Choose a word from a familiar context that features a letter sequence or word-study understanding. Draw lines representing each letter in the word.
– Provide a specific clue for the first letter in the word; for example, the first letter is a consonant in the second half of the alphabet. When students guess the correct letter, record it on the first line.
– Invite students to guess the remaining letters of the word.

– As they guess a letter, write any guesses that are incorrect but are possible sequences in a 'Could Be' column. Incorrect guesses that will not make possible sequences should be recorded in a 'Couldn't Be' column as single letters (not modelling incorrect letter patterns). When students guess a letter that could not be right, a segment of a mouse outline is drawn.
– Continue this until the correct letters are given and recorded on the lines.
– The game ends if the drawing of the mouse is completed before students complete the word.

As an extension, students can be challenged to find other words linked to the letter patterns identified in the game word; for example, if the chosen word is 'pneumonia', groups could be challenged to find words with 'pn' 'eu' or 'ia'.

Once Transitional readers are familiar with the game, encourage them to play What Comes Next? with a partner.

9 Word Back Spied Her

Word Back Spied Her can be used for a wide range of purposes; it is an excellent open-ended activity to support the development of sight vocabulary and word knowledge. A number of words, based on student needs or interest, are printed on sticky labels. A label is then placed on each student's back and the student is challenged to identify the particular word by questioning other students.

– Select the words to be used.
– Prepare a sticky label bearing one of the words for each student.
– Place a label on each student's back, ensuring that the word has not been seen.
– Provide each student with a complete list of the words.
– Discuss rules for questioning, such as these.
  – Questions need to be related to the features of the word; for example, Does my word have a prefix? Does my word have the letter pattern 'tion'? Is my word an adjective?
  – Responses can only be 'Yes' or 'No'.
  – A student can only ask another student one question before moving on.
  – A student who is unable to answer a question may say 'pass'.
– Teach students how to eliminate words from the list as they ask their questions.
– Direct them to move into designated groups as the words are determined; for example, according to parts of speech.

It is critical that either during or at the end of the activity students are given the opportunity to reflect and discuss the types of questions that were asked. This will help them to distinguish between useful and less useful questions to use in determining the words they have been given. Individualised lists can be created if necessary.

10 Cloze Activities

Cloze Activities encourage students to use context clues to predict the missing parts of a text; they are easily prepared by deleting words, parts of words, or punctuation marks.

When working with students to complete cloze activities, it is important to model how to gain the full benefit of context clues by always reading to the end of a sentence before trying to 'cloze' the gap.

It is beneficial for students to have the opportunity to discuss answers and justifications, allowing them to hear about strategies used by others, and alternative choices.

The following list provides options of cloze activities suitable for Transitional readers.

Punctuation cloze
Use sections from a text that students are familiar with and have read many times. Prepare a passage by deleting punctuation marks so that students can fill the gaps. This activity can be adapted by using removable stickers to cover key punctuation marks in a shared book session.

Word-parts cloze
Develop cloze activities by covering parts of words; e.g. **As a result of the volcanic eruption, the autumn sun___ was spectacular, or As the sun ____ly dipped towards the h__rizon, the sky was trans_____ into a stream of colour.**

Encourage students to complete the words by looking at the remaining word parts and using graphophonic and word knowledge.

Whole-word cloze
Prepare a passage, deleting any words that are chosen as a focus, such as subject-specific words, nouns, adverbs, signal words or contractions; always leave the first sentence intact. Encourage students to think of a meaningful replacement for each deleted word. Provide scaffolding questions, such as 'What could the next

word be? Does it make sense?' If necessary, support students by providing a list of words from which to choose.

For directions on preparing cloze activities, see the section 'Cloze Procedure' in Chapter 3.

11 Sound Hunter

Participating in Sound Hunter helps students to make connections between letters and sounds in words. They can become sound hunters in any context where they are involved with meaningful print. Texts such as books, charted songs and poems, magazines, modelled writing examples or written messages can provide contexts for Transitional readers to develop their graphophonic and word understandings by hunting for words.

- Choose a specific focus. For Transitional readers it could be:
  - any words with a particular letter pattern, such as words with 'ough';
  - any words with a particular sound, such as words that have a /shun/ sound.
- Choose texts that exhibit the chosen focus.
- Have students read the text for enjoyment.
- Encourage them to revisit the text to find and circle or underline words with the chosen focus; for instance, all the words that have a /shun/ sound. The words could then be written on pieces of card.
- Discuss the words.
- Ask students to sort them into subgroups; for example, according to the letter patterns that represent the /shun/ sound.
- Create a chart of the words, listing the groups into which they have been sorted. Leave room for more words to be added as they are discovered.
- Students may then be formed into groups and challenged to find other words from a selected subgroup; they might find them in specific texts, in class charts or on the word wall.
- Revisit, discuss and add to the chart on future occasions.

Different Spellings for the Same Sound

–tion	–cian	–cean	–sion
condition	dietician	ocean	tension
recognition	physician	crustacean	pension
exhibition			

Figure 7.15 A class-generated Sound Hunter chart

12 Word Origins

Word Origins involves students in investigating how words are related by examining the meaning of common parts. When beginning to use this activity, start with a word of which students know the meaning.

– Select a word from a current classroom context and highlight the focus part, such as aqua in <u>aqua</u>rium.
– Discuss the meaning of the word, referring to the text. If the meaning is unknown, it is provided (using a dictionary at this stage will undermine the final stage of the activity).
– Ask students to brainstorm any other words that have the highlighted part. List these words and their meanings; for example:
  – aquatic (growing or living in water);
  – aquamarine (a bluish-green colour like water);
  – aquaplaning (riding at high speed on water).
– From the collected definitions, have students infer the meaning of the focus word part.
– Refer them to a reference source to check the meaning and add any similar words they find there.
– Record the words and their meanings on a class chart.

13 Exploring Words

Exploring Words is an open-ended activity that provides students with an opportunity to work at their own level to create words. Transitional readers enjoy the challenge of creating as many words as possible using a given base word and selected affixes.

– Provide students with a focus base word and a selection of prefixes and suffixes.
– Establish guidelines for the creation of words; for example:
  – all words must include the base word;
  – the last letter of the base word may be changed or deleted when adding suffixes;
  – all words must be real words.
– Challenge students to make as many new words as possible in a given time, using the base word and adding prefixes or suffixes, or both.
– Provide time for them to share and reflect upon the words created.
– Record any patterns or rules the students discover.

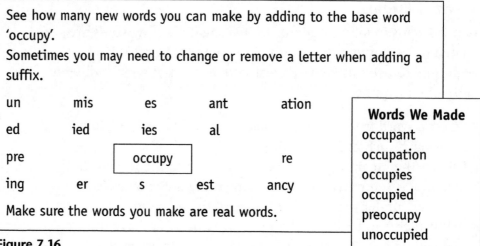

See how many new words you can make by adding to the base word 'occupy'.

Sometimes you may need to change or remove a letter when adding a suffix.

un	mis	es	ant	ation
ed	ied	ies	al	
pre		occupy		re
ing	er	s	est	ancy

Make sure the words you make are real words.

Words We Made
occupant
occupation
occupies
occupied
preoccupy
unoccupied

Figure 7.16

14 Making Words

Making Words (Cunningham 2000) supports the development of graphophonic and word knowledge, specifically helping students to focus on letters in the words. Making Words involves using letters to make words.

Prior to introducing the activity, the following steps need to be completed.

– Select a word from a current classroom context; for example, 'mountain'. This will be the secret word.

– Make a list of smaller words that can be made from the letters of this one, such as am, tan, atom, into, mount, union and nation.

– Choose about fifteen words from this list. They could include words:

– with a particular letter pattern to be emphasised, e.g. 'ain';

– of varying length;

– that can be made with the same letters in different places, e.g. **aunt, tuna;**

– that most students have in their listening vocabularies;

– that are plural.

Once the preparation is complete, the following steps apply.

– Provide each student with an envelope or tub containing each letter of the focus word on a card: 'a', 'i', 'o', 'u', 'm', 'n', 'n', 't' for 'mountain'. Have vowels and consonants on different-coloured cards.

– Direct students to make specified words one at a time. Select words from the list previously created. Ensure each one is written on a card.

- Start with two- or three-letter words and work up to longer ones.
  For example:
  - take two letters to make the word 'at';
  - add another letter to make 'ant';
  - add another letter to make 'aunt';
  - manipulate the letters in 'aunt' and come up with another word.
- Continue directing students to make words, discussing key
  features of each one.
- Challenge students to use all the letters to discover the 'secret word'.
- Use the words created to discuss patterns within them and use
  the patterns to generate new words, such as nation (from the
  original list), relation, station, foundation.

15 Word-Sorting Activities

Refer to Chapter 6: Early Reading Phase, p. 183.

16 Reading Plans

Refer to Chapter 6: Early Reading Phase, p. 191.

17 Share and Compare

Share and Compare provides students with the opportunity to
identify and compare the features of different texts; they work in
groups to sort a collection of texts into categories, then brainstorm
features of each category. The interaction and conversation allows
them to discuss and build on their knowledge of the text structure,
organisation and language features of different texts.

- Provide small groups with a collection of different texts, such as
  explanations and expositions. The texts should be related to a
  particular topic or theme being studied across the curriculum.
- Have students work together to sort the texts into categories.
  Discuss what influenced their choices.
- Ask them to explore the groups of texts more closely and to
  further analyse the features of each one. They can be encouraged
  to focus on examples such as the following.
  - The organisation of the texts: 'these explanations have
    headings, subheadings and diagrams'.
  - The language features of the text: 'in these explanations there
    are signal words indicating cause and effect, such as "as a result"'.
  - The text structure: 'these expositions had their ideas linked as
    problem and solution'.
- Invite students to share with the class what they discovered.
- Create a class chart, listing features of the texts that could be
  generalised to each form. The chart can be added to over time as
  students discover new features.

18 Looking for Clues

Looking for Clues provides students with an opportunity to analyse the language features used in different text forms.

- Provide students with a table format listing types of language features.
- As students read a text, have them record notes about the words used.
- Guide them to select words from each category listed in the table.
- As a whole class, analyse the words in each category. Discuss any patterns observed.
- Over time, provide opportunities for students to read and analyse similar text forms. Encourage them to look for further patterns and to make generalisations about language features particular to that form.

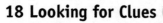

Looking for Clues		
Text: *Little Aussie Cookbook* Author: Form: *Recipe* Purpose: *To instruct*		
Language Features	**Words Used in this Text**	**Observation and Analysis**
nouns	1·5 cups self raising flour 23 cm square cake tin electric beaters	The nouns are factual and precise. They are specific to cooking and recipes
adjectives	melted serrated simmering	The adjectives are technical and specific
verbs	preheat sift brush beat pour	Action verbs started the sentences in the instructions
signal words	1, 2, 3	These words/numbers indicate what order you have to do things in

Figure 7.17

19 Signal Words

Signal Words focuses attention on the words authors use to signal different text structures; these are often called top-level structures. Once students know the type of structure in a text, it will help them to process information effectively and to select appropriate ways of summarising it.

- Introduce the class or a group to a particular type of structure in a text about to be read; for example, cause and effect.
- Using a sample piece of text, highlight the signal words. List and discuss them.
- Have students follow this procedure as they read another text with the same structure.

– Jointly construct a reference chart recording the text structure and signal words.
– As students' knowledge about text structure builds, add the information to the class chart.

TEXT STRUCTURE PATTERNS	SIGNAL WORDS TO LOOK FOR
Cause and effect	makes, causes, leads to, results in, forms, creates, because, so, consequently, so that, if, then, therefore, as a result
Compare and contrast	although, whereas, yet, however, compared with, unlike, like, different, similar, while
Problem and solution	dilemma, solution, to prevent, question, answer, solve, difficulty, trouble, crisis, explanation, resolution
Listing: logical or chronological sequence	in/on (date), not long after, before, after, when, to begin with, firstly, secondly, then, next, most important, for instance, as well, furthermore
Collection of details	several, many, some, as follows, such as, examples

Figure 7.18 A class-generated Signal Word cumulative chart

PROCESSES AND STRATEGIES

Major Teaching Emphases

- **Continue to build students' knowledge within the cues,** e.g. orthographic, world knowledge.

- **Consolidate known comprehension strategies and teach additional strategies,** e.g. synthesising, paraphrasing.

- **Consolidate word-identification strategies.**

- **Continue to teach students how to locate, select and evaluate texts,** e.g. conducting Internet searches, recognising bias.

- **Model self-reflection of strategies used in reading, and encourage students to do the same**

Organisation of the Processes and Strategies Substrand

The organisation of the Processes and Strategies substrand differs in several ways from that of the other substrands. Both the Teaching Notes and the Involving Students sections are located in Chapter 4 of the *Reading Resource Book*.

The rationale for this difference in organisation is that reading processes and strategies are not hierarchical, and therefore not phase-specific. A variety of processes and strategies need to be introduced, developed and consolidated at all phases of development.

What varies from one phase to the next is the growth in:
- the number and integration of strategies;
- the awareness and monitoring of strategies;
- the efficiency in use and selection of strategies;
- the ability to articulate the use of the strategies;
- the awareness of how the use of strategies help with making meaning;
- the ability to locate, select and evaluate texts.

Supporting Parents of Transitional Readers

ENVIRONMENT AND ATTITUDE

Transitional readers can recognise many words automatically and can therefore read familiar texts fluently and with expression. They use a variety of ways to work out unknown words, such as slowing down, re-reading, reading on and sounding out. Transitional readers change the way they read to suit different texts or purposes.

Supporting Transitional Readers in the Home

Transitional readers will benefit from a range of experiences, in the home setting. Ideas for providing appropriate experiences are available on Parent Cards located on the First Steps Reading CD-ROM.

Teachers can select appropriate cards for each Transitional reader from the Reading CD-ROM and copy them for parents to use at home. Also available on the CD-ROM is a parent-friendly version of the Reading Map of Development.

Parent Cards

1 General Description and How to Support Transitional Readers

2 Encouraging Reading

3 Reading with your Child

4 Selecting Texts

5 Reading and Writing Links

6 Supporting Oral Reading

7 Understanding How Texts are Read and Organised

8 Building a Love of Reading

9 Supporting Comprehension

10 Helping with Research Work

11 Using the Library

12 Building Word Knowledge through Games

CHAPTER 8

Proficient Reading Phase

Figure 8.1

Global Statement

Proficient readers have developed a multistrategy approach to identify unknown words and comprehend demanding texts such as subject-specific textbooks, novels and essays. They are able to select strategies appropriate to the purpose and complexity of the text. Readers have a greater ability to connect topic, grammatical, cultural/world and text-structure knowledge with what is new in the text. Proficient readers identify the target audience of a text. They draw on evidence from their own experience to challenge or question the text.

Proficient Reading Indicators

Use of Texts

◆ Reads and demonstrates comprehension of texts by:
- explaining how the main idea and supporting information relate to the author's purpose and the intended audience
- selecting events from a text to suit a specific audience
- linking ideas, both explicit and implicit, in a text, e.g. thesis and supporting arguments.

◆ Locates and evaluates appropriateness of texts and information in texts in terms of purpose and audience, e.g. validity, bias.

• Compares texts with a similar theme by organising information and ideas to provide evidence for a particular point of view.

• Uses information from a number of texts to make generalisations.

Contextual Understanding

◆ Recognises how one's values, attitudes and beliefs impact on the interpretation of text.

◆ Discusses the target audience for a specific text, and how the author has tailored the language, ideas and presentation to suit.

• Identifies the target audience for a range of texts.

• Recognises that particular societal groups are stereotyped in texts to serve the interests of other groups, e.g. surfers are long-haired layabouts.

• Detects positioning such as exaggeration, bias and prejudice in texts.

• Discusses the motives and feelings of characters/people in texts.

• Clarifies and justifies own interpretation of complex ideas and issues.

Conventions

◆ Recognises manipulation of text structure and text organisation, e.g. historical account written as a narrative.

◆ Recognises the selection of language features, such as:
- words to distinguish fact from opinion and bias, e.g. I think, It has been reported
- words/phrases that signal relationships, e.g. similarly — to compare, on the other hand — to contrast
- synonyms to denote connotations, e.g. thief, bandit, pickpocket.

• Recognises combined text forms with more than one purpose.

• Recognises an extensive bank of words automatically in many contexts.

• Identifies the role of structural and organisational features in an extensive range of text forms, e.g. chronology, paragraphing.

Processes and Strategies

◆ Selects from a broad knowledge base to comprehend, e.g. text structure and organisation, cultural/world knowledge, grammar, vocabulary.

◆ Selects appropriate strategies from a wide range to comprehend.

◆ Determines unknown words by selecting appropriate word-identification strategies.

• Selects and categorises key words in a text for a specific purpose.

• Discusses the selection and effectiveness of a range of cues and strategies used while reading.

Major Teaching Emphases

Environment and Attitude

- Create a supportive classroom environment that nurtures a community of readers.
- Jointly construct, and frequently refer to, meaningful environmental print.
- Foster students' enjoyment of reading.
- Encourage students to take risks with confidence.
- Encourage students to select their own reading material according to interest or purpose.

Use of Texts

- Provide opportunities for students to read a wide range of texts.
- Continue to teach students to analyse texts utilising information to suit different purposes and audiences.

Contextual Understanding

- Provide opportunities for students to discuss how the ideologies of the reader and the author combine to create an interpretation of the text.

- Provide opportunities for students to identify devices used to influence readers to take a particular view.

Conventions

- Continue to build students' sight vocabulary, e.g. technical terms, figurative language.
- Teach students to analyse how authors combine language features to achieve a purpose.
- Teach students to analyse how authors manipulate texts to achieve a purpose, e.g. structure, organisation.

Processes and Strategies

- Continue to build students' knowledge within the cues.
- Consolidate comprehension strategies.
- Consolidate word-identification strategies.
- Consolidate how to locate, select and evaluate texts.
- Model self-reflection of strategies used in reading, and encourage students to do the same.

Teaching and Learning Experiences

ENVIRONMENT AND ATTITUDE

Major Teaching Emphases

- **Create a supportive classroom environment that nurtures a community of readers.**

- **Jointly construct, and frequently refer to, meaningful environmental print.**

- **Foster students' enjoyment of reading.**

- **Encourage students to take risks with confidence.**

- **Encourage students to select their own reading material according to interest or purpose.**

Teaching Notes

An environment that supports Proficient readers is intellectually stimulating. Reading tasks need to challenge and motivate them by promoting meaningful engagement with texts. Personal reading preferences need to be acknowledged and encouraged; a broadening of these preferences can be promoted through collaborative activities such as book chats and book clubs. Also, Book Discussion Groups allow students to be involved in open-ended discussions where many different responses to texts are accepted and encouraged.

It is important to nurture the classroom reading community by sharing your own thoughts, genre preferences and knowledge about reading. These, along with student recommendations, offer an insight into different texts and each can be used to entice readers to broaden their own reading repertoire.

Exploring Print

Creating a print-rich environment is still important. The type of print available in the classroom will reflect a diversity of purpose.

Print that is functional and frequently referred to can be developed, based on student and classroom needs. It should be created by —

or in consultation with — the students in order to foster ownership and usage. Such print may include:

- procedural charts
- class reading recommendations
- questions and statements for book discussions
- strategies to be utilised.

Consider . . .
This book reminded me . . .
I wish the author would . . .
This character is like/unlike . . . because . . .
I predict that . . .
I was surprised by . . .

Confused?
- Re-read to see if the text now makes sense.
- Look for graphics on the page that may help.
- Try to summarise what you have read so far. Put it in your own words.

To Search the Internet
- Select the most appropriate search engine.
- Identify your key words.
- Type the key words into the space provided.
- Check the text selections in the search engine.
- If inappropriate, revise your key words. Try the search again.

Room 10's Top 10 Authors
Susan Cooper
Roald Dahl
John Marsden

Figure 8.2 Functional print for Proficient readers

Fostering Enjoyment and Challenging Readers

Reading to students is still important at this phase; it exposes them not only to skilled readers, but also to forms they may not otherwise experience. Reactions to texts and the pleasure derived from reading can also be shared with students. Modelled and Guided Reading are two invaluable procedures that allow teacher and students to demonstrate, analyse and discuss reading strategies they use throughout the reading process.

It is important that students at this phase be challenged. This can be achieved by:

- setting interesting and challenging reading tasks that students can complete successfully and within allocated times;
- establishing guidelines for a cooperative learning environment where risk-taking is respected and encouraged;
- promoting openness and sharing by minimising competitive situations;
- providing focused feedback that encourages, motivates and assists readers to make necessary changes to their reading strategies;
- listening and responding sensitively to students' comments;
- demonstrating how students approach reading and related tasks, including solving difficulties;

- valuing students as learners and experts, and inviting them to share their learning with their peers;
- recognising and valuing effort in the process of reading, not only in the product of reading;
- assisting students to set achievable reading goals that are based on realistic expectations, outcomes and timelines;
- discussing students' reading behaviours, and tailoring instruction to meet individual needs;
- facilitating learning that promotes reader independence;
- encouraging and praising students for trying new forms, topics or authors in their personal reading.

Proficient readers select texts according to purpose, use a variety of strategies to comprehend, and are able to evaluate their reading effectiveness. Teachers may not be able to provide them with all the necessary reading material they will require, so it is important to direct them to other sources such as the school and local libraries, the Internet, newspapers, CD-ROMs and everyday reading material. The class library needs to cater for individual preferences by providing a wide range of texts covering many different forms and topics. If this is done, the material available in the classroom will be more likely to cater for both interest and curriculum requirements.

As well as access to a wide variety of texts, the provision of time for independent reading of self-selected texts is critical for readers in this phase; this may involve both teacher and students in reading silently for a designated time. Teacher respect for and interest in student choices is the key to promoting both a nurturing reading environment and an enjoyment of reading.

Encouraging Risk-Taking

Proficient readers can become risk-takers if asked to:
- increase the diversity of texts they read, including non-preferred forms;
- critically analyse and respond to texts in a variety of ways;
- reflect on and discuss the success of their reading strategies;
- view incidents in texts from different perspectives;
- understand the links between reading and writing;
- build their knowledge base within the cues when necessary.

For further information about Environment and Attitude, see:
- *Linking Assessment, Teaching and Learning*, Chapter 5: Establishing a Positive Teaching and Learning Environment;
- *Reading Resource Book*, 2nd edn, Chapter 1: Use of Texts.

Use of Texts

Major Teaching Emphases

■ **Provide opportunities for students to read a wide range of texts.**

■ **Continue to teach students to analyse texts utilising information to suit different purposes and audiences.**

Teaching Notes

Proficient readers have often developed a personalised reading style and are capable of reading a wide range of texts for different purposes. They have refined the use of reading strategies, enabling them to read efficiently. Their reading is automatic, and only requires conscious processing as they encounter difficult or unfamiliar texts. It is important to encourage them to continually broaden their repertoire of texts read, while also pursuing their own particular interests.

The foci for helping Proficient readers in this substrand are organised under the following headings.
• Variety of Texts
• Analysing Texts
• Responding to Texts

Variety of Texts

These readers benefit from continued exposure to a variety of challenging texts and ample opportunities to interact with those texts at various levels.

There are many ways to continue to encourage the engagement of Proficient readers with a broad range of texts.
• Provide opportunities for independent reading time.
• Provide time for individual conferences where students can discuss aspects of their reading with peers or teacher.
• Organise buddy reading and paired reading events.
• Allow time for students to access reading material from a variety of sources; for example, time to search the Internet, time to visit the school library.
• Ensure that the classroom library has a wide selection of regularly updated reading material available.
• Allow students to contribute their own material to the class library, providing opportunities for them to explain their choices to the rest of the class.

- Arrange for authors to visit and discuss their craft.
- Set up Book Discussion Groups within and between classes so that students can openly discuss material they read and gain differing perspectives about a topic, author or event.
- Model the use of reading strategies, using texts from learning areas across the curriculum.

Analysing Texts

Proficient readers benefit from opportunities to analyse texts in a variety of ways for different purposes; this may be by studying the author of a text, or considering how authors construct their message through the use of text organisation, text structure, language features, theme or content. Students can also be encouraged to utilise information from texts to achieve different purposes; for example, to solve problems, make decisions, draw conclusions, broaden knowledge, share information with others or present a particular view.

Students can be encouraged to analyse texts in a range of ways.
- Provide opportunities to use reflective journals.
- Encourage students to identify and comment on differing points of view both within and between texts.
- Encourage them to question and challenge authors.
- Provide opportunities for them to access multiple sources and to synthesise information.
- Allow time for them to explore, analyse and articulate reactions and responses to texts.
- Demonstrate how to extract and organise information for different purposes and audiences.
- Assist students to analyse author styles and writing craft.
- Challenge them to interpret texts and transform them.
- Provide time for them to prepare information to present to an audience.

Responding to Texts

Teachers often have students answer questions or use prompts as a way to respond to texts. There are many ways of organising and discussing types of questions, e.g. **Bloom's Taxonomy (Bloom 1956), Question–Answer Relationships (Raphael 1986), Three Level Guides (Herber 1970) or Open and Closed Questions.** Whichever hierarchy is chosen, it is wise to include questions that require different levels of thinking. The focus in this phase should be on questions that promote higher levels of thinking.

Raphael (1986) categorises questions as Right There (Literal), Think and Search (Inferential), Author and You (Interpretive) and On Your Own (Critical/Evaluative), providing a useful framework for ensuring that different types of questions are used in the classroom.

Literal

Literal questions focus on what the author said. The answer is 'right there' in the text or pictures. Common literal questions begin with 'who', 'when', 'where' or 'what'.

Inferential

The answers to these questions can be found in the text but are not necessarily in the one place. These are the Think and Search questions. They show relationships such as cause and effect, sequence, or compare and contrast. These are also sometimes the 'how' and 'why' questions; the student has to 'put the answer together' from various sections or sentences in the text, asking questions such as 'How is . . . similar to or different from . . .?', 'What is the author trying to tell us here?', 'Was . . . an effective solution to the problem?'

Interpretive

These are the Author and You questions. They require the student to base the answer on the text, but also to draw on previous personal experience to reach a reasonable answer. The answer must not be a wild guess; it must be probable with reference to the text, not just possible based on personal experience. Examples are: 'From the evidence presented by the author, is it a good idea to . . .?', 'Based on what you have read so far, what do you think will happen when . . .?'.

Critical/Evaluative

These questions go beyond the text, asking for students' own opinions or judgements. They are the On Your Own questions, as the answers are not found in the text at all. The reader can answer the question without having read the text, although it does provide a starting point for discussions about the underlying messages or themes. Questions might be 'What do you believe about . . .?', 'What are your views on . . .?', 'What makes you feel that way?'

For further information about the Use of Texts substrand, see *Reading Resource Book*, 2nd edn:
• Chapter 1: Use of Texts
• Chapter 4: Processes and Strategies.

Involving Students

1 Reader Recommendations

Inviting students to make recommendations about texts read may encourage other students to read a wider range. When students complete Text Recommendation cards after reading, they are displayed for others to review. This is an effective process for sharing reactions to texts.

– After students have read a text, invite them to determine a rating, write a descriptive comment and identify the type of reader who might enjoy it.
– Recommendations can be placed inside the text, put on display or kept in a recommendation box.

```
┌─────────────────────────────────────────────────┐
│            TEXT RECOMMENDATION CARD               │
│  I rated _____ as _____   │
│  I would recommend it if you like _____   │
│  _____ │
│  _____ │
│  It's about _____ │
│  _____ │
│  _____ │
│  _____ │
│  Signature _____ │
└─────────────────────────────────────────────────┘
```

Figure 8.3

2 Verbed

Verbed is an activity in which students analyse texts using explicit and implicit information to draw conclusions. It involves selecting a verb that encapsulates the situation or outcome for each character.

This activity works best with newspaper or magazine articles, short informational texts and literary texts with strong characterisation. Literary texts may require a chapter-by-chapter analysis to account for a character's changing situation.

– Have a small group read a selected text and list the characters/ people in it.
– Students then work individually to generate a past-tense verb appropriate to each character or person listed.
– Invite them to share and justify their selected verbs. The group then discuss the words and choose the most effective. Discussion could revolve around:
   – justifying the choice of verb by referring to the text;

– the vocabulary used by the author;
– the perspective chosen — through whose eyes are the verbs
   selected?
– Have groups share their text and selected verbs, providing
   justification.

After reading a newspaper article about an oil spill off the coast of
Spain, the students selected these words to describe how the different
people were feeling.

Environmentalists — devastated
Fishermen — crippled
Shipping Company — embarrassed
Spanish Citizens — outraged
Volunteers — exhausted

Figure 8.4 A Verbed activity

3 Regrets and Rewinds

Creating Regrets and Rewinds allows students to analyse texts
and use information to draw conclusions about characters' or
people's actions. They identify actions or speech that may have
been cause for regret, and speculate on what the outcomes would
be if it were possible to rewind.

– Challenge students to identify perceived regrets while reading
   a text.
– Have them record and speculate on reasons why the character or
   person may regret the selected action or speech.
– Invite them to take on the role of the character or person,
   consider what they would do differently if they could rewind the
   text, and suggest how these changes might impact on the
   outcome.
– Invite them to discuss and compare their Regrets and Rewinds,
   justifying their decisions by referring to implicit or explicit
   information in the text.

4 Parting Gift

Parting Gift is an activity in which the reader decides on appropriate
gifts for the characters or people in a text. Considering what gifts
are appropriate for particular characters or people supports
Proficient readers in analysing texts and utilising information to
make and justify personal decisions.

- Allow time for students to read a text.
- Encourage them to discuss the needs and wants of selected characters or people; provide guidelines for the type of gift that may be appropriate for each one. Gifts may be:
  – concrete, such as a pair of shoes
  – abstract, such as a big shot of honesty
  – symbolic, such as a mirror for reflection.
- Provide time for students to individually create their lists of parting gifts for chosen characters or people. They should justify their choices by referring to the text and drawing on personal experience.
- Organise them in small groups to share their lists of parting gifts and justifications.

5 Transformations

Refer to Chapter 7: Transitional Reading Phase, p. 211.

6 Plotting the Plot

By Plotting the Plot (Burke 2000) Proficient readers are better able to identify the crucial parts of a literary text and to understand how a text is constructed. Students are asked first to read and analyse the text to identify the main events or critical parts, and then to rate each event according to how much impact it had on the outcomes.

- Arrange students to work in small groups to read and discuss the text.
- Have them list eight to ten crucial points, sequencing the points chronologically.
- Invite them to reach consensus on the single most crucial point; this should be rated with the highest positive or negative score.
- Direct students to allocate a number from 0 to 5 for each event according to the impact it had on the outcome: +5 = most positive impact, 0 = no impact, – 5 = most negative impact.
- Have them represent their group ratings on a line graph.
- Invite groups to share and discuss the patterns revealed.

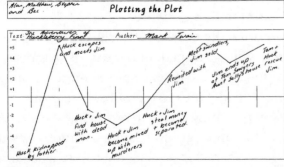

Figure 8.5

7 Re-connecting

Re-connecting is an activity in which students are encouraged to analyse texts and explore relationships between key characters or people. They are required to identify and record relationships between characters or people, then convey a message from one to another.

– After students have read a text, have them complete a sociogram, web or map to represent the relationships between the characters or people.
– Invite each student to choose two of the characters or people. Acting as one of these characters or people, the student selects a text form and constructs a message to send to the other one; the message must stem from the content of the text, but not (literally) be part of it.
– Encourage the use of innovative forms or formats including:
  – a greeting card
  – a text message
  – a last will and testament
  – an email
  – a postcard
  – a bio for a reunion website
  – a telephone conservation
  – a chance meeting.
  Where appropriate, the message may appear to be sent some time after the events in the text.
– Have students share their messages in small groups and discuss why a particular text form or format was selected.

8 Innocent until Proven Guilty

Innocent until Proven Guilty provides an opportunity for students to develop a deeper understanding of a text by drawing on implicit information to present a particular point of view. The activity involves a trial, with two small groups in a courtroom setting. Explicit information in the text must be adhered to during the trial.

– Once the entire class has read a text, have the students charge the main character or person with an offence.
– Have the class choose students to role play selected characters or people in the text who will participate in the trial as witnesses, and allocate each witness to either the defence or the prosecution team.
– Divide the remaining students into two groups. One group (the defence) has the task of preparing a case to show that the character or person is innocent; the other group (the prosecution) has the task of showing that the character or person is guilty as charged.

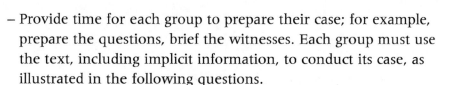

– Provide time for each group to prepare their case; for example, prepare the questions, brief the witnesses. Each group must use the text, including implicit information, to conduct its case, as illustrated in the following questions.
  – The prosecution might ask 'Did you, Goldilocks on the day in question enter the house without the owners' permission?' To which Goldilocks would have to say 'Yes', because it is explicitly stated in the text.
  – The defence, given a chance to question their witness, might ask 'Did you, Goldilocks, intend to steal or destroy any of the owners' possessions?'
– Provide the time and the setting for students to conduct the trial.
– At the close of the trial, summarise the key points established and determine a verdict of innocence or guilt.

9 Symbolism

This activity (Fredericksen 1999) requires students to analyse a text to create a new cover that uses symbols to convey the meaning of the text.

– Record on cards the titles of short stories, articles or any other text the class has read.
– Have each student select a card.
– Provide time, if necessary, for students to re-read their selected texts.
– Invite them to prepare covers for the texts by drawing pictures that symbolise main ideas. The actual title should not be included. Students also need to be prepared to explain their drawings and the symbolism behind them.
– Have them display their covers and invite other students to guess each title.

10 The Drammies

Refer to Chapter 7: Transitional Reading Phase, p. 215.

11 Dear Abby

Dear Abby is a partner activity in which students take on the role of either a character/person or an adviser to share or solve a problem occurring in a text. Participating in this activity encourages students to infer actions and behaviours, and to 'read between the lines' if asked to provide advice.

– Organise students in pairs. In each pair, one is allocated a character or person from the text; the other is to become the adviser (Abby).
– Allow time for students to begin reading the selected text. Direct them to stop reading at a point where there is a problem or issue for a character or person.

– The student being the character or person seeks advice from Abby. The student taking the role of Abby then responds, offering advice on what the other should do.

– Have students continue reading to a point where another problem or issue arises, and repeat the above process.

– If the whole class have read the same text, have students share requests and responses, and the way they relate to the original text.

12 Treasured Possessions

In completing Treasured Possessions, students have an opportunity to analyse texts and utilise information to make and justify personal decisions. They are required to assume the identity of an author and to bequeath a treasured possession to a character.

– After the reading of a text, have students discuss the characters, considering their actions and motivations.

– Pose this scenario: The author of this text is suffering from a fatal illness and is not expected to live much longer. He or she has a 'treasured' possession and wishes to leave it to one of the characters in his or her will.

– Ask each student to assume the role of the author, determine what is the treasured possession and consider which character will receive the bequest.

– Allow time for students to complete a Last Will and Testament, providing evidence for the decision.

– Invite students to share their work.

Figure 8.6

13 Responding to Texts

There are many ways in which students can respond to texts, and it is important to ensure that any response activity is purposeful and appropriate for the text being used. Responding in any of the following ways will assist students' understanding of the text. Thanks are due to Jack Thomson who contributed many of the following ideas to the *First Steps Reading Developmental Continuum* (1992).

Visual Responses

• Make a 'pictures only' text of the most important parts.
• Make a story map.
• Give an illustrated report, e.g. **postcards, drawings, maps**.
• Construct a stage and setting for a scene in the text.
• Create newspaper, magazine, radio or television advertising campaigns.
• Construct a visual timeline.

- Create a Venn diagram to compare different characters, events or processes.
- Create a Power Point presentation.

Oral/Aural Responses

- Debate issues raised by texts.
- Select background music for scenes in a text.
- Create a song for a particular character or for the text.
- Change the setting and discuss the effect of this on the behaviour and attitudes of the characters.
- Create a review of the text to be aired on radio.
- Conduct an interview with a character or with the author.
- Transform the text into a 'talking book', including sound effects.

Written Responses

- Write a different ending for the text.
- Add another chapter — at the end, in the middle or before the text begins.
- Write a lost-and-found advertisement for a significant object belonging to one of the characters or people in the text. Tell why the object was chosen, and its significance to the character or person concerned.
- Make a dictionary or glossary defining important terms used in the text.
- Assume the role of a character or person and write a diary with at least five entries.
- Rewrite a section of the text, assuming the role of an extra character.
- Create a new character. Tell how the text would change with this new character added.
- Write an unsigned letter from the point of view of a character and have the rest of the class work out who it is.
- Write an imagined biography of one of the characters or people.
- Write an account of what you might have done if you had been in one of the character's or person's predicaments.
- Write a letter to the author, sharing a response to the text.
- Write about a true-to-life incident similar to one in the text.
- Write an imagined dialogue between characters or people in two different texts.
- Write a newspaper report of an incident as it might have appeared in a newspaper in the time and culture of the text.
- Compare characters or people in different texts faced with similar problems.
- Research a historical text, distinguishing fact from fiction.

263

- Rewrite a scene in the text it as if it took place at a different time, in either the past or the future.
- Rewrite a scene in the text as if it took place in a different location, such as on a desert island, in Antarctica, on an ocean liner, or in your town.
- Create a newspaper report covering an event in the text as if you had witnessed it.
- Write a report as a private detective assigned to follow the main character or person over a certain time. Tell where this person went, who was seen and what was done. Draw conclusions about the character's or person's motives, values and lifestyle.
- Write a report as a psychologist offering advice to the main character or person. Explain what the problem is and what advice would be given.

14 Graphic Organisers

Graphic organisers are ways to represent written text in a diagrammatic form. They are completed by identifying key information and interrelationships between ideas, then transferring them to a suitable graphic for display and retrieval. Graphic organisers allow Proficient readers to provide organised and structured summaries appropriate to a variety of audiences and purposes. They also provide students with a framework for collating their interpretations and thoughts before, during and after reading a text. Readers are encouraged to look beyond the surface meaning to analyse texts.

Completing graphic organisers helps Proficient readers to:
- recognise and infer the major concepts;
- distinguish between concepts and important details;
- recognise and infer relationships between concepts.

It is important to introduce the students to a wide range of graphic organisers so that they can select the most appropriate way to retrieve and record information for a particular purpose.

Types of Graphic Organisers
- Labelled Diagrams
- Sequence of Illustrations
- Hierarchies
- Flow Charts
- Cycles
- Structured Overviews
- Retrieval Charts
- Venn Diagrams
- Tree Diagrams

Labelled Diagrams

Labelled Diagrams require students to draw a representation of an object described in the text and label the component parts.

The following information was used to create the labelled diagram in Figure 8.7.
- The receptacle at the base of the flower supports the reproductive parts.
- Stamens are made of two parts: the anther and the filament.
- Pistils are made of three parts: the stigma, the style and the ovary.
- The ovary contains the ovules.

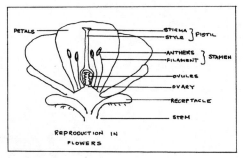

Figure 8.7

Sequence of Illustrations

A Sequence of Illustrations is created when a series of events in a text, steps in an experiment or instructions on how to do something are represented by a series of diagrams or illustrations.

Hierarchies

A Hierarchy is a pyramid in which information or characters or people in a text are ranked in order of importance; the most important information or character/person is at the top. A hierarchy can be recorded as a simple diagram, and may or may not have illustrations.

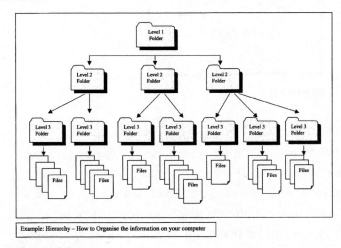

Figure 8.8

Flow Charts

In a Flow Chart, arrows are used to link important events and show the related time sequence. Flow charts can be used effectively to illustrate and clarify chronological order in a text.

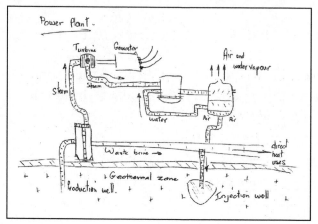

Figure 8.9

Cycles

A Cycle Diagram is a representation of a series of events that occur over and over again in the same order. Cycle diagrams emphasise both the sequence of events and the fact that they recur in a never-ending pattern; examples are the water cycle and the life cycle of a butterfly.

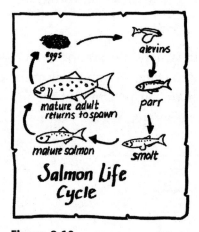

Figure 8.10

Structured Overviews

A Structured Overview is a visual representation of how concepts are presented in a written text. It shows the major concepts and the relationships between them. A structured overview can be used before, during or after reading, depending upon the purpose; as a before-reading activity it can be prepared by the teacher, providing the reader with an overview of the text content prior to reading.

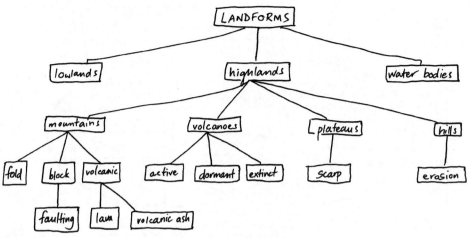

Figure 8.11

Retrieval Charts

A Retrieval Chart is used to organise information about a topic according to a number of categories, so that comparisons can easily be made.

Retrieval Chart						
Animal	Phylum	Locomotion	Feeding	Defense	Reproduction	Unique Characteristics
Nudibranch	Mollusc Gastropod	Poda	Radula, active feeder	Nematocysts, colouring	Sexual	Swallows anemones for their nematocysts, shelless
Sea Star	Echinoderm	Tube feet	Tube feet, oral disk, active feeder	Spiny skin	Sexual, regeneration of parts	Regurgitation of stomach to digest food.
Sea Urchin						
Sea Cucumber						

Figure 8.12

Venn Diagrams

Venn Diagrams consist of two or more overlapping circles; they can be used to compare and contrast events, characters, people, situations, ideas or concepts.

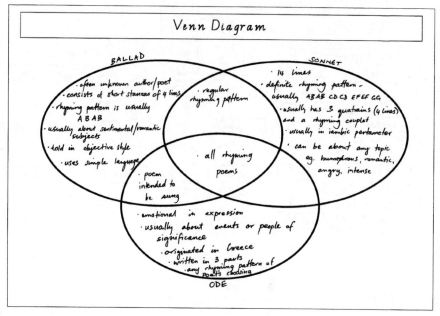

Figure 8.13

Tree Diagrams

Tree Diagrams are used to organise and categorise information, and show connections. They start with a focal point, such as a major theme or a main character, and subordinate information branches out from this point.

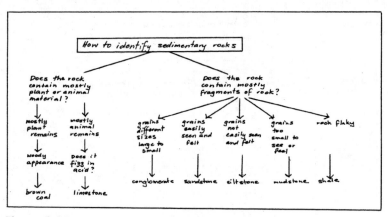

Figure 8.14

15 Note-making

The ability to make notes involves identifying and extracting important information from texts. Making notes helps students to understand content, to organise and summarise it and to record information for subsequent tasks. Note-making formats can be used to help students analyse texts for different purposes; they can be encouraged to use a variety of formats and to understand that particular formats are appropriate for specific questions or types of information.

Types of Note-making Formats
- Running commentary
- Chapter notes
- Character notes
- Using text structure or text organisation

Running Commentary

A running commentary (Thomson 1992) requires students to list events from the text in the left-hand column of a table. Commentary, speculation and connections with personal experience are recorded in the right-hand column.

Running Commentary	
Text: _____ Author: _____	
Events	Commentary

Figure 8.15

Chapter Notes

Chapter notes (Thomson 1992) provide an opportunity for readers to record main details from each chapter of a text. Jottings made under the headings of 'Who', 'When', 'Where', 'What' and 'Why' can be used as a springboard for discussions.

Chapter Notes					
Text: _____ Author: _____					
Chapter	Who	Where	When	What	Why

Figure 8.16

Character Notes

Character notes (Thomson 1992) allow students to become more perceptive about characterisation; they involve recording each main character's actions and speculating about motives. Students can also record predicted consequences of actions.

Character Notes			
Text: _____ Author: _____			
Character	Actions	Motives	Consequences

Figure 8.17

Using Text Structure or Text Organisation

Note-making formats designed around the structure of different text forms provides students with support in recording and retrieving key information. Formats can be created to suit the text and the purpose of the note-making activity.

Compare and Contrast	
Text: _____ Author: _____	
Topic: _____	

Figure 8.18

Persuasive Argument		
Text: _____ Author: _____		
Topic: _____		
Thesis	Argument 1	Argument 2
Argument 3	Argument 4	Conclusion

Figure 8.19

CONTEXTUAL UNDERSTANDING

Major Teaching Emphases

- Provide opportunities for students to discuss how the ideologies of the reader and the author combine to create an interpretation of the text.

- Provide opportunities for students to identify devices used to influence readers to take a particular view.

Teaching Notes

At the Proficient phase, students need to develop an understanding of how social values are constructed and communicated. Deconstructing texts allows them to better understand how authors use devices to influence readers to take a particular point of view; readers are then in a better position to accept, resist or challenge such messages.

The foci for helping Proficient readers to develop contextual understanding are organised under the following headings.
- Discussions about Ideologies
- Discussions about Devices Authors Use

Discussions about Ideologies

Readers in this phase benefit from being given many opportunities to explore and articulate their own ideologies, as these will have an impact on their interpretation of texts. Proficient readers can also be involved in investigating and discussing authors' backgrounds; this can lead them to speculate about how such backgrounds and experiences are reflected in text, and the author's motivation for creating the text.

As students read and discuss a text, have them explore the author's style and ideology by asking a variety of questions.
- What type of characters does this author usually create? For example, consider age, gender, culture and disposition.
- What types of settings does this author generally use? What seems to determine the setting in each text?
- What types of plots does this author develop? Examples could be linear or circular plots, or a plot within a plot.
- What devices does this author most often employ?
- What voice is used in each text?

- Are there similarities between the titles and book jackets of texts written by this author? Do you think these have an impact upon how the content of the text is perceived?
- Who or what is omitted from the text? How does this affect it? What do you think could be the reason for this?
- Whose point of view is being represented? What is another point of view the author could have taken?
- What social realities are portrayed? For instance, are the characters middle class, city dwellers?
- Who has the power? How does the author convey this?
- What assumptions does the author make? e.g. **conservationists are always anti-development.**
- What values does the author suggest? For example, the belief that girls should be quiet.
- What was most powerful for you in this text?
- How was your thinking influenced by the text?

Discussions about Devices Authors Use

Proficient readers are aware that a text is written for a particular purpose and audience. Discussions can focus on the devices used to target specific audiences. Discussing the reasons for these devices and their effectiveness will give Proficient readers a deeper understanding of how authors influence the construction of a particular view. At this phase of development, readers realise that it is the coming together of the prior knowledge of the reader and the craft of the author that creates interpretations of texts.

Devices used by authors include:
- choice of language, such as to create a positive or negative connotation;
- inclusion or omission of details;
- foreshadowing — giving a hint of things to come;
- irony, wit, humour, sarcasm, satire;
- flashback — interrupting the text to show something that happened earlier;
- understatement — downplaying the gravity of a situation;
- symbolism — objects used to represent something else;
- opinions disguised as facts;
- hyperbole — wild exaggerations;
- figurative language, such as similes, metaphors, analogy;
- generalising and drawing conclusions, such as 'Everyone knows . . .;
- personification — giving human qualities to inanimate objects;
- quoting statistics and experts;
- euphemism, such as saying 'passed away' instead of 'died';

- bias, propaganda, exaggeration, rhetoric;
- print size;
- font selection;
- design of pages.

For further information about the Contextual Understanding substrand, see *Reading Resource Book*, 2nd edn, Chapter 2: Contextual Understanding.

Involving Students

1 Reading Response Journals

A Reading Response Journal provides a place for students to record their personal expectations, reactions and reflections about texts before, during and after reading. Keeping a response journal provides opportunities for readers to recognise how they have combined their ideologies and those of the author to create an interpretation of the text.

– Explain the purpose and use of a reading response journal.
– As students read independently, have them consider and make notes on:
  – questions about the text they want or expect to be answered;
  – predictions they make about what might happen;
  – confirmation of predictions;
  – puzzles, confusions or unanticipated outcomes;
  – questions and points of interest they want to discuss with others;
  – connections they are making;
  – examples of author craft;
  – opinions and justifications.
– Provide opportunities for students to share their journal entries with peers or in teacher–student conferences.
– Invite them to re-read their journal entries periodically. Have them discuss and/or record what they have learnt about:
  – texts;
  – their use of cues and strategies;
  – their experience, knowledge and beliefs, and the impact of these on interpretation;
  – their cultural construction.

Quick Dip Reading Response Journal	
Consider	**Responses**
Questions	
Uncertainties	
Issues	
Connections	
Key themes	
Devices	
In less than ten words	
Predictions	

Reading Response Journal Questions

What is the significance of this particular detail/event/use of words?

How does it connect with other details/events/episodes?

What is this preparing the reader for?

What kinds of things might happen?

How does this event affect my interpretation of what has gone before?

What am I learning about this character and his or her relationship with others?

Why was she or he included in the story at all?

Whose point of view is being presented?

Why is the author offering this character's point of view here?

Figure 8.20

2 Stop, Think, Feel, Share

Refer to Chapter 6: Early Reading Phase, p. 168.

3 Conflicting Book Reviews

Conflicting Book Reviews involves students in exploring and analysing other people's views of books. The analysis of conflicting reviews becomes the stimulus for Proficient readers to clarify and articulate their own thoughts and reactions to books.

By identifying points in reviews that they agreed or disagreed with, students' own judgement of a book can become clearer. They may then be more confident in expressing and exploring their own interpretations.

– Have students read a selected book.

– Provide them with copies of conflicting reviews of the book.

– Ask them to read the reviews and use different highlights to mark places where they agree or disagree with comments of the critic.

– Have them share their reactions to the reviews as well as their own thoughts about the book.

– Ask them to prepare their own reviews of the book.

There are numerous websites that provide book reviews suitable for this activity, including:

• www.teenreads.com, www.kidsreads.com

• www.teenink.com (reviews written by teenagers).

4 Casting the Movie

In Casting the Movie, Proficient readers select actors to play the parts of characters in texts they have read. This activity encourages them to discuss actors they think would be appropriate for the roles and those who would be unsuitable, justifying their choices.

– From a previously read text, have students identify and record the characters on the Casting the Movie framework (see Figure 8.21).

– Provide time for them to discuss actors who would be suitable to play the characters. These should be recorded in the column 'Successful Applicant'.

– Encourage students also to consider actors who would be unsuitable for the roles. Record their names in the column 'Unsuitable Applicants'.

– Have students explain and justify their choices.

Casting the Movie			
TEXT: *Dancer : The Novel*		AUTHOR: *Colum McCann*	
CHARACTERS	SUCCESSFUL APPLICANT	UNSUITABLE APPLICANTS	JUSTIFICATIONS
Margot	Katherine Zeta Jones	Gwenyth Paltrow	Katherine has a dancing background + has starred in other dancing roles. She is the right colouring + statuesque to play Margot. Gwenyth is too young + frail, starred featured 'tutu-la ballerina
Rudolph	Paul Mecurio	Patrick Swayze	Paul is a fabulous dancer, also with past movie experience (dance film) Although also a dancer, Patrick doesn't have quite the presence of Paul. Also Paul Mecurio has the good looks and slight sense of arrogance/ self confidence required for the part!
Victor	Danny de Vito	Brad Pitt	His build + 'up front' nature along with his sense of humour suit the role of Victor. Brad is too young + good looking. Not known as a flamboyant person

Figure 8.21

5 Frictogram

A Frictogram is an adaptation of a sociogram, in which the relationships between characters or people are represented. However, while a sociogram is a general overview of relationships, a Frictogram represents only the friction between characters and participants. It is constructed and written from the perspective of each character or person.

- After students have read a text, ask them to list the characters or people on sticky notes.
- Have them arrange the notes on a page, placing characters that have a direct relationship close to one another.
- Direct them then to draw an arrowed line for each negative feeling generated by one character towards another. The lines can be varied (dotted, dashed, or having different thickness or colour) to show the intensity of each feeling.
- Direct students to describe the friction in a sentence that begins 'You . . . '. This should be written on the arrowed line.
- Invite them to share their Frictograms summarising the extent of friction between the characters.

6 Opinionnaire

An Opinionnaire helps students to access, reflect upon and focus their prior knowledge before reading a text. They are given a series of statements related to the theme, topic or issue of the text to be read and are required to decide whether they agree or disagree with each statement, providing personal justifications for their choices.

Opinionnaire about Love and Loyalty

Mark the statements with which you agree and put a cross next to the ones with which you disagree. Provide a reason for your opinion.

_____ Love at first sight is not possible.

Reason: _____

_____ There is no such thing as 'true love'.

Reason: _____

_____ If your family dislike the person you love, you should stop seeing that person to keep the peace.

Reason: _____

Figure 8.22 Adapted from http://www.sasked.gov.sk.ca/docs/mla/julie.html

– Prepare an Opinionnaire by creating a series of statements related to a topic, issue or theme of a text.
– Provide each student with a copy before they read the text. Direct them to read each statement and mark it to indicate whether they agree or disagree, recording a justification for each choice.
– Students then read the text.
– After the reading, invite them to compare their opinions with those presented by the author.

7 Hypothesising

Hypothesising is a form of predicting in which assumptions are made using information from both the text and the reader's prior knowledge. This activity encourages Proficient readers to explore and articulate their own ideologies, and discover how they impact on the interpretation of a text. Students are given a number of hypotheses for a text relating to characters, plot, setting or conflict. From these, they are required to select one and to provide personal justification for their selection of and response to it.

– Organise students in small groups.
– Present each group with a selection of prepared hypotheses cards related to their shared text.
– After previewing the cards have each student select one based on his or her own criterion, e.g. **most likely to happen, strongly disagree with, highly improbable.**
– Allow time for students to consider their selected hypothesis and their justification.
– Have students share their hypothesis with the group, giving reasons for their selection. Encourage them to question, challenge and discuss each other's hypotheses, drawing on the text and their own personal views for substantiation.
– Encourage them to generate additional hypotheses for the text.

8 Panel Discussion

Participating in Panel Discussions helps students to understand how the ideologies of the reader and the author combine to create an interpretation of a text. Panel discussions are based around one text, with the members of the panel either presenting their own views or being allocated a role. The remainder of the class, as the audience, make comments or ask questions of what has been presented.

– At the conclusion of a text reading, select panel members.
– Allocate roles to each member, such as the author, a teenager, an elderly lady and a critic.

- Provide time for each member to consider the text from the allocated perspective and write a short presentation of his or her view of it.
- During this time, have the audience brainstorm a series of questions that could be directed to each of the panel members.
- Invite each panel member to present his or her view.
- At the conclusion of the panel presentations, invite the audience to comment on them and ask individual members questions about what they have presented.
- Lead a discussion in which students can compare the different responses given by the panel members and speculate on how knowledge and experience influence the perspectives taken.

9 Text Innovation

Refer to Chapter 7: Transitional Reading Phase, p. 226.

10 Spot the Devices

In Spot the Devices, readers hunt for words, expressions or images that have been used by the author or illustrator in an attempt to position the reader. Newspapers, magazines and catalogues are ideal texts for this activity.

- Select an extract from a known text. Have students highlight words, expressions or images that have been chosen to position the reader.
- Invite them to discuss the highlighted text pieces, speculating about the author or illustrator's intent.
- Encourage them to suggest alternative words, expressions or images that would temper the impact, reverse its meaning or change the audience appeal.

11 Multiple-Text Approach

The Multiple-Text Approach uses a number of texts that are linked by theme, topic or issue to encourage readers to explore the way different authors have communicated their messages. Students compare the different messages and identify the devices authors have used to position the reader.

- Organise the class in groups of five or six.
- Give each group a different text on the same topic, theme or issue; these could include a chapter of a novel, a newspaper article or a history text.
- Have students read their allocated text, noting the key message presented and the devices used. Devices could include:

   – the author's choice of words to describe people, events or
     situations;
   – bias, exaggeration or assumption;
   – selection or omission of details;
   – opinions disguised as facts;
   – use of experts.
– Invite each group to report their findings to the rest of the class
  and use this information to make comparisons between the texts.
  Discuss how the devices used in each one influenced readers to
  take a particular view.

12 Deconstructing Texts

Deconstructing Texts involves Proficient readers in analysing a text,
section by section, to uncover the devices that have been used.

Deconstructing activities could include:
• identifying the language of character construction, such as the
  adverbs and adjectives used;
• identifying language that invokes the reader's sympathy or
  antipathy;
• identifying the author's viewpoint and the values being promoted
  or denigrated by it;
• comparing sections of different texts written by the same author
  to discover common devices used;
• identifying the devices authors use to communicate mood,
  emotion and atmosphere in specific passages;
• identifying the language that confirms or modifies previous
  expectations and interpretations;
• discussing the effects of, and possible motives for, specific
  revisions within several drafts of a professional writer's work.

Deconstructing texts in this way helps students to understand how
ideologies are constructed and communicated.

– Create small groups around previously read texts.
– Challenge each group to analyse their text, choosing activities
  from the above list.
– Provide time for sharing the analysis of texts. Encourage
  comments on what devices were identified and the impact they
  had on influencing a reader to take a particular view.

13 What's Missing?

Through the activity What's Missing?, readers recognise how authors have used omissions as a device to target specific audiences and to influence the reader to take a particular point of view. Students are encouraged to identify omissions from a text and discuss the impact they might have on the reader.

– Have students listen to or read a text. Pose the question, 'What's missing?'
– Students then record any notable omissions. For literary texts this might include omissions of orientation, resolution, character perspective, cause or effect. In informational texts, students may note omissions such as details, perspective, evidence, cause or effect.
– Encourage them to consider the following questions.
  – Do you think the omission was intentional or unintentional?
  – Who is the intended audience?
  – What impact does the omission have on the reader's point of view?
– Invite students to share their findings with the class.
– Discuss the effectiveness of using omissions as a device to influence a reader's construction of meaning.

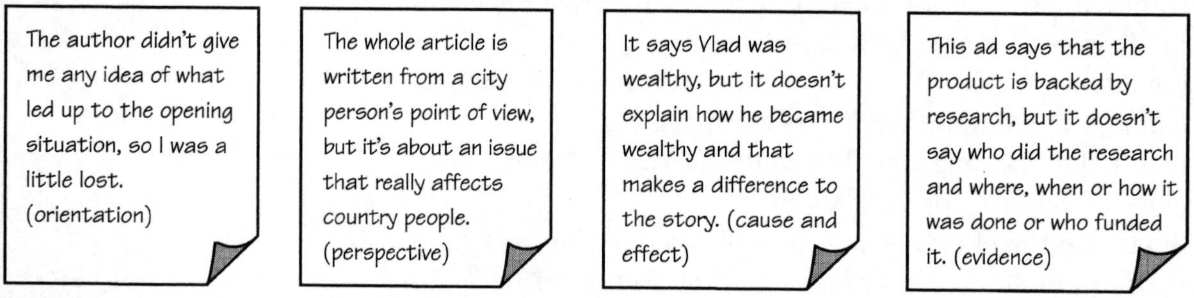

> The author didn't give me any idea of what led up to the opening situation, so I was a little lost. (orientation)

> The whole article is written from a city person's point of view, but it's about an issue that really affects country people. (perspective)

> It says Vlad was wealthy, but it doesn't explain how he became wealthy and that makes a difference to the story. (cause and effect)

> This ad says that the product is backed by research, but it doesn't say who did the research and where, when or how it was done or who funded it. (evidence)

Figure 8.23 What's Missing?

14 Change the Point of View

Refer to Chapter 7: Transitional Reading Phase, p. 223.

CONVENTIONS

Major Teaching Emphases

- **Continue to build students' sight vocabulary,** e.g. technical terms, figurative language.

- **Teach students to analyse how authors combine language features to achieve a purpose.**

- **Teach students to analyse how authors manipulate texts to achieve a purpose,** e.g. structure, organisation.

Teaching Notes

Proficient readers will be exposed to an increasing bank of words and varied text organisation and structures as they encounter complex texts in different learning areas. They benefit from opportunities to analyse a wide range of texts in order to consolidate their understanding of how meaning is constructed across a wide range of forms.

Modelled, Shared and Guided Reading procedures provide opportunities for discussion and analysis of the conventions used in a wide range of texts.

The foci for supporting Proficient readers to develop understandings about conventions are organised under the following headings.
- Sight Vocabulary and Word Knowledge
- Knowledge about Text Forms

Sight Vocabulary and Word Knowledge

Sight vocabulary is the bank of words a reader is able to automatically decode, pronounce and understand in the contexts in which they are used. Such words are called 'sight words' because efficient readers need to recognise them instantly on sight in order to maintain the speed and fluency required to make sense of the author's message. Many of these words have irregular spellings, making them difficult to decode.

While Proficient readers have become efficient at decoding and pronouncing words, some do not understand the meaning of all they can decode. Since it is not possible to teach students all the words they will need to understand, it is wise to invest time teaching them how to learn new vocabulary independently; this may involve analysing words by considering their component phonemes and morphemes, the context, or the grammatical function they serve.

Sight vocabulary for Proficient readers could include:
* words with either a literal or a figurative meaning, such as connotations and idioms;
* common words used in different learning areas, such as 'scale' as used in music, science or maths;
* technical terms.

It is important to teach students how to discover a word's meaning using:
* context clues — the sentence or sentences around the word;
* visual clues — pictures and diagrams;
* other resources — dictionaries and glossaries;
* structural analysis — considering prefixes, suffixes, word origins, foreign roots and derivations.

Knowledge about Text Forms

Providing text analysis opportunities allows students to examine the ways in which language is used to produce meanings and to communicate the author's purpose. Continuing to provide opportunities for students to analyse and discuss different text forms will help to consolidate understandings about the purpose, text organisation, text structure and language features of a wide range of texts.

Modelled, Shared and Guided Reading sessions provide an opportunity to discuss conventions in the context of authentic texts, and can also include a focus on texts that 'break the rules' to achieve a specific purpose and enhance impact.

When deconstructing texts with Proficient readers, the following points provide a focus.

Purpose

Texts are written to achieve a purpose. The purpose may be to entertain, as in a limerick, or to argue a point of view, as in an exposition.

Text Organisation

Text organisation refers to the layout. Proficient readers will benefit from understanding text-form frameworks; for instance, a narrative may include orientation, conflict and resolution. It is also important for these readers to understand the function, terminology and use of organisational features such as:

- headings and subheadings
- captions
- diagrams and other visual aids (photographs, flow charts, cross-sections)
- glossaries
- paragraphs
- bold or italic print
- illustrations
- hyperlinks
- Internet site maps
- spreadsheets
- website buttons, banners and dividers.

Text Structure

Text structure refers to the way ideas, feelings and information are linked in a text. These could include:
- problem and solution;
- compare and contrast;
- cause and effect;
- listing: logical or chronological sequence, collection of details.

Having an understanding of these patterns can assist Proficient readers to comprehend text.

Language Features

The term 'language features' refers to the type of vocabulary and grammar used. Each text form has specific features that are appropriate to that form. These include:
- tense, e.g. **past or present**;
- word choice, e.g. **precise technical adjectives, action verbs, words signalling different text structures**;
- style, e.g. **colloquial or formal**.

> For further information about the Conventions substrand, see *Reading Resource Book*, 2nd edn, Chapter 3: Conventions.

Involving Students

1 Challenge

Challenge is a word card game that helps Proficient readers to build their sight vocabulary. Students work in small groups to match adjectives, adverbs or verbs to characters or events in a text they have read; they are required to use inference, logic and effective argument to justify their matches.

– Select four main characters or events and place the names on a large grid (see Figure 8.24).
– On separate cards, list 20–30 descriptors. These can be adjectives, e.g. **loyal or vicious**; adverbs, e.g. **remarkably or intensely**; or verbs, e.g. **disappeared, destroyed.**
– All the cards are dealt out. Students then take turns to place one card on the grid next to the character or event it best describes.
– When a card is placed, the student must justify the choice by referring to the text. Any challenge made by other students to the appropriateness of the placement must be refuted logically and substantiated from the text.

Text: Call of the Wild	Author: Jack London
BUCK	JOHN THORNTON
DAVE	SPITZ

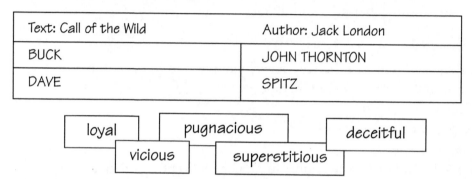

Figure 8.24 A Challenge grid and sorting cards

2 Analysing Literary Text Structure

There are a number of literary text sequencing structures that can be analysed.

- *Chronological* — events are written in the sequence in which they occur.
- *Retrospective* — the story starts at the end and then goes back to satisfy the reader's curiosity.
- *Flashback* — the story flashes back to events that have led to the present situation. This is often a useful way of developing a character.
- *Circular* — this starts at the climax, goes back to describe events leading up to it and then goes on to describe what happens next.
- *Double* — where two plots are running simultaneously, often leading to their combination at the climax of the book.

Analysing different structures helps students to become aware of the way authors manipulate texts to achieve a purpose.

– After students have read a text, provide them with the opportunity to identify the sequencing structure used.
– Invite them to work in pairs to create a visual representation of this structure.

– Provide time for them to discuss the author's purpose in choosing that structure and reflect on its effectiveness.

– Encourage students to use varying sequence structures in their own writing.

3 Meaning Continuum

Creating Meaning Continua encourages students to look at words and the nuances of meaning they may hold. Students also have the opportunity to generate and discuss alternatives to vocabulary presented in a text.

– Select an adjective or an adverb from a current text.

– Direct students to draw a horizontal line, placing the chosen word at the start of the continuum. A word that is opposite in meaning is placed at the end of the continuum.

– Students then brainstorm and list words related to those on the continuum.

– From this list, have students select several words to be arranged in order along the continuum, beginning on the left-hand side with the word closest in meaning and intent to the specified word and moving along the continuum to the opposite meaning on the right-hand side.

```
  ◁─── joyful   jubilant   happy   pleased   melancholy   gloomy   dejected   depressed   sad ───▷
```

Figure 8.25

– Challenge students to substitute some of the brainstormed words for the word in the text. Have them discuss the substituted words, identifying how the choice of a word can alter intended meaning.

4 Word Cline

Refer to Chapter 7: Transitional Reading Phase, p. 234.

5 Change the Organisation

Change the Organisation allows students to present factual information in a variety of ways. Asking them to present one piece of information as a graph, a table, a diagram or a written paragraph helps them to focus on and understand the impact that text organisation may have on the reader.

– Select a piece of text that lends itself to the information being presented in a variety of ways. Have all students read it.
– Invite groups to discuss the information in the text.
– Allocate parts of the text to each group.
– Direct each group to present their section of text in a specified way; for example, to change a written paragraph into a diagram, a graph into a table, or a diagram into a written paragraph.
– Invite groups to share their representations.
– Have students make comparisons between the original form of the information and the way the other students have reorganised it.
– Provide time for them to discuss the impact of organising text in different ways. Discuss when and for what purpose each form of organisation might be most appropriate.

6 Comparisons

Comparisons is an activity that invites students to analyse the type of language used by a number of authors. Collecting and comparing reviews of books, plays, restaurants, films, sporting events, concerts or live performances all on the same topic provides a context for examining the choice of words by different authors.

– Collect — or provide time for students to collect — a range of reviews on one topic by various authors. The Internet, newspapers, local magazines or television can be sources for these reviews.
– Have students work in small groups to analyse the reviews. They should highlight any words that indicate an author's opinion (either positive or negative) of the topic under review.
– Direct them to arrange the reviews in order from negative to positive, forming a continuum.
– Have them list the words that indicate each author's opinion. Speculate on the authors' choice of words.

The example in Figure 8.26 illustrates the choice of words used to express different opinions about the same film.

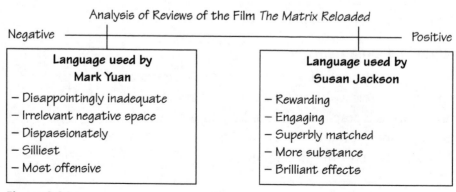

Analysis of Reviews of the Film *The Matrix Reloaded*

Negative ——————————————————————— Positive

Language used by Mark Yuan	**Language used by Susan Jackson**
– Disappointingly inadequate	– Rewarding
– Irrelevant negative space	– Engaging
– Dispassionately	– Superbly matched
– Silliest	– More substance
– Most offensive	– Brilliant effects

Figure 8.26

7 Speculate

This activity encourages students to think at the inferential level as they analyse and speculate on an author's choice of specific words. Discussing this helps them understand how authors use word selection to achieve a purpose and to help readers infer meaning.

– Have students read a selected text.
– From this text, select sentences or phrases describing an event, an action or a character.
– Select a word from each sentence and highlight it in some way.
– Have students speculate about why the author may have chosen to use the highlighted word in that sentence. Discussion could centre on the connotation of the word, on the intended message being given or on generating alternatives.

8 Character Descriptions

In this activity, students look closely at the language used by an author to describe characters. This helps Proficient readers to understand how authors combine language features to achieve a particular purpose.

– Have students read some descriptions of characters, individually noting key descriptive words or phrases; for example:
  – his nose is like an eagle's beak (use of simile);
  – his dapper London demeanour (choice of words);
  – leaned on a silver-handled cane (description of character action);
  – outsized flannel shirt, baggy tailor-made corduroys (description of possession and clothing).
– Form students into small groups and have them combine their key words and phrases into categories.
– Have them discuss what has been learnt about the characters from the author's words. Discuss which words were most powerful in building mental images of the characters.

9 Looking for Clues

Refer to Chapter 7: Transitional Reading Phase, p. 244.

10 Cooperative Controlled Cloze

The use of cloze activities encourages students to use context clues to predict missing parts of a text. These activities are easily prepared by deleting words or phrases.

It is beneficial for students to have the opportunity to discuss answers and justifications, allowing them to hear the strategies used by others, and alternative choices.

– Prepare a cloze passage by deleting words or phrases that would have several options for replacement.
– Have students read the text individually and record a word or a phrase appropriate for each space.
– Now organise the students in small groups.
– Direct them to go back to the beginning of the text and discuss the words they have chosen to fill the spaces. Encourage them to justify their choices on the basis of linguistic information, content or personal experience.
– Have them re-read their own work and compare it with the author's original text.
– Encourage them to discuss the impact of the choice of words, both their own and the author's.

11 Translations

This activity helps Proficient readers to identify figurative language in texts, to translate it into a common meaning and to speculate on the author's choice and use of the words. Figurative language analysed in this way could include idioms, clichés and similes; eye dialect, the use of non-standard spelling to represent the way a person speaks, can also be included. Students can often determine authors' opinions, values and prejudices by analysing the use and meaning of figurative language.

– Have students begin to collect examples of figurative language as they come across it in texts. Record these on a chart, noting the type of language and the translation.
– Once several examples have been identified and recorded, invite small groups to search for further examples of a particular type, such as metaphors.
– Ask the groups to share any examples discovered, providing the text, the identified sentence or phrase and the translation.
– Allow time to discuss the purpose and possible reasons for authors' use of the particular types of figurative language. Add further information to the class chart.

Text	What It Said	Translation	Language Feature	What's the Reason?
Sports section of the newspaper	'It's gonna be tough for our boys,' Coach Connolly said	This will be a hard game for the players to win	eye dialect	Using non-standard spelling gives the impression of speaking in a lower class way
'Boy', by Roald Dahl	His face was as still and white as virgin snow and his hands were trembling	He was very scared	simile	To create a vivid image in as few words as possible

Figure 8.27 A class-generated translation chart

12 Word-Sorting Activities

Refer to Chapter 6: Early Reading Phase, p. 183.

13 Word Origins

Refer to Chapter 7: Transitional Reading Phase, p. 241.

14 Collecting Words

Collecting Words helps students to build sight vocabulary and to analyse how authors use words to achieve a particular purpose. Collecting Words involves them in identifying and recording words they have read. The criteria for collecting words can vary according to the texts or the context in which the activity is being used, ranging from generic (such as interesting words) to specific (such as Latin roots). Proficient readers will benefit from collecting a range of words and justifying their choice.

- Decide on the time span for the activity and the criteria for word collection; for example, acronyms or onomatopoeic words.
- Create a space where the words can be recorded, such as on a class chart or a word wall.
- Ask students to add words to the lists from their reading in all learning areas, giving the source and the meaning of each one as they add it to the class collection.

15 Word Webs

Developing Word Webs helps Proficient readers build sight vocabulary as well as the concept and category knowledge needed to understand texts in different learning areas. Word Webs involve them in listing words related to a selected focus word according to given criteria. Students can create word webs before, during or after reading texts.

– Select a word from a current text that represents a concept students are studying.
– Place the word in the centre of a 'web' (see Figure 8.28).
– Surround the central word with organisational headings of the criteria so that students can record associated words.
– Have students work in small groups to record all possible connections to the central word.

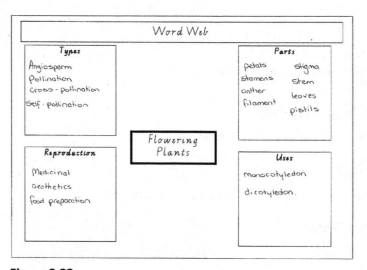

Figure 8.28

16 Semantic Association

Semantic Association is designed to extend students' vocabulary. It is an activity in which they brainstorm words associated with a topic, such as geothermal energy. Where necessary, additional words can be provided to introduce new vocabulary. The initial brainstorming activity can then be extended into a semantic association activity by inviting students to group and categorise the words into familiar subtopics with other known words, thus exploring the meanings of new vocabulary.

– Ask students to work together to list all the words they can think of related to a given theme or topic.
– Ensure that they discuss the meaning of any words unfamiliar to some students.
– Provide time for them to group and categorise the words.
– Direct them to attach a label to each category.
– Invite pairs or groups to share their words and categories.
– Encourage use of the new vocabulary in writing activities.

17 Concept/Definition Maps

Refer to Chapter 7: Transitional Reading Phase, p. 234.

18 Clarifying Table

Creating a Clarifying Table (Ellis & Farmer 2002) helps students to identify and define the way words are used in a specific context. This process can assist concept development by building a more complete understanding of the vocabulary.

– After students have read a text, select words representing concepts that are essential for them to understand in order to interpret the text; an example could be 'prejudice'.
– Lead a discussion about the word, eliciting a definition; a dictionary may be consulted if necessary. Record the definition on the clarifying table framework.
– To further clarify the meaning of the word, encourage students to discuss and record examples of where it is used or what it was used to describe in the text they have read.
– Direct them to draw upon their own background knowledge to add further clarifying statements; these can be added to the Clarifiers column.
– Invite any students who can make personal connections to the word to share their experiences. These can be recorded in the Connections column.
– Ask students to then consider examples or applications of where the word would not be used, or other concepts with which it should not be confused.
– Direct them to create a sentence using the focus word in the correct context.

Word

(prejudice)

Definition

an unfavourable opinion or feeling formed beforehand or without reason or knowledge

X **Use it to describe . . .** **Example of . . .**	**Clarifiers**	**Connections**
Use it to describe the way some people are treated because of their race, colour, religion or gender.	• when people are treated differently because of the group they belong to • making an unfair judgement about someone without knowing them • prejudice can lead to discrimination	In the song 'He's a Rebel' When an Aboriginal boy was attacked and run over the ambulance people thought he was drunk and didn't treat him properly and he died.
Don't confuse it with . . . X **Not an example of . . .**	Not an example of judgements based on fact or first-hand knowledge.	

Sentence

Prejudice occurs when you make judgements about people based only on the group to which they belong.

Figure 8.29 A Clarifying Table

19 Signal Words

Refer to Chapter 7: Transitional Reading Phase, p. 244.

PROCESSES AND STRATEGIES

Major Teaching Emphases

- ■ Continue to build students' knowledge within the cues.

- ■ Consolidate comprehension strategies.

- ■ Consolidate word-identification strategies.

- ■ Consolidate how to locate, select and evaluate texts.

- ■ Model self-reflection of strategies used in reading, and encourage students to do the same.

Organisation of the Processes and Strategies Substrand

The organisation of the Processes and Strategies substrand differs in several ways from that of the other substrands. Both the Teaching Notes and the Involving Students sections are located in Chapter 4 of the *Reading Resource Book*, 2nd edn.

The rationale for this difference in organisation is that reading processes and strategies are not hierarchical, and therefore not phase-specific. A variety of processes and strategies need to be introduced, developed and consolidated at all phases of development.

What varies from one phase to the next is the growth in:
• the number and integration of strategies;
• the awareness and monitoring of strategies;
• the efficiency in use and selection of strategies;
• the ability to articulate the use of the strategies;
• the awareness of how the use of strategies helps with making meaning;
• the ability to locate, select and evaluate texts.

Supporting Parents of Proficient Readers

GENERAL DESCRIPTION OF PROFICIENT READERS

Proficient readers use many ways to identify unknown words and comprehend texts. Reading is automatic, and when they encounter difficult texts they make decisions about the best way to deal with them. Proficient readers challenge and question information within texts; for example, they question validity and accuracy, compare characters with real-life people and link information to their personal experiences.

Supporting Proficient Readers in the Home

Proficient readers will benefit from a range of experiences, in the home setting. Ideas for providing appropriate experiences are available on Parent Cards located on the *First Steps* Reading CD-ROM. Teachers can select appropriate cards for each Proficient reader from the Reading CD-ROM for parents to use at home. Also available on the CD-ROM is a parent-friendly version of the Reading Map of Development.

Parent Cards

1 General Description and How to Support Proficient Readers
2 Encouraging Reading
3 Selecting Texts
4 Sharing a Love of Reading
5 Supporting Comprehension
6 Helping with Research Work
7 Using the Library

CHAPTER 9

Accomplished Reading Phase

Figure 9.1

Global Statement

Accomplished readers use a flexible repertoire of strategies and cues to comprehend texts and to solve problems with unfamiliar structure and vocabulary. They are able to fluently read complex and abstract texts such as journal articles, novels and research reports. Accomplished readers access the layers of information and meaning in a text according to their reading purpose. They interrogate, synthesise and evaluate multiple texts to revise and refine their understandings.

Accomplished Reading Indicators

Use of Texts

◆ Reads and demonstrates comprehension of texts using both explicit and implicit information to achieve a given purpose.

◆ Synthesises information from texts, with varying perspectives, to draw conclusions.

◆ Locates and evaluates appropriateness of texts and the information in texts in terms of purpose and audience.

• Uses information implicit in a text for a variety of purposes, e.g. to support or refute a viewpoint.

• Identifies and analyses main ideas and recurring themes in and between texts.

• Discusses layers of meaning in texts.

Contextual Understanding

◆ Discusses reasons why a text may be interpreted differently by different readers, e.g. personal background of reader, author bias, sociocultural background.

◆ Discusses how the context (time, place, situation) of an author influences the construction of a text.

◆ Analyses the use of devices such as rhetoric, wit, cynicism and irony designed to position readers to take particular views.

• Identifies how the author's values, attitude and beliefs have influenced the construction of the text.

• Analyses a range of texts for credibility, positioning, validity and accuracy.

Conventions

◆ Uses knowledge of one text form to help interpret another, e.g. literary features in informational texts.

◆ Recognises the effectiveness of language features selected by authors.

• Discusses the relationship between purpose and audience, text form and the media chosen.

• Associates specific conventions with text forms.

Processes and Strategies

◆ Consciously adds to a broad knowledge base, as required, to comprehend.

◆ Selects appropriate strategies from a wide range to comprehend.

◆ Determines unknown words by selecting appropriate word-identification strategies.

• Creates own organiser to demonstrate relationships between key words.

• Describes in detail how, when and why cues and strategies are used to construct meaning.

• Evaluates the selection and effectiveness of a range of cues and strategies.

Major Teaching Emphases and **Teaching and Learning Experiences** are not provided for this phase, as Accomplished readers are able to take responsibility for their own ongoing reading development.

Glossary

acronym	a word formed from the initial letters of other words, e.g. **SCUBA: self-contained underwater breathing apparatus**
adjusting reading rate	a reading strategy that involves the speeding up or slowing down of reading according to the purpose and/or text difficulty
affix	a letter or letters added to a word that affects the meaning, e.g. <u>un</u>happy, jump<u>ed</u>
alliteration	the repetition of the initial sound in consecutive words, often used to create tongue twisters, e.g. **She sells sea shells by the seashore**
analysing	a teaching and learning practice involving the examination of the parts to understand the whole
anecdotal notes	short written descriptions of an observation
annotation	written description recorded directly onto a work sample
antipathy	dislike or aversion
antonym	a word that means the opposite of another word
applying	a teaching and learning practice involving the independent use of a skill, strategy or understanding to achieve a purpose
assessment	gathering data about students
assonance	the repetition of vowel sounds often used in lines of poetry, e.g. **Ousted from the house, the mongrel growled and howled**
automaticity	bringing information to mind with little or no effort because a skill or understanding is so well known, e.g. **the fast, accurate recognition of single words when reading**
bias	a prejudiced view or a one-sided perspective
Book Discussion Groups	small groups who meet to discuss a text they have chosen to read
buddy reading	reading to younger students ('buddies') as a way of practising oral reading
choral reading	two or more students orally reading a text together with the intention of making a meaningful and enjoyable performance
cliché	a trite, stereotyped expression, idea or practice
cloze procedure	an instructional activity involving the completion of incomplete sentences
colloquial	denoting informal use of language, often seeking to replicate a conversational tone and possibly including slang or vulgarities
comparing	a reading strategy involving thinking about similarities and differences in what is known and what is portrayed in texts

compound word	a word as a single unit of meaning but made up of two complete words, e.g. **buttonhole, football**
comprehension strategies	thinking processes used by readers to prepare for reading, comprehend text, monitor reading and adjust reading when necessary, e.g. **connecting, comparing, synthesising, sensory imaging, predicting, paraphrasing, self-questioning**
concepts of print	understandings about what print represents and how it works, e.g. **has a consistent directionality, is made up of letters, words**
conjunction	a word used to link phrases or clauses to create compound or complex sentences, e.g. **and, but, however**
connotation	a meaning additional to one directly stated
consonant	one of all the letters of the alphabet except a, e, i, o, u
consonant cluster	a sequence of two or more consonants, e.g. **tr, shr, ng**
context	the broad linguistic, social and cultural experiences that are brought to a situation
context(ual) clues	information from surrounding text that enables readers to predict the meaning of unknown words
Contextual Understanding	a substrand of reading that involves an understanding of how the context affects the interpretation and choices made by authors and illustrators
Conventions	a substrand of reading that focuses on the structures and features of texts, including spelling, grammar, pronunciation and layout
conventions of print	rules that govern the customary use of print in a language, e.g. **punctuation, upper and lower case letters**
creating images	a reading strategy that involves the reader in using all five senses to create images before, during and after reading
critical literacy	the analysis and questioning of texts to reveal the values and beliefs that attempt to position
critical questions	questions that require the reader to evaluate information in a text based on personal knowledge or experiences, e.g. **What do you think about . . . ?**
critical thinking	logical thought processes based on sound evidence
cultural construction	one's view of the world shaped by cultural knowledge
cultural knowledge	a reader's experiences, values, attitudes and beliefs, and one's perception of these
decoding	a strategy used to identify an unknown word, e.g. **saying the sound represented by individual letters or letter combinations, blending them together and arriving at a pronunciation**
derivative	a word formed by adding an affix to a root or a stem, e.g. **happiness, unhappy**

determining importance	a reading strategy involving making decisions about what is important in a text and what is not
device	a technique used by authors and illustrators to influence the construction of meaning, e.g. **symbolism, metaphor, colour, size of characters**
digraph	two letters that together represent one speech sound, e.g. **ch, ai, ee, sh**
discussing	a teaching and learning practice involving the exchange of opinions on topics, themes or issues
evaluation (of student)	when judgements are made about students from data gathered
evaluative questions	*see* critical questions
explicit	something directly stated by the author or illustrator, e.g. **the information is in the words or the pictures**
familiar texts	those that have been previously read or that deal with aspects within the reader's personal experience; that is, the reader knows about the content, the topic, the language, the text structure or the author
familiarising	a teaching and learning practice involving raising awareness and activating prior knowledge
figurative language	language enriched by word images and figures of speech, e.g. **using metaphor, cliché, simile**
flexible grouping	forming and dissolving groups according to the goal of the lesson
fluency	reading aloud smoothly, easily and with expression, showing understanding of the author's message
focused observation	looking for specific behaviours or at particular students to gain an understanding of strengths and weaknesses
Global Statement	a written snapshot of a learner in a particular phase of development, which encapsulates the typical characteristics of that phase
grammatical knowledge	knowing about of the patterns of the language, e.g. **the order in which words are combined to make sentences and paragraphs**
graphic organisers	visual representations of concepts that enable a learner to visualise, record and retrieve information from a text
graphophonic cues	a source of knowledge that provides the reader with information about words, letters, combinations of letters and the sounds associated with them
graphophonics	the study of sound–symbol relationships
Guided Reading	a procedure that enables teachers to guide small groups of students reading a common text (assigned by the teacher) with the aim of teaching and practising reading strategies

Guided Writing	a procedure where teachers guide the students to construct a text with the aim of teaching and practising writing strategies
guiding	a teaching and learning practice involving the provision of scaffolds through strategic assistance at predetermined checkpoints in the learning process
homographs	words that are spelt the same but pronounced differently and have different meanings, e.g. **tear and tear, minute and minute**
homonyms	words that are spelt the same and pronounced the same but have different meanings, e.g. **scale (fish), scale (music)**
homophones	words that are pronounced the same but spelt differently and have different meanings, e.g. **here and hear, I'll and aisle**
ideology	the beliefs, values, symbols and devices that form the body of a doctrine, social movement, class or large group, e.g. **socialism**
idiom	an expression that does not mean literally what it says, e.g. **'pay through the nose'**
implicit	intended by an author or illustrator but not directly stated
Independent Reading	a reading procedure in which students are in charge of their own reading — they choose their own books, do their own reading and take responsibility to work through any challenges in the text
Indicator	a description of literacy behaviours on the *First Steps* Maps of Development
inferential questions	questions that require interpretation of information implied but not directly stated
inferring	a reading strategy that involves combining what is read in the text with the reader's own ideas to create their unique interpretation
informational text	a text that is more factual than creative in nature, presenting information in an ordered way, e.g. **a report, a biography, a recipe**
innovating	a teaching and learning practice involving the alteration or amendment of a text to create a new one
interpretation	inferring a meaning beyond what is literally stated
interpretive questions	*see* inferential questions
investigating	a teaching and learning practice involving finding, analysing, questioning and using information for a purpose
Key Indicator	a description of literacy behaviours that most students display at a phase on the *First Steps* Maps of Development
Language Experience	a procedure based on the idea that an experience can be shared, talked about, written down, and then read and re-read

language features	the grammatical structures and word selection appropriate for different text forms
linguistic cueing system	*see* three-cueing system
literal questions	questions that require recall of information directly stated in a text
literary text	a text that is more creative than factual in nature, usually consisting of characters, setting and plot; includes poetry
Major Teaching Emphases	teaching priorities appropriate to phases of development
making connections	a reading strategy involving making links between what is read and other texts, to oneself, or to personal knowledge about the world
metacognition	thinking about one's thinking
metaphor	a figure of speech in which a term or phrase is used to compare something to which it is not literally connected, e.g. 'The road was a ribbon of moonlight . . .'
miscue analysis	a detailed diagnostic procedure for recording, analysing and interpreting deviations from a text read aloud
Modelled Reading	a reading procedure typified by the teacher's selecting and reading a text to students, and thinking aloud selected processes being used
Modelled Writing	a writing procedure typified by the teacher's constructing a text for students, and thinking aloud selected processes being used
modelling	a teaching and learning practice involving explicit demonstration of the thinking behind how and why something is done
morpheme	the smallest meaningful unit of a word, e.g. 'un', 'reason' and 'able' in the word 'unreasonable'
nuance	synonyms with subtle differences in meaning, e.g. thief, bandit, assassin
onomatopoeia	the formation of a word that imitates the sound associated with what is being described, e.g. whoosh, plop, whippoorwill
onset	the part of the syllable preceding the rime (*see* rime): usually the consonant or consonant cluster that precedes the vowel, e.g. 'tr' in truck
orthographic knowledge	knowing about the spelling of words in a given language according to established usage
orthography	the study of the nature and use of symbols in a writing system, e.g. letter patterns
paraphrasing	a reading strategy involving reducing larger pieces of text to the most important ideas or messages
perspective	*see* point of view

phase	a clustering of behaviours along the *First Steps* Maps of Development
phoneme	the smallest sound unit of speech, e.g. /k/ in cat
phonemic awareness	the awareness of the individual sounds or phonemes that make up spoken words
phonics	a way of teaching that stresses sound–symbol relationships
phonogram	*see* rime; also known as word families, e.g. -at, -ame, -og
phonological awareness	an ability to recognise, combine and manipulate the different sound units of spoken words
playing	a teaching and learning practice involving the exploration of concepts and skills through imagining and creating
point of view	the stance an author has chosen to take that is revealed through devices used in the text, e.g. words and actions in a literary text or information included or omitted in an informational text
positioning	an attempt on the part of the author to influence the reader to take a particular point of view
practising	a teaching and learning practice involving the rehearsal of a skill or strategy
predictable text	a text featuring rhyme, rhythm and repetition of sentence patterns that make it accessible to beginning readers
predicting	a reading strategy involving the use of prior knowledge to anticipate what is going to occur in a text before or during reading
prefix	an affix added to the beginning of a word, e.g. <u>un</u>happy, <u>re</u>wind, <u>anti</u>biotic
primary information sources	raw material, including people and services, used when gathering information
print-rich environment	an environment filled with jointly constructed meaningful print
Processes and Strategies	a substrand of reading involving the application of knowledge and understandings to comprehend and compose texts
propaganda	the dissemination of particular ideas or information to help or harm an institution, person or cause
Read and Retell	a reading activity described by Brown and Cambourne (1987) involving students in predicting, reading, writing, sharing, listening and justifying
Readers' Theatre	the preparation and oral reading of a script where the focus is on interpreting the text rather than memorising it
reading conference	a structured conversation in which aspects of students' reading development are discussed

reading on	a reading strategy involving continuing to read when encountering difficulties or unknown words
Reading to Students	a reading procedure that involves the teacher reading aloud to students
reflecting	a teaching and learning practice involving the thinking back on the what, how and why of experiences
reporting	sharing learning with others
representing	the demonstration of learning in a selected way, e.g. by drawing a picture, constructing a graphic organiser or writing key words
re-reading	a reading strategy involving going back over the whole or parts of text to clarify meaning or to assist with word identification
rhetoric	the skilful use of language to influence or persuade an audience
rime	a vowel and any following consonants of a syllable e.g. 'ip' in 'trip'
root word	the basic part of a word that carries the meaning, e.g. read, health; a foreign root is the basic part of a word that carries the meaning but originates in a foreign language, e.g. auto, manus
scaffolding	strategic leads, prompts and support given to students in the form of modelling, sharing, guiding and conferencing with the aim of developing autonomy
scanning	a reading strategy involving glancing quickly through material to locate specific information
secondary information sources	texts such as encyclopaedias, websites, articles and magazines used to gather information
self-questioning	a reading strategy involving generating one's own questions before, during and after reading
semantic cues	the source of information that provides the reader with the knowledge associated with the overall meaning of a text, e.g. knowledge of the concept, topic
Shared Reading	an interactive reading procedure in which students see the text, observe a good model (usually the teacher) reading and are invited to read along
Shared Writing	an interactive procedure in which students see the construction of a text by a good model (usually the teacher) and are invited to contribute ideas and suggestions (the 'control of the pen' remains with the model)
sharing	a teaching and learning practice that involves the joint construction of meaning, e.g. between teacher and student, or student and student

sight vocabulary	the bank of words that a reader can recognise automatically; that is, can pronounce and know the meaning of the word in the context in which it is used
signal words	words often used to join phrases and clauses and also to indicate particular text structures, e.g. **because, on the other hand, similar to**
simile	a figure of speech making a direct connection, e.g. **as brave as a lion, as white as snow**
simulating	a teaching and learning practice involving the adoption of a role or imagining oneself in a hypothetical setting
skimming	a reading strategy involving quickly glancing through a text to get a general impression or overview of the content
sociocultural	a combination of social and cultural factors such as economic status, geographical location, beliefs and values
sociogram	a graphic representation of characters or people showing relationships among them
sounding out	*see* decoding
stereotype	a perception conforming to a set image or type based on culturally dominant ideas, e.g. **boys are tough, old people are a burden to society**
strand	one of four interwoven language modes, e.g. **reading, writing, speaking and listening, and viewing**
strategy	the mental processes 'you use to do something you want to do'
substrand	one of four interwoven lenses through which student performance in literacy can be monitored and supported, e.g. **Use of Texts, Contextual Understanding, Conventions, Processes and Strategies**
summarising	A reading strategy involving condensing information to the most important ideas
suffix	an affix added to the end of a word that affects the grammatical function or meaning, e.g. **jump<u>ed</u>, hesitat<u>ion</u>**
synonyms	words similar in meaning, e.g. **large, huge**
syntactic cues	the source of information that provides the reader with knowledge about the structure of the language, e.g. **language patterns and grammatical features**
synthesising	a reading strategy that involves bringing together pieces of information for different purposes during or after reading
targeted feedback	specific information given to direct, improve or control present and future learning
text	any communication from which meaning is gained, e.g. **books, videos, Internet website, conversation**
text form	a type of text, e.g. **recount, report**

text organisation	the way information is organised in a text — the layout, e.g. the text framework, paragraphs, diagrams, headings, subheadings
text structure	how ideas, feelings and pieces of information are linked in a text, e.g. compare/contrast, problem/solution, cause/effect, listing: logical or chronological sequence, collection of details
textual features	features of text used by authors to give emphasis, e.g. enlarged letters — HELP!, speech bubbles
three-cueing system	the sources of information a reader draws upon to make sense of what is read, e.g. graphophonic, semantic, syntactic
top-level structures	thinking patterns that provide frameworks for organising, sorting and storing information that enable connections and comparisons within a text to be made
transforming	a teaching and learning practice involving the re-creation of a text in another form, mode or medium, e.g. a story to a play, a book to a film
unfamiliar texts	texts that are sight unseen or deal with aspects not within the reader's personal experience; that is, aspects of the content, the topic, the language, the text structure or the author are unknown
Use of Texts	a substrand of reading involving the comprehension of texts
valid	sound, just or well-founded
vowels	the letters a, e, i, o and u, sometimes referred to as long or short: long vowels represent the sound of their alphabet letter name, as in b<u>ay</u>, b<u>ee</u>, b<u>oa</u>t; short vowels represent the sounds heard in b<u>a</u>t, b<u>i</u>t, b<u>e</u>t
word-identification strategies	thinking processes readers use in an attempt to identify unknown words
word knowledge	knowing about words, their meanings and how they work
world knowledge	*see* cultural knowledge

Bibliography

Allen, J. 2000, *Yellow Brick Roads, Shared and Guided Paths to Independent Reading 4–12*, Stenhouse Publishers, Portland, Maine, USA.

Allen, P. 1992, *Belinda*, Puffin Books, Ringwood, Victoria, Australia.

Anderson, J. 1989, *Here Today, Everywhere Tomorrow? The Effects of Introduced Plants and Animals on Australia*, Bookshelf Publishing Australia, Gosford, NSW, Australia.

Amber, J. 1999, *Spiders and How They Hunt*, Heinemann Educational Publishers, Oxford, UK.

Beierle, M. & Lynes, T. 1993, *Teaching Basic Skills through Literature: A Whole Language Approach for Teaching Reading Skills*, Creative Teaching Press, Cypress, CA, USA.

Beecher, B. & Arthur, L. 2001, *Play and Literacy in Children's Worlds*, PETA, Newtown, NSW, Australia.

Beers, K. 2003, *When Kids Can't Read What Teachers Can Do: A Guide for Teachers 6–12*, Heinemann, Portsmouth, NH, USA.

Belanger, C. 1988, *The T-shirt Song*, Shortland Publications, Auckland, NZ.

Bender, L. 1989, *The Body*, Aladdin Books, London, UK.

Bloom, B. S. (ed.) 1956, *Taxonomy of Educational Objectives: The Classification of Educational Goals: Handbook I, Cognitive Domain*, Longmans Green, New York, USA.

Bolton, F. & Cullen, E. 1987, *Animal Shelters*, Ashton Scholastic, Gosford, NSW, Australia.

Brian, J. 1991, *Natural Disasters*, Magic Bean, Martin International, Flinders Park, South Australia, Australia.

Bromley, K., Irwin-De Vitis, L. & Modlo, M. 1995, *Graphic Organizers: Visual Strategies for Active Learning*, Scholastic, New York, USA.

Brown, H. & Cambourne, B. 1987, *Read and Retell*, Heinemann, Portsmouth, NH, USA.

Burke, J. 2000, *Reading Reminders, Tools, Tips and Techniques*, Boynton/Cook Publishers, Portsmouth, NH, USA.

—— 2001, *Illuminating Texts*, Heinemann, Portsmouth, NH, USA.

Carle, E. 1969, *The Very Hungry Caterpillar*, World Publishing Company, Cleveland and New York, USA.

Carter, M. 1992, *Possum Goes to School*, Childerset Publishers, Cairns, Qld, Australia.

Clay, M. M. 1993, *An Observation Survey of Early Literacy Achievement*, Heinemann, Portsmouth, NH, USA.

—— 2000, *Running Records For Classroom Teachers*, Heinemann, Portsmouth, NH, USA.

Bibliography

Comber, K. 1991, *Cousteau: An Unauthorised Biography*, Magic Bean, Martin International, Flinders Park, South Australia, Australia.

Comet 2002, Pearson Education Australia, Melbourne, Australia, Issue 1.

CSIRO Education 2001, 'Scientriffic — get your hands on science', Sept/Oct, no. 15, Dickson, ACT, Australia.

Cullen, E. 1986, *An Introduction to Australian Spiders*, Ashton Scholastic, Gosford, NSW, Australia.

Cunningham, P. M. 2000, *Phonics They Use*, Addison-Wesley Educational Publishers, New York, NY, USA.

Dahl, R. 1982, *The BFG*, Puffin Books, Ringwood, Victoria, Australia.

—— 1984, *Boy: Tales of Childhood*, Puffin Books, Ringwood, Victoria, Australia.

Dolch E. W. 1939, *A Manual for Remedial Reading*, Garrard Press, Champaign, Illinois, USA.

Duffelmeyer, F., Baum, D. D. & Merkley, D. J. 1987, 'Maximizing reader–text confrontation with an extended anticipation guide', *Journal of Reading*, 31, pp.146–150.

Education Department of Western Australia 1994, *Supporting Linguistic and Cultural Diversity through First Steps*, Perth, Western Australia, Australia.

Elkonin, D. B. 1973, 'USSR', in *Comparative Reading*, ed. J. Downing, Macmillan, New York, NY, USA.

Ellis, E. S. & Farmer, T. 2002, 'The clarifying routine elaborating vocabulary instruction', http://www.ldonline.org/ld_indepth/teaching_techniques/ellis_clarifying.html, 16 July.

ERIC Clearinghouse on Reading, English and Communication, 'A developmental path to reading', *ERIC Review*, vol. 7, issue 2, Bloomington, IN (downloaded from the web).

Fountas. I. G. & Su Pinnell, G. 1996, *Guided Reading*, Heinemann, Portsmouth, NH, USA.

Fox, M. 1983, *Possum Magic*, Omnibus Books, Adelaide, Australia.

—— 1988, *Guess What*, Voyager Books, Orlando, Florida, USA.

—— 1988, *Koala Lou*, Puffin Books, Ringwood, Victoria, Australia.

—— 1989, *Night Noises*, Omnibus Books, Norwood, South Australia.

—— 1993, *Time For Bed*, Omnibus Books, Norwood, South Australia.

—— 1995, *Wombat Divine*, Omnibus Books, Norwood, South Australia.

——. 2001, *Reading Magic: How Your Child Can Learn to Read before School — and Other Read-Aloud Miracles*, Pan Macmillan, Sydney, Australia.

Fredericksen, E. 1999, 'Playing through: Increasing literacy through interaction', *Journal of Adolescent and Adult Literacy*, vol. 43, no. 2, October, IRA, USA.

Fry, E., Kness, J. & Fountoukidis, D. 1984, *The Reading Teacher's Book of Lists*, Prentice-Hall, Paramus, New Jersey, USA.

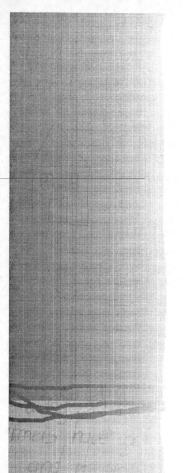

Glasson, T. 1997, *Heinemann Outcomes English 3*, Rigby Heinemann, Melbourne, Victoria, Australia.

Goodman, K. 1996, *Ken Goodman On Reading: A Common-sense Look at the Nature of Language and the Science of Reading*, Heinemann, Portsmouth, NH, USA.

Goodman, Y. M. & Burke, C. L. 1972, *Reading Miscue Inventory Manual: Procedure for Diagnosis and Evaluation*, Macmillan, New York, NY, USA.

Gray, L. M. 1995, *My Mama Had a Dancing Heart*, Orchard Books, New York, NY, USA.

Griffiths, A. 2002, *The Day My Bum Went Psycho*, Pan Macmillan, Sydney, NSW, Australia.

Guile, M. 1996, *Revenge of the Green Genie*, Ashton Scholastic, Gosford, NSW, Australia.

Hancock, J. (ed.) 1999, *The Explicit Teaching of Reading*, International Reading Association, Newark, Delaware, USA.

Harney, S. 1992, *A Dinosaur Directory*, Jacaranda Press, Milton, Qld, Australia.

Heald-Taylor, G. 2001, *The Beginning Reading Handbook: Strategies for Success*, Heinemann, Portsmouth, NH, USA.

Herber, H. L. 1970, *Teaching Reading in Content Areas*, Prentice-Hall Englewood Cliffs, NJ, USA.

Hill, S. 1990, *Readers' Theatre: Performing the Text*, Eleanor Curtain Publishing, South Yarra, Victoria, Australia.

Holdaway, D. 1980, *Independence in Reading — a Handbook on Individualized Procedures*, 2nd edn, Ashton Scholastic, Gosford, NSW, Australia.

Hoyt. L. 2000, *Snapshots*, Heinemann, Portsmouth, NH, USA.

—— 2002, *Make It Real*, Heinemann, Portsmouth, NH, USA.

http://www.kidsreads.com

http://www.sasked.gov.sk.ca/docs/mla/julie.html 'Exploring Love and Loyalty: Romeo and Juliet' Grade 9, accessed 06/03

http://www.smartdraw.com Power Plant

http://www.teenreads.com

http://www.teenink.com

Hughes, M. 1998, *Stone Soup*, Ginn & Company, Aylesbury, UK.

Hutchins, P. 1987, *Rosie's Walk*, Scholastic Inc., New York, USA.

Jennings, P. 1987, *Quirky Tails*, Puffin Books, Ringwood, Victoria, Australia.

—— 1989, *The Paw Thing*, Puffin Books, Ringwood, Victoria, Australia.

—— 1998, *Singenpoo Strikes Again*, Puffin Books, Ringwood, Victoria, Australia.

Johnson, T. D. & Louis, D. R. 1987, *Literacy through Literature*, Heinemann, Portsmouth, NH, USA.

Jose, E. & Andersen, H. C. 1999, *Little Match Girl: A Classic Tale*, Phyllis Fogelman Books, New York, NY, USA.

Keene, E. O. & Zimmermann, S. 1997, *Mosaic of Thought: Teaching Comprehension in a Reader's Workshop*, Heinemann, Portsmouth, NH, USA.

Kitching, K. & Wansborough, C. 1996, *Storytime Topics: Traditional Tales Used as the Starting Point for Classroom Activities with Children from Five to Seven Years*, Belair Publications, Twickenham, England, UK.

Lee, D. 1987, *Alligator Pie*, MacMillan, Toronto, Canada.

Little Aussie Cookbook 1995, Murdoch Books, Sydney, NSW, Australia.

London, J. 1903, *The Call of the Wild*, Prentice-Hall, Englewood Cliffs, UK.

Luke, A. & Freebody, P. 1999, *A Map of Possible Practices: Further Notes on the Four Resources Model*, Practically Primary, Primary Teachers Association of Australia, Sydney, NSW, Australia.

McAlexander, P. & Burrell, K. 1996, Helping students 'get it together' with synthesis journals, paper presented at the annual conference of the National Association of Developmental Education, Little Rock, AR, USA.

McCann. C. 2003, *Dancer: A Novel*, Metropolitan Books, New York, USA.

McLaughlin, M. & Allen, M. B. 2002, *Guided Comprehension: A Teaching Model for Grades 3–8*, International Reading Association, Newark, Delaware, USA.

Marshall, V. & Tester, B.1988, *Bernard Was a Bikie*, Ashton Scholastic, Gosford, NSW, Australia.

Martin Jr, B. & Carle, E. 1967, *Brown Bear, Brown Bear, What Do You See?*, Henry Holt & Co., New York, USA.

Miller, D. 2002, *Reading with Meaning: Teaching Comprehension in the Primary Grades*, Stenhouse Publishers, Portland, Maine, USA.

Ministry of Education, Western Australia 1987, *Reading to Learn in the Secondary School: Teachers Notes*, Department of State Services, State Supply, Perth, Western Australia.

Morris, A. & Stewart-Dore, N. 1984, *Learning to Learn From Text: Effective Reading in the Content Areas*, Addison-Wesley, North Ryde, NSW, Australia.

Mudd, S. & Mason, H. 1993, *Tales for Topics: Linking Favourite Stories with Popular Topics for Children Aged Five to Nine*, Belair Publications, Twickenham, England, UK.

Munsch, R. 1980, *The Paper Bag Princess*, Scholastic Australia, Sydney, NSW, Australia.

Numeroff, L. J. 1985, *If You Give a Mouse a Cookie*, HarperCollins, New York, NY, USA.

Ogle, D. 1986, 'KWL: A teaching model that develops active reading of expository texts', *The Reading Teacher*, International Reading Association, Newark, Delaware, USA, February.

Opitz, M. F. 2000, *Rhymes and Reasons*, Heinemann, Portsmouth, NH, USA.

—— & Ford, M. P. 2001, *Reaching Readers: Flexible and Innovative Strategies for Guided Reading*, Heinemann, Portsmouth, NH, USA.

Owocki, Gretchen 1999, *Literacy through Play*, Heinemann, Portsmouth, NH, USA.

Parsons, M. & James, M. 1996, *Heinemann Outcomes Science 2*, Heinemann, Port Melbourne, Victoria, Australia.

Pask, R., Butler, J., McMeekin, T. & Wiber, M. 1998, *Heinemann Outcomes Geography 2*, Heinemann, Port Melbourne, Victoria, Australia.

Patterson, K. 1977, *Bridge to Terabithia*, HarperCollins Juvenile Books, New York, NY, USA.

Pearson, P. D. 1976, 'A psycholinguistic model of reading', *Language Arts*, vol. 53, pp.309–14.

Raphael, T. E. 1982, 'Teaching children question-answering strategies', *The Reading Teacher*, International Reading Association, Newark, Delaware, vol. 36, pp.186–91.

—— 1986, 'Teaching question–answer relationships, revisited', *The Reading Teacher*, vol. 39, no.6, pp.516–22.

Rhodes. L. (ed.) 1993, *Literacy Assessment: A Handbook of Instruments*, Heinemann, Portsmouth, NH, USA.

—— & Shanklin, N. 1993, *Windows into Literacy: Assessing Learners K–8*, Heinemann, Portsmouth, NH, USA.

Richgels, D. J., Poremba, K. J. & McGee, L. M. 1996, 'Kindergartners talk about print: Phonemic awareness in meaningful contexts', *The Reading Teacher*, vol. 49, pp.632–42.

Riley, P. 1998, *Vehicles — the Inside Story*, Ginn & Company, Aylesbury, UK.

Rivalland, J. 1990, *Zoom Notes 2: Spelling, English Language K–7 Syllabus*, Education Department of Western Australia, Perth, Australia.

Robb, L. 1996, *Reading Strategies that Work: Teaching Your Students to Become Better Readers*, Scholastic, New York, USA.

—— 2000, *Teaching Reading in Middle School: A Strategic Approach to Teaching Reading that Improves Comprehension and Thinking*, Scholastic, New York.

Rohl, M. & Milton, M. 2003, How children learn literacy: Processes, development, difficulties, course notes LAN 5124, Edith Cowan University, Perth, Western Australia.

Routman, R. 1996, *Invitations: Changing as Teachers and Learners K–12*, Heinemann, Portsmouth, NH, USA.

—— 2000, *Conversations: Strategies for Teaching Learning and Evaluating*, Heinemann, Portsmouth, NH, USA.

—— 2003, *Reading Essentials: The Specifics You Need to Teach Reading Well*, Heinemann, Portsmouth, NH, USA.

Rubenstein, G. (comp.) 1988, *After Dark: Seven Tales to Read at Night*, Omnibus Books, Norwood, South Australia.

Rylant, C. 1988, *Every Living Thing*, Aladdin Paperbacks, New York, NY, USA.

Schwartz, R. M. & Raphael, T. 1985, 'Concept of definition: A key to improving students' vocabulary', *The Reading Teacher*, International Reading Association, Newark, Delaware, vol. 39, no. 2, 198–205.

Scieszka, J. 1989, *The True Story of the Three Little Pigs*, Puffin Books, New York, NY, USA.

Shea, M. 2000, *Taking Running Records*, Scholastic, New York, NY, USA.

Sheldon, D. & Blythe, G. 1990, *The Whales' Song*, Random House Children's Books, London, UK.

Snow, C. E., Burns, S. & Griffin, P. 1998, *Preventing Reading Difficulties in Young Children*, National Academy Press, Washington, DC, USA.

Taback, S. 1977, *There Was an Old Lady Who Swallowed a Fly*, Penguin, Ringwood, Victoria, Australia.

Taberski, S. 2000, *On Solid Ground*, Heinemann, Portsmouth, NH, USA.

The Sunday Times 2003, *Fishing WA*, Part One: Southern WA, Perth, Australia.

Thiele, C. 2001, *The Monster Fish*, Southwood Books, Sydney, NSW, Australia.

Thomson, J. 1992, *Independent and Advanced Phases, Reading Developmental Continuum*, Ministry of Education, Perth, Western Australia.

Tovani, C. 2000, *I Read It, but I Don't Get It: Comprehension Strategies for Adolescent Readers*, Stenhouse Publishers, Portland, Maine, USA.

Turner, A. (ed.) 1992, *Patterns of Thinking: Top-Level Structure in the Classroom*, PETA, Newtown, NSW, Australia.

Twain, Mark 1989 (1885), *The Adventures of Huckleberry Finn*, Doherty Tom Assoc. LLC, New York, NY, USA.

Vacca, R. T. & Vacca, J. L. 1989, *Content Area Reading*, 3rd edn, HarperCollins, New York, NY, USA.

Vaughan, M. K. 1984, *Wombat Stew*, Ashton Scholastic, Gosford, NSW, Australia.

Wagner, J. 1977, *John Brown, Rose and the Midnight Cat*, Puffin Books, Ringwood, Victoria, Australia.

Wilde, S. 2000, *Miscue Analysis Made Easy: Building on Student Strengths*, Heinemann, Portsmouth, NH, USA.

Wilhelm, J. D. 2001, *Improving Comprehension with Think-Aloud Strategies*, Scholastic, New York, USA.

——, Baker, T. N. & Dube, J. 2001, *Strategic Reading: Guiding Students to Lifelong Literacy, 6–12*, Boynton/Cook Publishers, Portsmouth, NH, USA.

Wilson, L. 2002, *Reading to Live: How to Teach Reading for Today's World*, Heinemann, Portsmouth, NH, USA.

—— 2003, Opening address, Australian Literacy Educators Association, Western Australian State Conference, Perth, Australia, May.

Yopp, H. K. 1992, 'Developing phonemic awareness in young children', *The Reading Teacher*, vol. 45, no. 9, May.

First Steps Second Edition Professional Development Courses

The *First Steps* **Second Edition** materials form a critical part of the *First Steps* professional development courses that promote a long-term commitment to educational change. Together, the professional development and the materials provide a strategic whole-school approach to improving students' literacy outcomes.

First Steps offers a full range of professional development courses that are conducted at t he invitation of a school or education sector. Given the breadth of literacy, schools generally choose to implement only one strand of literacy at a time. A strand should be selected on a needs basis in line with a school's priorities. Schools can select from two-day courses in any of these strands:
• Reading
• Writing and Spelling
• Viewing
• Speaking and Listening.

Each participant who attends a two-day course receives:
• a Map of Development in the chosen literacy strand
• a Resource Book
• the *Linking Assessment, Teaching and Learning* Book
• a course book of professional development reflections
• practical activities for classroom use.

Within each stand, a selection of additional sessions, beyond the regular course, will also be available to meet the needs of teachers in different schools and contexts. These additional sessions can be selected in consultation with a *First Steps* Consultant.

For further information about or registration in *First Steps* courses contact your nearest STEPS Professional Development Office.

UNITED STATES OF AMERICA
STEPS Professional Development
and Consulting
97 Boston Street
Salem
Massachusetts USA 01970
Phone: 978 744 3001
Fax: 978 744 7003
Toll free: 1866 505 3001
www.stepspd.org

UNITED KINGDOM
STEPS Professional Development
and Consulting
Shrivenham Hundred
Business Park
Majors Road
Watchfield SN8TZ
Phone: 01793 787930
Fax: 01793 787931
www.steps-pd.co.uk

AUSTRALASIA
STEPS Professional Development
65 Walters Drive
Osborne Park WA 6017
Phone: 08 9273 8833
Fax: 08 9273 8811
www.ecurl.com.au

CANADA
Pearson Professional Learning
26 Prince Andrew Place
Toronto, Ontario M3C 2T8
Phone: 416 447 5101
Fax: 416 447 3914
Toll free: 1888 867 7772
www.pearsonprofessionallearning.ca

Professional Development Notes

Professional Development Notes